Mickey Walker

The Toy Bulldog and His Times

MICKEY WALKER

The Toy Bulldog and His Times

by Mickey Walker
With Joe Reichler

Random House   New York

To My Wife
Marci
And all the others
Who have helped me

Mickey Walker

The Toy Bulldog and His Times

CHAPTER ONE

I was born dead, with a black eye, but even that early, I must have been too stubborn to quit. I had to fight even before I drew my first breath, and I grew up fighting. I fought my way through childhood and through school, and fighting cost me every job I ever had—till I learned one day that doing the thing I liked best could earn me more money than any job a lad my age could ever have.

But fighting, once I'd turned pro, brought me much more than money (about five million dollars after managers' cuts, in seventeen years) and ring championships and fame. It put me on center stage during the wildest, whackiest, most wonderful two decades this country has ever known.

Looking back on it now, I must have been as wild and whacky and screwball as the times. But I wouldn't trade the memories for any part of the millions I earned and spent. Memories of the tough guys, the managers, the dolls, the drunks, the dudes, the gossip and intrigue, the shenanigans in the hotel rooms and lobbies and training camps—and the nearly two hundred fights I had in four divisions.

In those days it was easy for a guy like me to live violently, as if there were no tomorrow. I'm not looking for either glory or sympathy. I'm no hypocrite. If ever a guy enjoyed raising hell, it was me. And few guys raised more hell or had more fun while doing it.

If I was a sinner, I sinned happy.

3

I couldn't have picked a better time to be born—even if I did come close to being counted out before I ever got started.

The doctor who brought me into this world gave up on me. I first heard this story years later, twenty-one to be exact, when I won my first world championship. Doctor Timothy Reilly, who delivered all three children born to Elizabeth Higgins Walker, told me about it.

Liz—we all called my mother Liz—had a tough time with me; I weighed twelve pounds. I was so darned big Doc had to use instruments to pull me into this world. That's how I got the black eye, my first of many. Though I showed no signs of life, the doctor did all he could. He shook me, spanked me, massaged me, and breathed into my mouth. I did not respond. So he made up his mind that I was dead, bundled me up in a blanket and laid me aside so he could work on Liz.

Doctor Reilly got the surprise of his life a few minutes later. He had just succeeded in reviving Liz when I let out a howl.

"Mike," he beamed at my old man after he had recovered from his surprise, "it looks like you got yourself a family."

I was born in the three-hundred-year-old industrial city of Elizabeth, New Jersey, which then had a population of around 50,000. It adjoins Newark to the south. Like all good-sized cities, Elizabeth is divided into distinct neighborhoods. At the turn of the century, many of these neighborhoods were tough. The one I was born into was the toughest. It was called Keighry Head, and still is.

Keighry Head is largely colored now, but in my time it was an Irish community where skull-cracking was the favorite sidewalk sport, just as "potsie" was the big game in other cities.

As an infant, I was practically teethed on shillelaghs. I had to fight in order to grow up. Grandma's house, in which I was born, stood at 905 Magnolia Avenue, just two doors away from Bob Cooper's saloon. Cooper's Corner, they called it, and it was the hangout for almost everybody in Keighry Head.

It was a middle-class neighborhood, not a slum area. In fact, there were some expensive and imposing residences there—good-sized homes seated on spacious, valuable sites. Grandma's house, which still stands, was one of those. It is a big white frame building with blue trim and shutters. The stable behind it also remains to this day, and that was kept as sparkling clean as the house itself.

There were grapevines and fruit trees of all kinds in back of the stable. The stable itself was a beautiful brick building. It was a mansion compared to the house. I could never understand why the horses lived better than the humans in the Higgins household. But no man had a greater love for horses than my mother's father.

Grandpa Patrick Higgins then owned work horses, but at one time he had owned some of the finest thoroughbred racers and trotters in the world. Among them were the famous trotter Hitchings, and Salvator, the greatest race horse in the country in the 1890's. He was the Man o' War of his time. Grandpa even imported Isaac Murphy, the celebrated jockey from Ireland, to ride Salvator. Murphy was colored.

Gramps was a building contractor. He also built up a

man-sized family. Ten children kept things humming in the Higgins home, which was surrounded by twenty acres of lawns and fields. That was before my time, though. What I remember best about the house is the back yard, where Uncle Daniel, the oldest of five sons, erected a punching-bag stand.

I punched that bag as far back as I can remember. I couldn't reach it at first, so Uncle Joe would hold me up. Later on, when I got a little older, I would stand on a soap box to punch the bag.

Besides Daniel, Joe and Liz, there were Aunts Maggie, Nellie, Katie and Mamie, and Uncles Pat, Big John and Little John. Only one is alive today. That's Aunt Maggie. She was easily the liveliest, the glamour girl of the family. She's about seventy-eight now, an attractive woman, who dresses in style, likes to go to dances and night clubs and is active in community life. She likes her beaux, but she considers anyone over fifty too old.

Uncle Daniel, who was to have a great influence on my life, was a fine architect. He was also a fine athlete, having at one time been the State's amateur featherweight and lightweight champion. Uncle Joe was the one who took me in hand my first year as a fighter. He became my self-appointed trainer and arranged my first training camp. Of the entire Higgins clan, Little John probably had the strongest personality. He was very handsome, very reckless and a two-fisted drinker—who was usually very drunk. He did the most amazing things. As a soldier in the First World War, he broke every rule in the Army but he wound up with a medal for knocking out a German machine-gun nest singlehanded. He was gassed in that action.

After the war, Uncle John received a veteran's bonus check of fifteen hundred dollars from the government. He purchased a car and went on a toot. Three weeks later, he received another fifteen-hundred-dollar bonus check. With this money, he extended the bender and wrecked the car he had bought with the first check. He had about nine hundred dollars left and he took care of that by drinking a gin mill dry. When all the money was gone, the Higginses had a visitor . . . a government agent. It seemed that the second bonus check had been sent to John Higgins in error, so would he please hand over the fifteen hundred? Little John sobered up in a hurry then. He didn't have fifteen hundred cents, let alone a grand and a half. As far as I know, the government never did get its money back.

Anyhow, that's the kind of County Kerry Irish clan Mike Walker got himself mixed up with when Pat Higgins consented to let him take the hand of his spirited daughter Elizabeth in holy wedlock. Liz was eighteen and had known Mike only a few months. The year was 1899.

Mike was born in an old Irish section in Holyoke, Massachusetts, called The Flats. A bricklayer by trade, Mike was known for his exceptional physical strength but he hated fighting. It was his ambition to work for God. Mike was twenty when he took a job in Boston. There he met John L. Sullivan, then heavyweight champion of the world. At different times, John L. worked as a laborer, keeping his body fit and strong for the prize ring. He and Mike became fast friends. John L., as did others, took notice of Mike's unusual strength and he invited Mike to work out with him. Mike's natural boxing skill and his powerful punch amazed Sullivan, and the great man, backed by his trainer, William Muldoon, tried repeatedly to persuade Mike to become a professional fighter. Mike wouldn't listen. He wanted no part of the fight game. He would box only with his friend, John L. Sullivan.

John L. was still trying to convince Mike he ought to enter the ring when Mike was offered a good-paying job as a bricklayer with the Pat Higgins Construction Company in Elizabeth, New Jersey. "I'll take it," Mike told the old champ. "I'll work there for six months. Then I'll quit and begin serious study for the priesthood."

When Mike was ready to leave, John L. accompanied him to the station, where they arrived a few minutes before train time. "Mike, you're a fool," Sullivan said. "Ever since the first day we put the gloves on, Bill Muldoon has said you've got what it takes to be a champion. It's two years since I hung up the gloves. Bob Fitzsimmons is champion now. With a couple of fights under your belt and with me to help you a little, I'm sure you can lick him. What do you say, Mike? Will you change your mind and come back with me?"

Mike raised his powerful right arm and let it fall on Sullivan's shoulders. "John," he said slowly, "I boxed with you because I respect you and am proud to be in your company. But to fight with fists for money or vengeance . . . I'll never bring myself to do it!"

Later, as he was about to board his train, he turned again to Sullivan. "John," he said, "after I get settled in Elizabeth, I hope to become a priest . . . but I will never forget you."

Their hands clasped. "Be on your way then," John L. said. "And God bless you!"

Mike's dream of priesthood was knocked out of his head by—of all things—a horse. A few months after he had begun work at the new job, he was approaching the Higgins house when he heard flying hooves. Before he had

8

a chance to dodge out of the way, he was knocked flat on his face. While trying to get the mud out of his eyes, he heard a peal of girlish laughter. He looked up in anger.

"I can't help laughing," said the girl on the horse. "You look so funny lying there. I do hope you're not hurt. And I suppose it's no use for me to say I'm sorry."

Mike struggled to his feet. "Why aren't you more careful . . ."

"Me? Careful? You're the one who should be careful. Do you know the horse you nearly knocked down is the finest race horse in the country? You could have hurt him . . . Say, what are you doing here, anyway? What do you want?"

"I'm here to see Mr. Higgins. I have a message for him from the foreman."

The girl's face softened. "Papa isn't home now," she said. "I'm Liz, his daughter. Won't you come in?"

Mike nodded his head.

Later, when he thought of it, he couldn't remember exactly at what moment he had first fallen in love with her. He couldn't really remember much of anything except the way she looked, the way she smiled, the way she threw her head back when she laughed. It was a wonderful, contagious laugh. It made him feel so good that he wanted to laugh, too. It seemed that when Liz laughed, the whole world was happy.

In the weeks that followed, Mike and Liz saw each other every day.

One evening as Mike was leaving the Higgins home, Liz's father grabbed his arm and said, "Come on, Mike. Let's go to Cooper's and have a beer."

At Cooper's, as the bartender was filling their glasses, a thick loud voice from the other end of the bar rang out:

9

"Higgins, why don'cha come down here and drink with a real man."

Stillness settled over the saloon. Higgins looked calmly at the speaker. "I'm *with* a real man, Roone," he answered.

Roone swaggered toward Mike and Pat. "So says you. If he's a man, why don't he prove it? I'll bash his face in."

Higgins tried to push the fellow away. "Go home, Roone. You're drunk."

Mike hadn't said a word. He just kept drinking his beer slowly. When he finished, he took Higgins by the arm and said, "Let's get out of here."

Once outside, a worried Higgins tried to explain the demanding code of Keighry Head. "Mike, you'll never be able to live down the insult you just swallowed in there. The people of Keighry Head despise a coward. I don't blame you for not accepting Roone's challenge. He's a professional prize fighter. He's known as the heavy-weight champion of New Jersey. But I'm afraid the men in there won't be as understanding as I am."

Mike listened quietly. "I hate fighting," he said. Then he explained that before meeting Liz he had hoped some day to become a priest. He was now, he said, so much in love with Liz that he no longer knew his own mind. "What should I do, Mr. Higgins?"

"We'll see Father Floriene, Mike. He'll be in his rectory after Mass next Sunday. He can tell you what to do. In the meantime, don't mention a word of this to Liz."

Father Floriene listened attentively as Mike told his story. He explained what had happened at Cooper's saloon; he told of his feeling about fighting, of his spiritual desires—and of his love for Pat Higgins' daughter.

Father Floriene rose slowly from his chair. He clasped his hands behind his back and paced the floor. Then he stopped in front of Mike.

"There are many ways to serve God," he said. "I've no doubt you would have made a fine priest, for you have a sincere love for your fellow man. But the Lord must want you to serve him in other ways, or else he never would have sent you to Pat's daughter."

Father Floriene paused. He allowed a slow smile to appear on his kind face. "I can only help in spiritual battles," he said. "I'm sure if you ask the help of St. Michael, the Fighting Angel, he'll show you the way."

Mike's mind was at ease as he left the rectory. He knew what he had to do. Within a week, arrangements were made for a fight to the finish between Mike Walker and Pat Roone, winner take all. A fifteen-foot ring was roped off in the back room of Cooper's saloon. On the night of the fight, the place bulged with Keighry Head inhabitants. Both fighters were stripped to the waist. Cooper, the referee, called the fighters to the center of the ring. Then he gave the signal to start fighting.

Roone came forward with a rush, his arms swinging wildly. Mike stepped to one side, carefully measuring his opponent. Suddenly he let go with a right. The blow caught Roone flush on the chin. The sound of bone meeting bone was plain above the crowd's shouting. Roone fell flat on his face. His body quivered for a few seconds, then lay perfectly still. The crowd, so noisy a minute ago, stood silently watching. Thirty seconds passed and Roone still hadn't moved a muscle.

Mike lifted Roone and dragged him to his corner. As he turned to leave, Mike said quietly to Roone's second, "When he comes to, give him the purse."

Mike and Liz were married a few months later by Father Floriene.

I came along on July 13, 1901 . . . the first of three

11

children. Marie, my sister, was born a year later—a beautiful girl, like her mother, and as gay and full of life as Liz. We didn't have the blessing of her goodness long enough, though. In 1919 she drowned while swimming off the beach at Staten Island, New York. She was only seventeen.

Joseph was born in 1910, eight years after Marie. He's the solid one in the family; he is a graduate of Fordham University, where he studied law. Now he is Chairman of the New Jersey Boxing Commission and is Recreation Commissioner of the State.

The first thing I remember about myself was my long, golden curls. These curls were my mother's pride and joy. Mom spent more time on my hair than on her own. Each morning she would fuss with them, then dress me in a Little Lord Fauntleroy outfit and send me out to play. Her reasoning was odd. She thought I wouldn't get into fights in such an outfit. I'd have been better off if she had given me brass knuckles.

With my Irish mug, you can imagine how I looked. Those curls were everybody's target whenever I stepped out of the house. Somebody would always pull my curls and then, sure as hell, he'd get a punch in the nose.

I really blended into the Keighry Head scene—like a sore thumb—standing there in front of Cooper's saloon in a black velvet suit, white brocade collar, short pants, long curls . . . and a cigarette dangling from my lips. I was smoking at the age of seven.

I hated those curls but I had to wear them. I'd go out dressed immaculately, my curls carefully arranged, and in an hour I'd be back, my clothes torn, my face dirty and my hair in a mess. I know Pop didn't like the sissified way I was dressed but he never opened his mouth. The old man was a six-foot, two-hundred-twenty-pounder, but Mom was the boss.

He took me to a bricklayers' outing one Sunday afternoon and like all Irish picnics this one wound up in a riot. Pop got a bag on and got into a fight. Naturally, I got into it, too. I tried to help him by biting the leg of the nearest guy but wound up being heaved into a large tub that had held the iced beer. The ice, by that time, had melted and the water came over my head. My suit, brand new for the occasion, shrank and the belt became a necktie. We took a trolley home and Pop warned me to watch out for Mother. He knew he'd get hell from her for getting drunk in public and not taking care of me.

We got off at Reade and Magnolia, several blocks from our house, and walked the rest of the way home. The old boy could hardly navigate on his own and I had a heck of a time holding him up. We had just reached Henry Street, around the corner from where we lived, when who should spot us but Mom. She hadn't lived with Pop all those years without knowing every one of his tricks.

Taking the whole thing in at one glance, she made a beeline for us, grabbed Pop and spun him around. Holding him up with one hand, she lifted up her skirts a bit with the other, raised her right foot, and planted her shoe with the pointed toe right on Pop's fanny.

"Look what you've done to Edward's curls," she screamed.

Poor Pop. He didn't mind the kick so much. It was the laughing and jeering of the boys on Cooper's Corner that really shamed him. He stayed away from the saloon for a week.

CHAPTER TWO

I went to Sacred Heart School, where I was a better-than-average student but hardly a delight to the Sisters. I had a trigger temper and the minute one of the other kids would say or do something I didn't like, I'd haul off and hit him on the chin.

Mother Regina, the principal, was very understanding, even when she punished me with a few flicks across the knuckles with her pointer or ruler. More often, she'd look at me in that wise, all-knowing way of hers, smile tolerantly and say:

"Please, Edward, no more fights."

I kept getting in trouble, however, and one day she decided that maybe the curls were the reason. So she took me into her office and sheared them off with a big pair of scissors. I was happy but Mom was furious. She was going to beat Mother Regina's brains out, nun or no nun.

The cure didn't work. I kept brawling. I guess I had gotten into the habit. Mother Regina would call me into her office, time after time, and tell me I was getting a reputation as a troublemaker. How she knew every time I got into a fight I never found out, but after each one, there I would be in her office trying to give an explanation.

Somehow, I could never lie to her. Not that I was above lying, but I sensed that she'd see through any lie I might tell.

"Can't you see where all this is leading you, Edward?" she would plead with me. "Once you get a reputation as a fighter, anyone else who wants to make the same reputation will challenge you. You'll spend the rest of your life fighting."

It turned out she was right. I became the toughest kid in a very tough neighborhood. And when a challenger from another neighborhood wanted to muscle in on Keighry Head to show *how* tough he was, my pals—all tough guys themselves—chose me to fight the challenger. I seldom lost.

My best pal, in those growing-up days, was Oliver Petrie. He used to cheat in crap games and I had to save his neck. As soon as somebody challenged him, I'd step in and put the guy to sleep. I found out then how hard I could hit. The crap games and the fights were endless.

I would not steal money. That I considered a sin. I never went along with some of the others who broke into stores or robbed people. I wasn't afraid. It's just that I wasn't a thief. Once, years later, I had to make a choice between fighting a guy for ten bucks or taking a thousand dollars to stick up a bootlegger. At that time, a grand was all the money in the world to me—but I fought the guy to get a tenner, instead.

Keighry Head was 90 percent Irish but there was one Jewish family, the Sampsons. Mrs. Sampson ran a grocery store on Bond Street next to a bakery owned by an Irishman, John Cullen. We had a law: Never steal from Mrs. Sampson. That was because she sold groceries to our folks on trust. We called it "tick." She never pressed for the money. She could leave her bread box wide open and we'd never touch a thing. But sure as hell we'd rob Cullen clean out—if he left his showcase open.

15

For some reason, I never thought of that as stealing.

Cullen's cakes were delivered in a horse and wagon by Hartman's Bakery. While the driver was making a delivery in the store, five or six of us would raid the wagon and swipe as many cakes as we could carry. One day, the driver took longer than usual and we just about cleaned out the wagon.

We had to pass Cooper's Corner on the way home and the neighborhood loafers there grabbed us and took away our loot. Ten minutes after devouring the goodies, those oafs were sick, doubled up in pain. All were stricken with diarrhea. The driver had set a trap for us, loading the cakes with jallop, which was a 1912 version of a Mickey Finn. I laughed my head off watching those big, tough weisenheimers crying with pain and crawling on their knees—and begging to be next in Cooper's john.

Through the years I've been mixed up with the worst kind of mobsters and hoods, but I've never carried a knife or gun. I think I know why. It stems from an experience I had around 1910. There was a place in Keighry Head which was a camping ground for hobos and it was called The Dumps. There was a freight yard nearby, where these bums would drop off every day to gather in The Dumps.

There was one mean customer, a sandy-haired, skinny guy with an evil face and droopy mustache. We later called him "Jack the Ripper" because he got into a fight with another bum and, when he was taking a good pasting, pulled a knife and ripped open the other man's stomach.

This happened in a field near where we were playing baseball. Most of the kids ran away in fright but three of us tried to help the poor victim, once Jack had left. We dragged him three blocks looking for a doctor but

16

he was bleeding terribly and crying for a priest. So we dragged him to the church, only to have him die in our hands on the steps to the rectory. The priest rushed out and gave him the last rites.

The police questioned all the witnesses but we stuck to the code of the neighborhood and wouldn't squeal: nobody knew a thing. But Jack the Ripper disappeared completely from the face of the earth, and I've always believed that Keighry Head caught up with him and dumped him into Wilde's pond.

We used to go swimming in a creek called The Hole, during the summer vacation. It was about five miles from Cooper's Corner and we walked both ways. One day, as a practical joke, I pushed Cheese Kennedy's brother Joe into the creek when he was sitting on the bank. Joe began to flounder in the water, bobbing up and down.

"Save him, Mickey!" Cheese yelled. "He can't swim . . . Save him!"

I jumped in and with Cheese's help, managed to get Joe ashore. The minute he reached safety, he ran all the way home naked—not even stopping to pick up his clothes. The next day I was on the carpet before Mother Regina, who dealt with her boys even when they did wrong things during vacation. I had a hard time convincing her that it was only a joke and that I wasn't trying to drown Joe.

I was twelve when I pulled my first important "deal." A guy named Big George hired about twenty of us kids to distribute circulars advertising soaps and household goods. Big George was always around Cooper's Corner, wearing a derby hat and a big sparkler in his tie. He never was without a fat cigar which sat rakishly under his handlebar mustache.

I got a quarter for delivering the circulars and for six

weeks did a profitable business. I'd sneak around the corner and throw them down the sewer. I had just finished disposing of a batch one day, when a huge shadow loomed over me. I looked up and saw my father.

"What are you doing?" Mike wanted to know.

I told him and was kind of proud of myself for out-witting Big George. I bragged about it.

"Well, you'll have to give back all the money," Pop said. "That's out-and-out cheating."

Funny, I hadn't considered it dishonest—just smart business. I had long since spent the quarters and knew I'd have to work to pay them back. Fortunately, my troubles were washed away two days later when a big rainstorm came up and flooded Spring Street. Thousands of circulars were swimming all over the neighborhood. The other kids had "delivered" theirs the same way. But Big George turned out to be a bigger cheater than the rest of us. He had been allotted two dollars a week for each boy and was giving us only a quarter.

The police charged him with contributing to unsanitary conditions in the city and he pleaded guilty at the trial. He knew he wouldn't be safe in Keighry Head if he put the blame on the boys.

I don't remember ever being a kid. I always seemed to have problems. At twelve, I was a man, with a man's problems and a man's decisions to make. One of those had to be made when I was fighting Patty Donahue and it served as a yardstick in life for me ever after.

Patty was seventeen and was thinking of the prize ring. He had moved to Keighry Head from another neighborhood where he was used to shoving smaller kids around, and the first thing he did was to look for the kid who was supposed to be able to lick his weight in wildcats. He had heard of the Keighry Head tradition, and he laughed when I was pointed out as the boy he had to fight.

"That's the big, tough guy I came over here to give a licking to?" he sneered. "Why, he's just a baby."

Jimmy Gleason stepped out from our group. "You're a fresh bastard," he said. "Don't worry. We'll get someone bigger for you to fight."

I made up my mind in a flash. Nobody was going to fight for me. My right hand was already on its way before I even got to Patty Donahue. It landed flush on his jaw—and the greatest street fight of my life had begun.

After five minutes of toe-to-toe slugging, a large crowd gathered. Men and women ran from their porches and poured out of stores and saloons. Mike, my dad, was one of them. He stood on the side, watching.

Fifteen minutes passed . . . twenty minutes. Patty and I kept swinging. We were both getting very tired; our wallops were losing force. We were both bloody and I was sick and dizzy. I had no more power in my blows and was about to pass out. Maybe I would have taken the first excuse to do so if Patty hadn't said, "Do you want to quit?"

Quit? Me quit? Never! Patty's words seemed to give me new strength. I knew he felt as awful as I did—and I'd been looking for a chance to get out of the fight. I bent over and, with what strength I had left, rammed my right fist into his belly.

The breath seemed to squoosh out of him. He crumpled slowly to the ground and lay still. I stood wavering over him, fighting to keep from falling at his side. Suddenly I felt Mike's hand on my shoulder. The crowd moved back and made a path for Mike and me and we walked slowly down Magnolia Avenue, his arm on my shoulder.

At Sacred Heart, I managed to resist the teachers until the eighth grade before being expelled for good. It was examination time, a week before graduation. I sat in the back of the room at a little table and chair all my own. I had no desk because Sister Anselma kept me apart from the other kids, believing I'd get in less trouble. Some people are born that way, she used to say . . . always the center of controversy, no matter what they do.

On this particular day, we were supposed to draw a map of South America and, since I liked drawing, I was working away carefully when Leon Griffin, who sat in front of me, whispered over, asking to see my map. Even in those days, they could see that I was pretty fair in the drawing department.

Sister Anselma, who could hear a mummy breathe, caught Leon cold. She stormed down the aisle and belted him on the nose, striking him with her ring. Whomp! The blood spurted out.

Leon grabbed his bloody beak and when he saw all the red stuff in his hand, screamed, "I'm bleeding to death, I'm bleeding to death!"

The whole thing struck me so funny that I let out a roar. Sister Anselma headed for me. Meanwhile, Leon leaped out of his seat to run out the door. She stopped, undecided which kid to go after, then started toward him. By this time, the whole class was roaring.

Emily Riley sat up front. She was the brightest kid in the class. With the Sister out of the room, I figured this was a good time to compare my drawing with hers. I bent over her desk and Joe Easton, a kid from my block, took his pen and jammed the point into my rear end.

"Ouch! My ass!" I shouted, jumping a foot high. As I came down, facing the door, there stood Sister Anselma with Mother Regina. Their faces were blazing red. The room was in an uproar.

"Get your books and leave this classroom immediately," Sister Anselma ordered. "And don't come back!"

After that, Mother Regina informed my parents that I was enough to try the patience of a saint and—since there were no saints teaching at Sacred Heart School—I was expelled. I didn't care because I thought I'd had enough school. I didn't even accept Mother Regina's invitation to return for the graduation exercises.

Although I was booted out, I never had any grievance against the Sisters. I liked them and I think they liked me, too. Years later, even after all my divorces, I went back to visit those of them who were still alive and I was welcome. Some of the Sisters are now at a private school on Elizabeth's North Broad Street.

During my fighting days I made it a point to visit Mother Regina every time I came back to Elizabeth after a bout. I always welcomed her wise counsel. She had a great influence on my life. I felt a personal loss when she died. I loved her. In her own way, she was just as much of a fighter as anybody in Keighry Head.

So is Sister Anselma. She is Mother Anselma now, at the same private school. I always feel purified after a visit with her. I'll never forget the first time I went back to see her after winning the welterweight championship of the world. It was seven years after she told me never to come back.

"Edward," she said, "I just knew you were going to be a champion fighter some day."

CHAPTER THREE

I took expulsion from school in stride, but my folks didn't. I was fourteen at the time, so Mike figured that if school didn't agree with me, maybe work would. He talked it over with Uncle Daniel Higgins, who was head of the firm of Higgins and Eggers, Architects, on Fifth Avenue. Uncle Dan was a fine architect and they hoped that architecture might be in the family blood . . . mine, anyway.

He placed me in the architectural office of George B. Post and Company, at 101 Park Avenue. I began as an errand boy at thirty dollars a month and my immediate superior was a Mr. Houston, the office boss. To supplement my daytime learning, I was sent—balking like a steer—to the Mechanics Institute in the evenings. I endured this day-and-night deal for over two years and have always considered that the lowest point in my life. Release came in a manner you might expect.

I'd been with Post about a year and a half when I was promoted to a job which called for filling in drawings, which actually is part of a draftsman's work. Six months later, I passed an exam to enter night school at Columbia University.

I hated the job but didn't dare quit. Dad thought it was a great opportunity. I suppose it was, but I couldn't see it that way even when I did make progress within the company.

I never had any money. I used to give my entire salary

to Mom. She'd let me have fifteen cents a day for lunch and pay my train fare.

To save money, I'd walk blocks to where I could get lunch for a nickel (a sandwich for three cents and coffee for two). Sometimes, when I'd gotten enough dimes saved up that way, I'd play hooky from work and have dates. Babe Moser was my first girl, a pretty blonde. We met at a movie in Elizabeth when I was fifteen. I couldn't afford many dates though, with no money. Anyway, between work and night school, I usually didn't get home to Elizabeth until ten o'clock each night.

Babe and I enjoyed the movies together. No talkies then . . . the silents. My favorites were Douglas Fairbanks, William S. Hart, Harold Lloyd, Charlie Chaplin and Viola Dana.

Another coincidence: Babe later married Joe Orsini, brother and manager of Dominic Orsini, the first boy I ever fought as a professional.

I never thought much about girls until I was a teenager and found out that in order to be important, you had to have a girl. All the big boys had girls.

When I started working, I was a "dese, dem and dose" guy. I picked up polish and my diction and grammar improved. Also I was really coming along as a junior architect. In my third year with Post, I had my own table and was one of forty draftsmen. One morning, a short, muscular fellow named Weisberger called me over, handed me a milk bottle and a dime and said, "Walker, go out and get me a dime's worth of radium."

"Right you are, sir . . . be right back," I sang out and left for nowhere in particular to get the stuff. I had never heard of radium but that made no difference. I went from store to store, drug stores, groceries, hardware stores. The merchants went along with the gag, telling me they were fresh out, or that they were cooking up some or they weren't handling it any more. Finally, one druggist sent me to the drug store in Grand Central Terminal with the assurance that they always had it.

Then I knew I was being taken. That had been the first place I'd gone to. I was tired and disgusted and felt like a fool. When I got back to the office with the empty milk bottle, the other draftsmen began to laugh. Weisberger had let them in on the joke. I didn't think it was funny and floored Weisberger with a right hook to the chin. He made a loud noise as he hit the floor, but he quickly bounced up again. Weisberger's name isn't in the ring record books as an opponent of mine but he was as game as most I've met. He walloped me on the nose, bringing blood. Then Mr. Houston came in and stopped the fight.

He led me to the office of Mr. Post. There were actually three Post brothers. They conferred, and then the head brother came over to me and said, "Mickey, we'll have to discharge you. We cannot have anyone in our employ who settles things with his fists."

"That's okay with me," I said. "Just give me a letter to my parents. I don't want them to think I quit."

Actually, another of the brothers, realizing I wasn't entirely wrong, came over and said they'd take me back if I'd quit fighting. "Oh, no," I pleaded. "I've got another job."

I beat it out of there before he found out I was lying.

It was 1918. I was seventeen then. The United States was at war and I wanted to join up. I wanted to join the Navy because I believed those posters about joining the Navy and seeing the world. At the recruiting station, I

24

told them I was eighteen—the legal minimum—but they said I looked younger and would have to have my parents' approval. Mom wouldn't give it, and I was out of luck. Many years later, I tried to enlist again in another war and was again turned down—too old.

There were lots of jobs open and I had many in the next six months. I usually got into a fight and was fired. I worked at a leather goods factory in Elizabeth, and during an argument with a big fellow named Teddy, I conked him with a left hook and broke my hand. The floor was concrete, and his head hit it hard. When he came to, he told the boss I'd hit him with an ax or some instrument. I showed them my busted mitt and said, "No ax. Just my hand."

The boss didn't believe me and the next morning I was reading the Help Wanted signs.

My next job involved not an ax but a sledge hammer. I went to work on Staten Island, at Berley's Shipyard, where there was a fierce rivalry between the men from Elizabeth and those from Staten Island.

A rigger named Eddie McGill, who was a professional fighter, decided to needle the freckle-faced newcomer. He pulled a couple of gags to annoy and embarrass me. I told him to lay off, or I'd knock him into the middle of next week.

He accepted my challenge and we agreed to settle it in front of the shipyard after we knocked off work. Eddie was fighting prelims around Staten Island but I didn't know it—not that it would have made any difference.

Word of the fight got around and the Staten Islanders figured he'd teach me a lesson. There must have been five thousand men working there; it was one of the biggest shipyards in the East. Almost all of them were on hand to see this bare-fisted battle.

It lasted about fifteen minutes before I knocked McGill flat on his back and left him gazing up into the Staten Island sky.

The next day, I was down in the bow of a ship fitting in what they called a liner. It is a wedge-shaped piece of steel about a foot long, and four or five inches wide on the broad side. It fits in where the big iron sheets overlap and helps to make the hull tight. Each one weighed about ten pounds. While I was down there, one of them was dropped on my head.

I was knocked down but not out. They took me to a doctor who bandaged my head and sent me home. The Elizabeth boys heard that one of Eddie's Staten Islanders had dropped it, and a riot between the two factions resulted. The company officer blamed me and I was fired. He said I was impeding the progress of the war.

After that, I got a job in Moore's Shipyard in Elizabeth as a "heater." One day a big ironworker knocked over my forge, causing the coals to fall on me and burn my legs. I shouted at him and he sneered, "Hey, kid, keep out of the way of men who're trying to work."

I let him have it right on the chin and he hit the deck like a clap of thunder. They dragged him to the hospital and I was given the sack. I was making $110 a week then —twice as much as I had ever made before—and I hated to lose that job. Actually, it turned out to be a great break. If I hadn't gotten fired, I might have made shipbuilding my trade and never gotten into the prize ring.

At the time, of course, I couldn't know that. I was out of work. That was all that mattered. The war had just ended, which made it even tougher for me to get a job.

The streets were full of doughboys, all in the same spot I was . . . looking for work. What chance did I have? Everybody was still singing "Over There" and waving the Red, White and Blue. The boys in khaki were still heroes and I was just a punk civilian kid.

I was out of work for almost a year. There just weren't any jobs. The idleness got me down. I felt useless, unwanted. I had very little money and that hurt, too. I was disgusted and blue.

I became a neighborhood loafer. Mom, a regular guy, was considerate of her "poor Edward," but the old man kept hounding me to find work. It burned him up to see me hanging around the house. To avoid arguments, I started killing time with the boys around Cooper's Corner.

On a cold March day in 1919, I was feeling fed up with everything. No job, no money, no future. What's going to become of me, I wondered. I thought of the jobs I'd had—four in less than a year—and I'd blown them all. I was a hot-head, but not a troublemaker. Yet trouble always seemed to be around me.

I thought of this as I leaned against a lamppost on Cooper's Corner, smoking a cigarette. Where do I go from here? I thought. A large colored advertising poster in Cooper's window attracted me. I walked over for a closer look. The sign read: "All-Star Boxing, Forester Athletic Club."

Underneath, in smaller print but in bright red, it listed the names of the main-event boxers.

That gave me an idea. Why not become a fighter? I'd always been quick with my fists.

I recalled Mother Regina's words during one of those times when she'd tried to straighten me out.

27

*Can't you see where all this is leading . . . You'll spend
the rest of your life fighting . . .*

Fighting?

Why not? I loved to fight. There was money in it and
I sure needed dough. Why not take a shot at it? Why not
get paid for fighting?

I read the poster again. This was to be the first legal
boxing card in Elizabeth. The State of New Jersey had
just passed a bill to legalize professional boxing. They'd
had some boxing bouts in Newark but they were amateur
four-rounders. Now they were going to have eight-round
professional fights.

Always impulsive, I made up my mind I was going to
be a boxer and put my fighting on a business basis.

I flipped away my cigarette and turned to the fellows
with me.

"Hey, you guys," I almost shouted. "I'm going to be a
fighter, a real prize fighter."

Up to this time, I had never seen a prize fight in my
life, although I followed the fight game in the papers.
Jack Dempsey, then heavyweight champion of the world,
had been my idol ever since he knocked out the giant
Jess Willard for the title. At the time I stood five feet, six
inches and weighed 118 pounds. Although I probably belonged in the featherweight class, I didn't look like a little
man. I had the shoulders and the arms of a heavyweight.
I even looked like a fighter, with my pug nose and heavy
jaw.

When I went home for supper I told my mother about
my idea. "All right," she said, "if you think you can fight.
But don't let your father know."

I borrowed some money from Mom and bought a pair
of boxing gloves, shoes and a few other things I needed.

Mom sewed up a pair of black tights for me. Those hand-made black tights became my luck charm. I never fought without them. In all my fights I refused to wear any but this old pair of black tights. In later years, I patched them up and sewed them together, but I would no more think of entering the ring without them than I would think of fighting Jack Dempsey with one hand behind my back. I always kept them in my private gymnasium in back of my house. I think I would have killed anyone who attempted to steal them. They still are my most precious possession.

There used to be a Commission ruling in New York which required one man to wear black tights, red belt and red side stripes down the thighs. I had a red belt stitched at the top of those old tights for the heavyweight championship battle with Jack Sharkey at Ebbets Field. Jack wore the purple colors with the blue belt. I also wore a sweater my mother knitted for me, a purple sweater buttoned to the top. I wore it going into the ring in place of a robe. When I retired I gave it to one of Jack Kearns's fighters as a good luck charm and wished him the same luck I had had with it. The poor guy got knocked out in the first round of his first fight.

All set now, I waded into something I knew nothing about. I got advice from various guys in the neighborhood. We had some good fighters at that time in Keighry Head. For instance, they told me I had to train. I never did like training, although later I had intensive training under careful management. I couldn't see much sense in training for a few rounds of boxing. Gosh, didn't I fight for an hour at a time in the street? But soon I was to learn the difference between the two kinds of fighting.

I went to the YMCA on East Jersey Street with another

fighter, Jimmy McCann, who was training for a comeback. I got the low-down from him. I didn't know what to do in a gym. I just stood there, in my new shoes and tights, watching the other fellows train. I felt lost. I recognized Georgie Ward, Willie Davis and others. The Y was filled with fight fans watching the boys work out, as prize fighting was something new in Elizabeth.

A man came over and asked if I would box with his brother. I was just his weight, he said, about 118 pounds.

"Sure," I said.

I was nervous when I climbed into the ring but I wasn't afraid. Seconds after they had put the gloves on me I got hit on the chin with a right hand. I went down, more surprised than hurt. I lost all self-consciousness. I got up and let everything go, to make up for my ignorance of boxing.

The spectators thought they were at a real fight. They cheered us on. It was real, as far as I was concerned. I tore into my opponent and knocked him down with a left hook to the chin. As soon as he got up, the YMCA physical instructor, a fellow named Wilfred McCann (later New Jersey Boxing Commissioner), jumped into the ring and made us take the gloves off.

"There'll be no grudge fighting here," he growled.

It was not until then that I was introduced to the boy with whom I had just finished boxing. I recognized his name, Dominic Orsini. I had read of his fights in Staten Island.

The matchmaker from the Forester Athletic Club in Elizabeth was in the audience. He was a former fighter named Howard Smith, and he had fought against Abe Attell, the featherweight champion of the world. He came down to the shower room and asked me if I would fight Orsini for him.

"My card is filled for next Monday," he said, "but it's the first fight night in Elizabeth. I want to give 'em their money's worth. I'll put you on as an added special."

He said he'd pay me ten dollars. It was to be a four-rounder. Georgie Ward, my friend, was fighting in the feature bout. That Monday night the Keighry Head fans gathered on Cooper's Corner and marched down the middle of the street to Elizabeth Port, where the fight was to take place. We were three hundred strong.

Orsini came from an Italian section called Peterstown. Of all the neighborhoods in Elizabeth, the two strongest rivals were Keighry Head and Peterstown. It looked like there would be plenty of fighting—and not all of it in the ring. The excited residents of Keighry Head shouted that one Irishman could lick five Italians, and the people of Peterstown swore their favorite could take on all the Micks, one each night. The two Elizabeth papers, the *Journal* and the *Times*, gave our fight more space than they gave the feature bout. The police sent down reinforcements in case of a riot.

My first fight almost didn't come off. The fight club had distributed posters advertising the star bout (Georgie Ward vs. I-forget-who) and the "Elizabeth Thunderbolt" Mickey Walker vs. Dominic Orsini. My father, whose name was Mickey Walker, too, of course, never saw those posters until one day on Broad Street when he was going to work and met a friend.

"For shame, Mike," said the friend, "a man of your age goin' in for fightin'. Achone! If I hadn't seen it on the billboard with my own eyes, I never would have believed it."

31

My father was the strongest man I have ever known but the most easygoing. "Patrick," he replied, "you're either drunk or crazy. I haven't had a fight in twenty years, and you know it."

"Then tell me," demanded Pat, "why should they have your name plastered all over town? 'Mickey Walker' it says in letters as big as your hand. What did they call you? The 'Elizabeth Thunderbolt.' Come with me. I'll show you the billboard in the window of Turley's saloon."

So they went down to look at the poster. Mike read it and light dawned on him.

"It must be Edward," he said.

My father didn't go to work that day. He turned around and came straight home. He had several things to say to his son and none of them were pleasant. I was out of the house doing some road work, but he sat down and waited. I got a couple of steps into the house, breathing hard from running, and there was my father.

"I'll have a few words with you," Pop said. "Is it you that is being the Elizabeth Thunderbolt?"

"Gee, Pop, *I* didn't make it up . . ."

"You go right to these people and tell them that no son of Michael Patrick Walker will ever become a professional prize fighter!"

I started to protest but Mom came to my rescue. "If the lad wants to fight," she said quietly, "he ought to have the chance. Besides, nobody can beat our Edward, Father."

Pop hesitated. "Well, since he's already promised this fight," he conceded. Turning to me, he said more sternly, "Now, my little thunderbolt, we won't say any more. As long as you've signed for the fight, you'll have to go through with it. But it's your last fight. And you'd better win because if you lose, you'll get a worse licking from me."

I let out a whoop of delight. "Don't worry, Pop," I said. "I'll win, all right."

CHAPTER FOUR

My first fight for money! I'll never forget it. Orsini versus Walker. There it was on the big poster stuck on the corner street post. Peterstown versus Keighry Head. The city of Elizabeth was our oyster. As we were marching down Broad Street, Jimmy McCann started talking.

"Listen, Mickey," he said, "you oughta have a manager."

"What's a manager?" I asked.

"A manager," said Jimmy, "is a feller who handles you, keeps track of you, looks after your interests."

"Okay," I said, "get me a manager."

Outside the fight club Jimmy met a friend named Oscar Lamb and elected him my manager. This Lamb fellow, a short guy in his thirties, was trying to crash the gate. He agreed to be my manager, probably because it meant he wouldn't have to pay his way in to see the fight. It didn't matter to me who was my manager. All I was interested in was fighting. It didn't take Oscar any time at all to take over. I was eating raisins when we were introduced. As I shook his hand with my right, I shoved some raisins down with my left.

"What're you doin' with them raisins?" Oscar asked, still shaking my hand.

"Oh, my mother read in a book on health foods that raisins are good for the wind. She loaded me down with three boxes before I left the house."

Oscar grabbed the raisins. "You must be nuts," he said, "eating them things before a fight."

My new manager took me down to the dressing room and put me through his rigmarole. I did everything he said. About ten minutes before the fight, he laid me out on a table, poured some liquid on me and started to rub me with it. The stuff burned like fire. "Hey," I screamed, "what are you doing?"

"Quiet," Oscar ordered. "I am rubbing you down, like all the best fighters."

"What's this stuff?" I asked. "It burns like hell."

"This is my secret formula," Oscar declared.

I got to do what my manager tells me, I thought, but this stuff burns. When he got it all over me, I couldn't lie still.

That first fight lasted only twelve minutes, but it seemed like twelve years. It was the first bout of the evening. The first round wasn't so bad, but in the second I started to sweat in earnest and Oscar's secret formula kept running into my open pores. I had to do a marathon around the ring to cool off. I was afraid it would get into my eyes and blind me. At the same time, I was feeling sick in the stomach from the raisins.

It was a good fight and I won the "newspaper" decision. In those days fights were not judged. Barring a knockout, there was no official winner. The majority opinion of the reporters covering the fight determined the winner.

In the third round, I had Orsini groggy when suddenly I heard a noise of broken glass and a shower of it came

34

tumbling down into the ring. My mother had followed far behind the crowd, climbed onto the roof of the club and set up a one-woman claque on the skylight directly over the ring.

Women weren't permitted to attend fights in Elizabeth in those days. But Liz found a way. She literally "crashed the gate."

She had managed to restrain herself through the first two rounds, but when I had a chance to knock out Orsini in the third, she just couldn't control herself any longer. She began to swing her arms, trying to help me. One of the wild swings connected with the window and sent the glass crashing down on the ring. The cops had to climb up and help Mom off the roof.

Pop didn't go to the fight. In fact, he never saw me in the ring until after I had won the welterweight championship. Even when he went, he would duck out during the fighting and come back between rounds. On the other hand, Mom went to many of my fights. She loved them and was my biggest and loudest booster.

I licked Orsini but when the bout ended, I expected trouble. I thought for sure there'd be a riot. Instead, the Peterstown gang joined the Keighry Head boys in cheering Mickey Walker. They adopted me as their own and became great fans of mine from then on. After all, weren't we all from Elizabeth?

I was a sick champ, though, after the fight. Going down to the dressing room, my manager was all excited over my victory. "Boy, oh boy," he said, "you got the makings of a champion in you."

"Say," I said, "what is your secret formula made of?"

Oscar grinned. He held up the bottle so I could see the label.

"Horse liniment," I read.

"We're gonna make you a champ," Oscar said.

"You're fired," I said. He left, and I got undressed and went under the shower. Pretty soon he came back. "I got our dough," he called out. "Our dough?" I repeated. "You mean *my* dough. Hand it over."

Oscar took some money out of his pocket and counted out eight dollars. "Hey," I complained, "I was promised ten dollars for the fight. Where's the rest of it?"

"Well, kid," he said, "ain't I your manager? Those two bucks are my cut."

No sooner were the words out of his mouth than he made a dash for the door. He had seen the look on my face. I dropped the towel I was drying myself with and tore after him. He headed out of the building and into the street.

What a picture that must have been, me chasing him down Broad Street without any clothes on! I never got those two bucks back, and I never saw Oscar Lamb again.

Keighry Head was wilder than usual that night. My pals had backed me against Orsini and went right to Cooper's Corner and other saloons to celebrate. They spent their winnings and then some, toasting Mickey Walker, the Elizabeth Thunderbolt. There was just one thing missing—me.

Not that it mattered much to them. They were out to get plastered and they did. This was the last year of legal drinking in the United States for many years. The Volstead Act had been passed by Congress in January and was to go into effect the following year, January 16, 1920. That was the Eighteenth Amendment—Prohibition.

It was like giving the Cooper's Corner crowd a Mickey Finn. Keighry Head without a saloon? No booze on Saturday nights? No joints where the gang could hang out? It was like a funeral which had no ending.

Prohibition meant nothing to me. At eighteen, I had never even tasted hard liquor. We always had beer around the house and as kids we used to take a sip or two with permission from Liz. I didn't even drink much beer after I had grown up.

Looking back, I really can't tell you the real reason why I didn't drink then. I just never had the urge. I didn't care if others did. Perhaps it was because I was a good athlete and felt I should stay in condition. It was bad enough that I smoked. That habit I'd had almost before I started school and I've never shaken it.

I was in no mood for any kind of celebrating that night, anyway. I was sick. The upset stomach from the raisins, the burning skin from the horse liniment, the whims of a fight manager . . . eight dollars wasn't enough for that ordeal. I didn't care if I ever saw another boxing glove.

But the next day I read the papers. Mom had gone out and brought back the *Times* and *Journal*. My name was on top of the sports page in letters an inch high. The stories described my footwork in the ring as the speediest seen in years. They didn't know that I was just trying to cool off. My fight got the headlines over the main bout.

Gone was the burning sensation. My stomach felt better. My father didn't thunderbolt me. Those big headlines softened him up a little. People regarded me in a different light. They looked at me with new respect. The kids pointed me out. All of a sudden Mickey Walker was somebody. Maybe those boxing gloves had something, after all.

I was ready to fight again.

This is where my Uncle Daniel Higgins stepped in again. He had seen the fight. He was a fine architect but he was also a good judge of boxing and boxers. When he was the State amateur featherweight and lightweight champion, the smart managers tried to get him to turn professional, but he boxed only for sport.

Uncle Daniel thought I had possibilities. He insisted I go under the wing of Johnny Anthes, a former amateur all-round athlete. He and Uncle Dan had run in long-distance races with Longboat, the great Indian runner, and Durando, the Olympic champion. At the time, Anthes had a confectionery store on Spring Street and he also had the newspaper route for Elizabeth.

If a fighter can be made, Johnny Anthes made me one. He took over and watched me like a mother hen. He watched my training, my food, my habits, my everything. He watched me closer than my own mother. He made sure I did road work, running ten miles a day; sometimes he ran with me, himself.

Every afternoon, Johnny would take me into the back room of his confectionery store and teach me the finer points of boxing. He saw I had a natural left hook and he worked with me for hours to perfect that hook. It was my best punch.

My ability to hit hard with my left came about through an accident. I was about ten or eleven when Ed Malone and I hitched a ride on the back of a milk wagon as it was passing Cooper's Corner. I jumped off right in the path of a moving motorcycle and was thrown sky high. I wound up in the hospital with a broken collarbone.

My ambition then was to be a major league baseball player. I was in a cast for a couple of months, and I had a terrible fear that my right arm would be useless. So I started to develop my left. I started throwing and batting left-handed. I got so I could throw left-handed as well as right-handed. That, I'm sure, is what gave me that good left hook in the ring.

Uncle Daniel had Anthes draw up a contract—Johnny was the only manager I ever had a contract with—but it was never needed. We were great pals and remained so until Johnny died in 1956. If a fighter and his manager aren't pals . . . what's a contract?

My first fight under Anthes was with a champion, the featherweight champ of New Jersey. His name was Jimmy McCran, not to be confused with my old pal, Jimmy McCann. This fellow knew me from the shipyard.

"Mickey Walker?" he sneered. "I'll teach him a lesson for even thinking of fighting the New Jersey champ. I'll murder him."

My first fight under a real manager . . . it felt good. Made me feel important. I was beginning to feel my oats.

It took me two rounds to put the Jersey champ in a flat position. Now I was really getting somewhere. My name was in the Jersey papers; even the big Newark papers were giving me some space. I was the featherweight champ of New Jersey, and my hat was getting too small for me. It was a great feeling while it lasted. But it didn't last long. Just until my next fight.

I was getting very popular around Elizabeth. It was something that came home to me, something I had always looked for. It felt great. Popularity! It's a thrill that is difficult to explain. It's a feeling of importance a man gets from being successful, a feeling of being someone special. You feel it when people recognize you and give you a big hello or a cheer everywhere you go. While you're fighting, you long for that stuff. You think it's important. The public spoils you. And like most fighters, I took the applause seriously.

I loved to have someone yell, "There's Mickey Walker! Hi, Mickey, old boy!" And in no time I'd be buying drinks all around. I was young and tough and I didn't know that the guy who cheered me after I won the title would give me the brushoff when I lost it.

Now Uncle Joe Higgins took me in hand. He became my trainer and took it upon himself to teach me how to box. He didn't know a left jab from a right hook but he could punch. We used to box every night. Everything would go along all right until he hit me a hard blow. Then I would tear into him and really slug it out. Once I hit him on the nose and flattened it.

Uncle Joe was a handsome man, and those bouts with me didn't do his looks any good. He was a cute one, though. It didn't look right for the nephew to lick the uncle, so whenever I'd have him groggy, he'd stop the fight saying, "Aw, Mickey, you're not doing it right. Won't you ever learn?"

Uncle Joe's training methods were a little crude, but they helped put a strong foundation under me for my tough fights later on.

Overnight I had become the best drawing card around Elizabeth because of my following. Matchmaker Smith wanted me to fight for him. Anthes, realizing how much I was in demand, asked for one hundred dollars. Smith argued I wasn't that good, that I didn't rate so much money because of my lack of experience, but Anthes insisted. Forced to yield to Johnny's demands, Smith went out and got a real tough opponent to fight me: Phil Delmont. The boy had sixteen knockouts out of seventeen fights.

Talk about being overmatched. I barely lasted a round. A right punch put me on the floor and the referee had reached the count of eight when the bell rang. The minute's rest between rounds seemed more like a second. I hardly heard the gong starting the second round. It sounded like it was miles away. I was trying to get up to fight but my manager wouldn't let me. It was ruled a first-round technical knockout.

It was a terrible letdown for me, after being a big shot for a couple of weeks. I was really deflated. But I had no thought of stopping. I was even more determined to become a fighter.

In a small way I got back at Delmont. In his next fight, he was knocked out by a fellow named Lou Urban. Smith, still sore at Anthes, matched me with Urban. I knocked him out. That was some sort of vindication, I felt.

Years later, at the Astor Hotel in New York, I was the guest speaker at a sports dinner. A fellow came over to the head table. "You don't remember me," he said. I looked him over carefully. "Sure," I said, "your face is very familiar . . ."

"Well, it ought to be." This fellow grinned. "I'm only the guy that once knocked you out. The name's Delmont."

Johnny Anthes and I were partners for a couple of years. Johnny was wise enough to know that at first I needed plenty of seasoning, and for a while I fought almost every week. He never overmatched me again. All my early fights were for six rounds, and except for Delmont he picked my opponents carefully. I seldom lost one.

Finally, though, he took a chance and matched me with a guy named Benny Cohen, who was being groomed for the lightweight championship. The fight took place in Newark in 1920. Cohen was a knockout king in his own right and the fight was a slam-bang affair. Benny wasn't letting his chance at the lightweight crown go to an

Irishman—not without giving it all he had, anyway. We were both on the floor a couple of times. Cohen knew how to handle himself and he could hit, too. At first I thought he'd brought a hatchet into the ring with him, but then I saw that my left hook was doing as much damage as his right. We were hitting like sledge hammers, like pile drivers. The fans were standing on their seats.

The newspapers gave me the decision—unanimously. I got a five-hundred-dollar purse, the most money I had ever earned for one fight up to that time. It seemed like a million dollars.

Shortly after, Johnny and I split up. He matched me against a fellow whose name I can't remember now. Anyway, the fight never came off. A couple of days before the fight, my grandmother took sick. Now, my grandmother was one of the most important people in my life. She lived on the street next to ours, and I spent as much time in her house as in my own. She was like a second mother to me, a lady of the old school and full of wise sayings from the old country. She knew about the Banshee and Robert Emmett in the Wigelow Mountains. She had treasures she would show me, like a real Irish shillelagh, or the pipe smoked by my great-grandfather.

When I heard she was sick, I ran around to her house, met the doctor there, and asked how sick she was. The doctor looked me straight in the eye. "Your grandmother," he said, "is in a fair way to die."

I rushed to Johnny's store. "Johnny," I said, "you gotta call off this fight. My grandmother is sick."

"Ah, the old story," Johnny said.

"Listen, Johnny," I said. "Maybe you don't realize how serious this is."

"This fight is a sellout," Anthes said. "The advance sale

shows we'll be in the dough, and the promoter is hinting about making you a big boy."

"You mean I can't be with my dying grandmother?"

"No fighter of mine stops training for any relative—grandmother, uncle, cousin—sick or well," replied my manager firmly.

"Call off the fight," I insisted.

"The promoter won't allow it," Johnny said.

"Call it off," I said.

"Not me," said Johnny. "You fight tomorrow night, or else . . ."

"Johnny, you need a new fighter," I said and walked out.

A little later, a neighborhood boy rapped on the door and handed me a note. It was my contract with Johnny. Written on it were just two words: "Good Luck."

My grandmother died a few days later.

Johnny never said so but to this day I'm convinced he decided to split us up for what he honestly felt was *my* own good. You see, I didn't realize my potential but Johnny did.

I was like a ham. I wanted an audience—big-time recognition, to have people point me out and say, "That's Mickey Walker, the fighter."

Johnny, I realize now, had no ambition to become a big-timer in the sports world. He knew he could not cope with such sharpshooters and shrewd manipulators as Leo P. Flynn, Billy Gibson, Pete Reilly and Jack "Doc" Kearns.

He felt he would be a handicap if he remained with me. The grandmother incident gave him the excuse he needed to bow out. He took it. Later, Johnny became a New Jersey internal revenue man and he collected my taxes. So, in a way, he was still taking a bite out of my earnings.

I was on my own for a few weeks. I knew I needed a manager and had plenty of chances but I wanted someone I could trust, someone who would look out for me—who would also be a pal. I talked with Leo P. Flynn and others. None appealed to me. They were all too businesslike. I felt no warmth for them. I wanted someone I could regard as a friend as well as a manager. I visited Gripp's gym in New York one day and spoke to Tom O'Rourke, a very sharp manager of the period.

"I'll be glad to take you on, son," O'Rourke told me. "I'll get you a fight right away with Panama Joe Gans."

At the time, Gans was the hottest thing in the welterweight division—too hot for me. "Some other year," I said, giving him a quick good-bye.

I did all my training at Great Kills, on the southern tip of Staten Island, which is the borough of New York City closest to New Jersey. Uncle Joe set up the camp for me. Actually, the camp was a big tent supported by trees and decorated with blankets. It looked more like a place to hold auctions than a training camp, but it was very colorful. Uncle Joe also put together a dummy for me—a sailor's duffle bag filled with rags—which I used for a punching bag. Road work was rough because all my running was done in soft sand. That's hard on the ankles. But I owe my strong legs to that sand.

It was there that I fell in love for the first time. Olga Olson, a Swedish blonde with a gorgeous figure, was the most popular girl on the beach. We were both excellent swimmers and got a great kick out of each other. I was eighteen and she was twenty-one, and she made me feel important.

44

I was sure it was love but I found out differently—and fast. One night I had a date with her and was right on time. I was dolled up like a Christmas tree on the outside and shaking like a leaf inside. She was late and I worried that something had happened to her.

I waited almost two hours and was really panicky. I paced up and down nervously, imagining her under the wheels of a truck or hurt in a trolley car accident.

Uncle Joe saw I was upset. "You waiting for Olga?" he asked.

"Yes," I gulped. "I've got a date with her."

"Well, Knockout"—he grinned—"you'll have to take her husband along, too. She just got married an hour ago!"

From the beginning, I guess, I just wasn't fated to hold on to my women.

I was still without a manager, and on returning home from my training camp one night, I found a stranger waiting outside my house. He recognized me and extended his hand.

"I'm Jack Bulger," he said. "Where can I find your manager? I can line up good fights for you."

Bulger was the matchmaker at the Laurel Athletic Club, a fight club in Newark. I had heard of him but had never met him. He was a little fellow, well dressed and personable.

"You can't find my manager," I answered, "because I don't have one."

"Kid, you got one now," he said. "I'm your manager!"

I blinked. Wait a minute, I thought. What kind of a fast shuffle is this?

He saw me begin to back off and quickly added, "Why don't we go into the house and talk it over?"

45

It didn't take very long. I just took to the man. I liked his style, his direct approach and straight talk.

In less than fifteen minutes, I was sold. We shook hands.

That was the start of a fine partnership and friendship. We never had a contract. We didn't need any written piece of paper between us. A handshake was good enough.

CHAPTER FIVE

Bulger had a lot of class. He was a smart-looking little guy, loved to gamble and considered himself quite a ladies' man, but he was as honest as Abe Lincoln. Bulger loved the bright lights of Broadway and could get rid of money as quickly as any of the so-called free spenders, but I never saw him take a drink. It was he who introduced me to Broadway and the night life. Jack had worked in vaudeville and in motion pictures before he got into the fight game. He worked with John Bunny, the old Vitagraph comedian who was regarded as one of the greatest funnymen of the silent pictures.

Bulger loved the company of the Broadway big shots and the Ziegfeld Follies girls. He would use me as his introduction card, and he would move in and take over. It was through Bulger that I met the beautiful dancer, Ann Pennington, the hottest little bundle of personality on Broadway. I also met Texas Guinan, Fanny Brice, Jimmy Durante and—Polly Adler.

I was in a different world. I wasn't a champ yet, but I was important, and it felt good.

The life of a fighter in his heyday is a little like a whirl-wind. Looking back, it is hard to remember each time I fought in Rochester, Kankakee, Kalamazoo or Peoria through the years. Jack and I were catching trains and putting opponents down all over the place. I was still growing and had moved up to the welterweight (147 pound) class.

Jack and I were a team. When he took me over, he promised to make me champion of the world within a year—and he didn't miss it by much. He guided me with cunning and caution. He was careful not to overmatch me, but before long I was fighting the best in the division. Finally, he signed me up for an over-the-weight non-title match with welterweight champ Jack Britton. It was scheduled for Newark, on a twelve-round, no-decision basis.

Bulger had me believing that Britton was an old man and all I had to do was go in and hit him and it would all be over, but Britton acted very queerly for an old man. He must have caught up with his second childhood that night. For eight rounds I saw more boxing gloves and tasted more of them than in my whole boxing career up till that time. But champion Jack started to tire in the ninth. He would back up against the ropes and sit on the middle one, taking a rest. And all the time he was talking to me.

"Mick," he'd say, "I hear you can punch with your right, but I think it's a lot of baloney."

This kind of talk would get my nanny, and I would wind up to give him one. When it came, Britton could see it coming a mile off and all he would do was move his head a half-inch.

"You couldn't break an egg with that," Britton taunted. "Do I have to show you how to do it?"

"I'll show you, you donkey," I muttered, winding up again. I would graze his head, that was all.

"What a weak one," Britton jeered.

The champ talked his way out that night. He was smart; he was experienced. He never let me hit him with my favorite punch after he had me on the floor in the first round. When the fight was over, the newspapermen gave me the edge. But since it was an over-the-weight no-decision fight, Britton was still champion.

During the rest of 1921, I fought my most persistent rival, Dave Shade, twice, knocking him out once and outpointing him the other time. I also knocked over a string of palookas and went through the year without a defeat.

In 1922, Bulger began to groom me for the championship. He moved me into better company, including Lou Bogash, Jock Malone, Georgie Ward, Pal Reed and Soldier Jake Bartfield—I fought Bartfield three times in less than two months. I won most of these bouts and lost a couple, but all the time I was gaining experience and a record.

I fought Shamus O'Brien four times. He was a good fighter with a large family—and it seemed every time I fought him, his wife presented him with another kid. Each new addition seemed to make him just that much tougher. The last time I fought him, O'Brien had twelve kids. Bulger thought he'd be a soft touch by then, but he made me work as hard as I did in any fight I ever had. I think that one ended in a draw. Finally, I told Bulger to knock him off my list. He was getting too tough.

Bulger was a gambler—one of the biggest. His favorite sport was shooting craps and he knew every gambling joint around New Jersey and New York. I remember the

48

first spot he took me to. It was in June of 1922, and I had just fought Lou Bogash in Boston. Bogash outweighed me by 18 pounds and took the decision. My purse was five thousand dollars. Bulger asked me whether I'd like to run the roll up to twenty, twenty-five thousand, and I said sure.

One of the biggest crap games in those days was run over the Palace Theater on Market Street in Newark. Underneath the theater was a night club, which was run by the mob. The gambling joint was run by Joe Regan. There was a crap game already going on when we got there. One of the players was Niggy Rutkin, a partner of Longey Zwillman, one of the biggest racketeers in the country.

Nobody paid any attention to me. I was just a punk kid. Bulger would never let me gamble or smoke or drink or even go around with girls. He made sure I lived a clean life and he watched me like a hawk. He had an idea I was one of those goodie-goodie boys. He thought I didn't know a pair of dice from dominoes. If he had only known I'd been shooting craps almost from the day I learned to walk.

Me a goodie? That was a laugh. I was a natural-born hell-raiser. I enjoyed life. Although Jack was strict, I did manage to get away from him a few times and find a girl, or hang around with the Keighry Head toughs.

If anything, I was getting too big for my britches. At twenty-one, becoming famous and on the way to the big dough, I thought the world had been made just for me.

I didn't mind risking the whole five-grand purse but I didn't enjoy standing around like an innocent babe while Bulger was doing the rolling and getting the kicks. I itched for action but was afraid to offend Bulger by demanding to play.

Jack started to lose right from the beginning. The dice were cold for him and his luck got worse as he went along. Before long, our bank roll was pretty thin. Rutkin was another big loser.

I was getting impatient. In fact, I was sore as hell. I knew I was a pretty good crap-shooter and was sure I could win if I could get the dice in my hands. I asked Bulger to let me take over but he paid no attention to me.

What worried me most was what my mother would say if I got home without any money. I always gave her half of my purse. She never asked me what I did with my half, but hers she insisted on getting. Most of the time my half was gone before I got home, but I never failed to give Mom her share.

Our roll was now down to three hundred dollars. I was in a sweat. I grabbed Bulger's arm again.

"Look, Jack," I begged, "your luck's been bad all night. Why not change it? Let me try it. I might be lucky."

"Why not?" Bulger said finally. "You could have beginner's luck."

Beginner's luck? Keighry Head's best crap-shooter? Back in the old neighborhood I handled the dice as well as any of the veteran crap-shooters. I was an expert pad-roller. A pad-roll could be used only on a carpet or a cloth-covered table. You couldn't pad-roll, for instance, on the sidewalk. The concrete was too smooth. In order to be a good pad-roller, you have to hold the dice a certain way and you sort of push the bones out with your thumb, making sure they have no spin on them. You just let the dice slide out. I had learned all the tricks as a kid.

I made my first point. "Hey," exclaimed Bulger, "what did I tell you? Beginner's luck."

I made my next point, and the other gamblers smiled

knowingly. They all took me for a beginner. That was all right with me, especially when they waived the rule that the dice had to be bounced off the cushion on the far end of the table. That was a break. Now I could slide the dice out easy-like without hitting anything. That's just what I'd hoped they'd allow me to do.

When Niggy and the other "wrong" betters saw me making my points, one after another, they switched to my side, betting "right," along with me. That put the entire burden of fading the shooter on the house. Well, inside of thirty minutes I had won forty thousand dollars and Niggy Rutkin had gained back his losses and won some money besides.

I was still holding the dice when Joe Regan announced that the house was broke. He knew what I was doing but he was afraid to make an issue of it because all the tough guys in the joint were backing my play.

After paying off everybody, Joe called me into his office and drew a gun. He pointed it at my head and growled, "Lissen, you little punk. You got away with it this time but if you ever show that mug of yours in here again, I'll blow your brains out."

Bulger looked at me in a different light after that. He knew then that I wasn't so wet behind the ears. It didn't change our relationship a bit, though. He bore down on me as hard as ever, making sure I stayed in line and kept in top condition. He never let me forget that my job was fighting.

When Jack finally got me a title fight, it was with Britton and I was more ready for the old champ than I had been the first time we fought. Tex Rickard promoted the championship bout at Madison Square Garden—the old smelly one on Twenty-third Street, on November 1, 1922.

Britton had won the welterweight title from Ted "Kid" Lewis in 1917. He was one of the shrewdest ring generals the game ever saw. Though not a hard hitter, he was so accurate and rapid in his punching, so clever in defense, that few men anywhere near his weight had been able to beat him during eighteen years in the ring. He was the champ and I was a kid and here we were—going to fight fifteen rounds with the welterweight championship at stake.

Britton started out as a 2½ to 1 favorite but the odds wavered, slipped. On the day of the fight, the people of Elizabeth and nearby New Jersey towns barged into New York with ready money to bet on their boy. The odds suddenly shifted, with me the favorite. Britton was thirty-seven and I was only twenty-one.

When we entered the ring they were betting 8 to 5 that Mickey Walker would be the new champion. This sudden switch in odds aroused the suspicions of William Muldoon, then the Boxing Commissioner in New York State, and he ordered Joe Humphries, the famous ringside announcer, to inform the crowd that all bets were to be declared off. It was the only time, to my knowledge, that such an announcement was ever made from a prize ring.

The person responsible for all this was Arnold Rothstein, the big-shot New York gambler. Neither Rothstein nor anybody in New York knew much about me. Up to the time of that match, I had done no fighting in New York. All my fights had been in Boston, Philadelphia and the New Jersey cities. To get the New York fans interested in me, they had given me a tune-up fight against one Artie Bird in a New York fight club, and I'd knocked Bird out in eight rounds.

That meant nothing to Rothstein, who made Britton the

favorite. My New Jersey, Pennsylvania and Massachusetts supporters grabbed all available bets and pretty soon, with so many people still eager to put money down on me, the odds shifted and I became the favorite.

Rothstein was no chump and he wanted to get out from under. He passed the word that the fight was fixed. It wasn't, of course, but people believed him. In order to get a crack at the title, Bulger had agreed to a deal whereby we would take 50 percent of the net and pay Britton a guarantee of thirty thousand dollars for laying his title on the line and coming in at the weight. That was the custom in those days. Yet rumors persisted that the fight was fixed.

I won the fight without any trouble. In one of my scrapbooks, I recently came across an article by a fight reporter, Harry Newman of the New York *News*, who wrote: "Poor Jack Britton! The old champion cried in the center of the ring while the crowd gave him probably the greatest ovation that ever was accorded a fallen champion. Three times during the conflict, Jack was pounded to the floor by his youthful opponent. In the 10th round, Britton was battered down and only the bell saved him from a knockout. A left hook to the chin scored most of the knockdowns. Walker used the left with deadly effect through the fight. Mickey gave Britton an awful pounding throughout the entire journey and there was no hesitancy in the end when the officials declared in favor of the Jerseyite. Youth had to be served."

When the decision was announced, Britton, arm-and-leg-weary, with two black eyes, walked over and shook hands.

"I hope you hold it as long as I did," he said chokingly.

I felt sorry for him. He was standing there, tears in his eyes, as I left the ring with his title.

CHAPTER SIX

Champ . . . I soon found out what being a champion meant. I was surrounded by new friends. Kids followed me in the streets. Their mothers and fathers stopped me to shake my hand and ask for autographs for their children.

I was to find out later how fickle people can be.

I got a taste of what was to come only hours after I copped the title. Bulger had arranged a big party for me at Bill Duffy's Silver Slipper, a night club on Forty-ninth Street and Seventh Avenue. A celebration. But I didn't want to go. I was a champ, true, but I didn't know how to take all this adulation. So I sneaked out of the dressing room by a back door and grabbed a cab to Penn Station.

I wanted to see my mother, not a lot of Broadway well-wishers. I got on the train without being recognized by pulling my coat collar up and my cap down. I tried not to be conspicuous as I sat down in a corner seat, the cap over my eyes. Pretty soon, after the train pulled out of the station, I overheard a couple of fight fans talking about me. They were seated right in front of me. Their voices were loud and I couldn't help hearing them.

"Boy, that Walker! What a lucky bum!" one of them said. "He won't hold the title long. Who did he beat? Britton's an old man. Anybody could have taken him."

"I'll bet there's a half-dozen kids in the neighborhood that could murder Mickey," said the other.

I was sensitive then, and I resented this talk. I was getting madder by the minute. As they kept taking me apart, I felt like getting up and knocking their heads together. But I was smart enough not to start a fuss on the train. I figured I'd wait until we got into the Elizabeth station. Then I'd fix both their wagons. As I was figuring out the best place to pop them, the train came to a halt. I made a beeline for them. They saw me coming and recognized me immediately. One of them grabbed me by the hand and shook it vigorously.

"Hey, fellers," he shouted, "look who's here. The champ himself. Hi, Mick. You were great tonight. You murdered the bum. We knew you'd do it, Mickey, boy. You're the greatest fighter in the world."

Gone was all my planning.

The others recognized me, too, and pretty soon I was being slapped silly. A couple of guys hoisted me on their shoulders and the crowd followed. I was carried down Broad Street all the way to Keighry Head, with the mob growing larger block by block. I'll never forget the impression it made on me. Here were a couple of guys calling me a bum one minute and carrying me on their shoulders—a hero—the next.

When we finally stopped in front of my house, it seemed all Elizabeth was there. What a house party we had. All the neighbors were there . . . the Cullenses, the Sampsons, Tim O'Leary, Cal McCarty and so many others. Cooper sent over beer; Sampson, the grocer, sent over bread and cakes; Cohane, the butcher, supplied the meat. Everything on the cuff. No strings attached. It was the biggest impromptu celebration Elizabeth ever had. And to top it off, the city gave me a parade through the streets the next day.

My life changed from then on. I no longer was just Mickey Walker, the prize fighter. I was a champion of the world. I became a symbol of the town. From then on, if I did anything wrong, it was a reflection on the city. If I did anything good, it brought credit upon the people of Elizabeth. They were really proud of Mickey Walker, the former Elizabeth Thunderbolt!

Three years in the ring and I had a world's title. Bulger decided we ought to cash in on it, so he accepted an offer to go on the stage for a couple of weeks. We did a funny bit difficult to describe. Our opening was at the Howard Theater, a famous old burlesque house in Boston, where all the champions from John L. Sullivan to Jack Dempsey had appeared.

We decided to give a party at the Copley Plaza Hotel, where we were staying. The Copley normally didn't take in prize fighters. We invited the girls from the show at the Howard Theater. It wasn't a very good idea, for it didn't take the girls long to start a battle among themselves. It developed into a free-for-all and the next day we left the hotel—by request.

After our vaudeville appearance, we returned to New York and Bulger threw another party for me. It was a delayed celebration of my taking the title. Among the guys there was Dempsey. Jack and I had been friends for two years. We're still good pals today.

I had met him first in the winter of 1920 while he was in training for his title defense against Bill Brennan. Dempsey had taken the heavyweight crown from Jess Willard eighteen months earlier. From the very first, Jack was my idol. I copied his style of fighting and felt proud when some writer referred to me as "The Little Dempsey."

I enjoyed watching him fight and he used to come and see me in the ring, too. One night I fought Jock Malone in Newark, with Jack at ringside. Dempsey's presence seemed to bring out the best in me. I was inspired and poor old Jock didn't have a chance. I pummeled him all over the ring and then, as if it were rehearsed, I belted Malone over the ropes and into Dempsey's lap. I glowed all over when Jack flashed me a warm grin.

One time I came close to boxing Jack. In 1922, before I won the welter title, Dempsey came to Newark on an exhibition tour. Without consulting me, Bulger rushed to Loew's Theater, where the heavyweight champ headlined a vaudeville bill, and got Jack Kearns, Dempsey's manager, to agree to an exhibition on the stage between Dempsey and me. Bulger figured it would get nation-wide publicity.

The first I knew of this ingenious stunt was when Bulger said to me, "Hey, Mick, hold your hat. I got you a fight with Dempsey at Loew's Theater."

At first I thought Bulger was joking. When I realized he meant it, I howled.

"Look," I protested. "You know I'm not afraid of any human being, but this guy isn't human. Not the way he can punch. I've seen a few of Dempsey's stage exhibitions and I always left with the feeling that he held a grudge against anyone wearing boxing gloves. No, sir. I'm not going into any ring with him. I figure if he hits me on the chin, he'll knock my head off."

"Goddamn you," Bulger snarled. "If he hits you, hit him back. You'll flatten him."

He believed it, too.

57

I finally promised I'd box Dempsey. The day of the scheduled exhibition, I went over to my old neighborhood and gathered a dozen of my Keighry Head toughs. We headed for the theater in Newark and when we got there I told them to wait outside the stage door. I gave them instructions to jump Dempsey the minute he stepped outside after the bout. I was certain he would flatten me and that's how I was going to get my revenge.

It was a stupid idea, I realize, but I used to get some silly notions in those days.

Fortunately, it never happened because the exhibition was called off.

"The Boxing Commission won't permit you and Dempsey to box," the theater manager told me.

I was so happy over the news that I didn't bother to ask why. It came like a reprieve. If the fight had come off, Bulger might have gotten the publicity he was after, all right, but I might not have been around to read it.

A month after my fight with Britton, Bulger and I were sitting at a table in Lindy's Restaurant on Broadway when the waiter leaned over and whispered that Arnold Rothstein wanted to talk to me.

"Okay, send him over," I said.

The guy looked at me as if waiting for me to say I was only kidding, that I'd be over to see Mr. Rothstein right away. When he realized I meant it, he shook his head slowly and walked even more slowly to Rothstein's table. I had never seen Arnold Rothstein, but I knew who he was, of course, a top-money gambler, who was supposed to have been the engineering force in the World Series fix of 1919.

"Hi'ya, Champ."

I looked up at a dark-haired, handsome man with blazing black eyes which bore right into me. With him was a skinny, sallow guy. They sat down at our table without waiting for an invitation.

Rothstein didn't waste any time.

"You know, kid," he said, "you almost cost me a good chunk of dough when you beat Britton. I stood to lose six hundred thousand. That's how much I had going against you that night. Lucky I knew some people. If I didn't have connections, I would have blown all that dough."

I glared across the table at him. "So you're the bum who called off all the bets."

Rothstein just laughed. He was supposed to be the bank for the underworld. He'd loan money for anything no matter how crooked it was, and he was then at the peak of his power.

"Look, kid," he said quietly, "you're a great little fighter and you're going places. You're going to make a lot of money. But you can make more if you team up with me. All I want you to do is to take it easy once in a while, and let me know about it. There are lots of suckers around and if we have a sure thing we can clean up. I'll let you know when I want you to go easy and I'll cut you in on the bets."

I was getting ready to hit him with a left hook when his skinny pal pulled a gun from inside his coat. It was a big black one and must have been a foot long. But I was so mad, I didn't give a damn. I was getting set to let that fancy-dressing little punk have it, too, when Bulger jumped up, grabbed my arm and got between us.

Rothstein didn't even get up out of his chair. He just kept smiling. "Put it away, Legs," he ordered. Then he looked levelly at me.

"You're a game little pepperpot, but a dumb Mick," he

59

said, without raising his voice. "It's no skin off my nose if you don't want to wise up."

He got up to leave. "Legs" got up, too. "It's okay, kid," Rothstein said, putting his hand on my shoulder. "Know what? I'll make money on you anyway. I think I'll bet on you every time you fight."

After they left, Bulger asked me if I knew who the skinny guy was. I shook my head.

"That's Rothstein's bodyguard, Legs Diamond," he said. "You're lucky the trigger-happy son-of-a-bitch didn't shoot you down right here."

The next year, 1923, my feud with the Latzo family began. The Latzos came from the Pennsylvania coal district. They were all athletes and were stars in boxing, baseball and football. Several of them—John, Mike, Steve and Pete—had turned to the ring. John and Mike had retired from the game, Steve was getting along pretty well and Pete was just reaching his stride.

I took Steve pretty handily in Philadelphia, knocking him out in the third round. Pete was anxious to avenge the family honor. We boxed in Newark and although he lasted the twelve rounds, he absorbed a pretty good shellacking. He wasn't discouraged, though.

"I'd like to try you again some day," he said through cracked lips.

"Sure, any time," I assured him. "Whenever you say."

Now that I was a champion, my father took a different attitude toward my fighting. He still couldn't bring himself to watch me in the ring, but nobody—except maybe my mother—was prouder of my success. Not long after I won the welterweight title, he started on me to fight in his home town, Holyoke, Massachusetts. He wanted to show his old cronies what a great son he raised, and he wouldn't give me a minute's rest until I promised.

Holyoke didn't go in for boxing in a big way, but the fans supported a small club, with about 800 members. My manager didn't want anyone too tough under those conditions, so the promoter got me an opponent called Wildcat Nelson. I had knocked the Wildcat out once before, so we went to Holyoke.

It did my heart good to watch my father. My old man walked around his home town with his chest stuck out so far they had to move the buildings back. He introduced me to all the relatives, and it began to look like I was related to all the Irishmen in Holyoke.

Well, Nelson got sick or something, and we had to bring in a substitute in a hurry, so we sent for Harlem Eddie Kelly. I hadn't seen Eddie since I boxed him a couple of years before. He was a good fighter then, but he had had to quit and had taken to driving a taxi.

It was a shock to see him. He looked like a fat man from the circus, and was in no shape to climb into the ring. Of course, I didn't want to go too hard on him, and the people in Holyoke didn't like that at all—especially since there was a substitute in the first place. Kelly didn't help matters much by going down in the second round without being hit. The next thing I knew the people were throwing chairs. I guess they didn't like the fight.

As soon as we could, Bulger and I made a mad dash for the dressing room, grabbed our clothes and beat it for the railroad station. Mike was right behind us.

"Well, boys," he apologized, "there must have been some out-of-town people there."

As a new, young and eager champion I was a manager's delight: light-hearted and easy to handle. I loved to train, loved to fight. Bulger kept a tight check on me. He was especially strict about girls. He himself loved his women, but he said dames were no good for a fighter.

He banned automobiles because he figured it would be too easy for me to sneak off on a date.

"I'll never be able to keep an eye on you if you have a car," he told me.

Jack himself owned a big Cole eight and had his own chauffeur. That was the only car he let me ride in. If he wasn't around, the chauffeur played watchdog. It was rugged discipline and at times I felt like balking. Yet I never really got up on my hind legs and defied him. I realized he loved me like a son and wanted to keep me on top as long as he could.

Despite their constant supervision, I did manage to work in a date once in a while. Jack couldn't keep romance out of my life entirely.

I was training in Rumson for a fight. Bulger had chosen a quiet country home owned by Annie Blaicher, wife of a Rumson policeman. Annie rented rooms to special friends during the summer, since Rumson was then largely a summer resort on the Jersey shore. I took a room there and trained on the grounds.

A steady visitor to my training camp was Jack Kelly, an enthusiastic fight fan. He was about my age and we became friends. One Sunday I met Kelly in church. He was with an attractive, blond young lady and after Mass, he introduced us:

"Mickey, meet my sister, Maude."

She was twenty-one, and lived with her mother in Brooklyn but spent the summers in Rumson, where the family had a summer home.

They invited me to their house. Maude and I were attracted to each other immediately and from that day on, we saw each other constantly. Some of my pals jokingly insisted I called for her while I still had the boxing gloves on my hands after training sessions. It was a wonderful summer and we knew we were in love. A year later we married. That was in June of 1923. We rented a house in Elizabeth, across the street from my mother's.

I had been champion only a few months when the Elks Club of Elizabeth talked Bulger into letting me fight in my home town. The money—after our purses had been taken out—would go to charity. My opponent was Jimmy Jones, no stumblebum. In fact, he was recognized as welterweight champion by the New York Athletic Commission at the time. New York had taken the title away from me because I hadn't defended it there within the six-month limit.

Bulger refused to have me fight in New York because he felt at that time there were no real money matches in the big town. I didn't need New York anyway. I was doing much better in Chicago, Philadelphia, Newark and Boston.

The fight with Jones was scheduled to take place in June, 1923, in Dreamland Park. Lots of tickets were sold. I had a couple of tune-ups and in the last one I broke my hand. The fight had to be postponed.

Bulger wanted to put it off until mid-winter and hold it indoors in the Elizabeth Armory. But the Elks people insisted the fight go on in September because they had a big advance sale and if the fight were switched indoors, much of the money would have to be refunded and charity would be the loser. So, despite my bad hand, I agreed to fight in September.

I didn't think it was too bad a fight, but the referee

and the fans did. It was scheduled to go ten rounds but the ref tossed both of us out of the ring in the ninth and declared it no-contest. He ruled we weren't trying. The Elks Club, sore as the dickens, claimed I let my home town down and refused to release my purse. I was out $24,000.

I got burned and decided to hell with the Elks Club and everybody in Elizabeth. If my own people could pull a rotten trick like that on me, then I didn't want to live in their crummy town. I had been spending a lot of time in Rumson anyway, so I decided to live there permanently.

Late in 1923, I bought my mother-in-law's home in Rumson, and she came with the house. I paid her nine thousand dollars. It was a two-bedroom house when I bought it. I added three more bedrooms, tore down the porch and changed it from a plain, wooden frame house into a colonial with white pillars. I built a wing, adding a sun parlor, a dining room and a recreation room. I also had a gymnasium built over the garage. Finally, the entire house was painted white and it really was pretty. The total cost went up to fifty-two thousand bucks.

CHAPTER SEVEN

In Rumson, I met the best people—and the worst. Rumson, at that time, was one of the wealthiest places in the world. As champion, I was tolerated and sometimes invited to the Rumson Country Club where I played golf, tennis and even polo with the members. These ultra-

rich guys came to my camp to watch me train and presented me with gifts, such as bulldog puppies.

The bootleggers and rum runners rode high in those
days and I was in a position to cut in on their racket. As
big and powerful as they were, they had to have help
. . . at the local level—the "fix." Which is where I came
in.

Rumson, Seabright, Deal, Asbury Park . . . towns
along the Atlantic Coast on down to Barnegat Bay. These
were the watering spots for people with ready cash, as
well as rum-ports for the runners.

In those days, bootlegging was a big business in America and the bootlegger was accepted as a businessman.
He was a powerful figure on the American scene. After
all, what was a party or a weekend without hooch?

Millionaires rubbed shoulders with racketeers at my
training camp—and shared the "good stuff" from the
same hip flasks. There was the sporting crowd. There were
gamblers, bookies, Broadway guys and dolls, politicians—
and the bootleggers. In those days, many were prouder to
know Owney Madden or Al Capone than the mayor or
governor.

I got to know the crooks and the cops, and so it was
only natural that I'd be the guy to handle the "ice," as
they call it today. Then it was known as "graft."

We laughed at the federal government's attempts at
enforcing prohibition. The big operators got so bold that
they went out and refitted ships which could outrun the
Coast Guard cutters.

The liquor, mostly Scotch and Irish whiskey, was
brought from Bermuda and the Bahamas and landed on
the beaches at night, mainly at Seabright and Atlantic
Highlands. Then it was distributed to various points by

truck. The trucks had to go through Rumson and Red Bank.

The bootleggers were the sole suppliers to plush night clubs, private clubs such as golf and yacht clubs, neighborhood delicatessens and speak-easies. Anybody could get a drink—if he knew "Joe" or "Benny" and had the money. Price was no object. Even though the bootleggers charged five times as much for a case as did the legitimate distillers before Prohibition, they had no trouble selling it. In fact, they couldn't smuggle in enough to satisfy America's thirst.

From coast to coast there was a market, but the stuff had to come in somewhere, and I happened to be right where a lot of it was coming in.

Owney Madden and Bill Dwyer controlled the traffic in New York (they "imported" from Long Island beaches). In Jersey the bosses were Pete Reilly, Larry Coyle, Big Red Dempsey and Herman Black. I got to know them well. In fact, Reilly managed Jack Delaney, the light-heavyweight champ. Coyle owned a night club in Brooklyn called—believe it or not—Cave of the Fallen Angel. Black owned the Connors Hotel in Atlantic Highlands.

Madden, the most powerful boss in the East, was an Englishman who came to this country when he was eleven and settled in an Irish neighborhood on New York's west side. It was the area in the mid-Thirties between Tenth Avenue and the Hudson River. A tough neighborhood then, it still is no place for a boy who can't fight.

Madden went into the bootlegging and boxing rackets in 1923. He moved fast. In partnership with Bill Duffy, a fight manager, he bought the Cotton Club, then one of the top night spots in New York. Madden was also the undercover manager of many big-name boxers. He controlled

Primo Carnera, Maxie Rosenbloom, Bob Olin, Ace Hudkins, Pancho Villa, Jimmy Braddock and Leo Lomski, among others. He also had the top managers of the day, including Joe Jacobs and Joe Gould, fronting for him.

So, you see, Frankie Carbo didn't originate the bit. He just copied a master.

Big Bill Dwyer was a tall, dignified man with a friendly smile. His blue eyes were lively behind horn-rimmed glasses.

He, too, loved sports and rackets—and blended them well. It was Dwyer who brought ice hockey to New York. He organized the old New York Americans and footed half the bill to put an artificial ice plant into Madison Square Garden. He owned a stable of race horses and had a piece of four race tracks: Tropical Park in Miami, Rockingham in New Hampshire, Mount Royal in Montreal and Coney Island in Kentucky.

He was one of the first bootleggers to unload liquor in New York and New Jersey. Bill started with little fishing boats and wound up with big ships. He bought a submarine chaser and refitted it to bring in the Scotch.

Twenty miles off Rockaway Beach, Long Island, it would rendezvous with the ocean-going freighters which brought the stuff from Scotland.

Income tax trouble finally cut him down, as it did Capone. He went to jail in 1939 after the government obtained a judgment against him for $3,700,000 for taxes dating back to 1922. When he died in 1946 he was practically a pauper. I believe Madden or some other of his former associates was supporting him at the end. Still, he was a proud man. I remember walking around Miami with him one night. There were two others with us. We went to Tom Henney's bar, but Dwyer wouldn't let any-body else buy the drinks.

In the early twenties, the bootleggers would pick up the liquor from ships ten miles out to sea and load the stuff on fishing boats in the middle of the night. Later they would cut it by mixing a quart of good liquor with a quart of grain alcohol and bring it into the beach at Seabright or the Highlands. Everything went well until the stuff was brought ashore. Then the local police would some-times give them trouble.

One day Reilly approached me after a workout. He made me a proposition. Would I help his boys get the booze through? I was legitimate and I was friendly with the local police as well as the city authorities. Nobody would bother me. All I had to do was handle the cops and politicians in the area so that the boys could get their liquor safely on the beach and out of Seabright to Rumson and Red Bank.

I agreed. Prohibition was a joke anyway. People were going to drink no matter how they got it, and I grabbed a chance at some easy dough with very little personal risk.

I acted as go-between and took care of certain police. That was easy in those days. When they learned that a legitimate guy like me was connected with it, they were delighted. They knew they'd be taken care of and they could trust me.

The liquor was left on the beach at Seabright, where trucks picked it up and took it along Rumson Road to Red Bank, some ten miles west. Once they got to Red Bank, the drivers were out of danger. They had plenty of bought protection from Red Bank to other points.

I received seventeen dollars for each case that was

brought in. Ten of it was for me, five dollars went to police and the other two went to higher-ups.

I made a lot of money out of bootlegging, but I never took an active part in it. I didn't even collect the money. Jimmy Duryea, who acted as sort of a valet, chauffeur and bottle washer for me, was my pickup man. He was supposed to split the ten in half but, often as not, he short-changed me. I didn't really care. I was making so much money, what was a few bucks more or less? Everybody was happy. The bootleggers were getting their hooch through, some city officials were getting their cut, and the rich Rumson clientele were being supplied with whiskey, the imported kind. Nobody complained. Everybody knew what was going on. It was no secret.

Strangely enough, the only bit of violence occurred between me and my chauffeur. At first, I didn't mind his clipping, but when I learned that he had become the new owner of the food concession in the Molly Pitcher Hotel in nearby Red Bank, I decided to check some figures with him. Sure enough, I caught him red-handed. My take at the end of a particular month was supposed to be forty thousand dollars. He gave me sixteen thousand dollars. That was too big a difference to ignore.

I called Duryea on it. We got into an argument and he pulled a gun. He had done so much business with the mob that he fancied himself one of them. He found out he wasn't so tough when I hit him over the head with a beer bottle. I fired him as my chauffeur but when he went broke later on, I felt sorry for him and took him back.

Our "good thing" lasted three years. Then other mobsters began moving in on the Madden and Dwyer monopoly early in 1926 and it became rough. Dutch Schultz, the maniac killer from the Harlem section of New York, declared himself in. With him, he brought hoods and guns and before long there was shooting and killing. I wanted no part of that. I valued my hide too much. I never wanted to be a gangster.

My mind was made up for me one day. I received a visit from one of the Brooklyn mob . . . Little Augie Pisano. (I knew him as Al Capone's chief lieutenant and had got to know him well during his visits to my training camp.)

"You'd better get out of the bootlegging racket, Mickey," Little Augie said. "The Big Fella is moving in. He told me to tell ya he'd hate to see ya get hurt."

I was glad to take the hint. He didn't have to draw a map for me. There was no doubt about who the Big Fella was . . . Scarface Al. I had met Capone the first time I fought in Chicago in 1923. I was in the Chez Paree, celebrating a knockout victory over Morrie Schlaifer, a local hot-shot. I wasn't drinking in those days but that didn't prevent me from enjoying the night life. I liked to dance; no one did a meaner Charleston.

We were enjoying the show when Bulger noticed Capone sitting with a group of his mugs at a nearby table. How Jack managed to be friendly with all the racketeers as well as Broadway and Hollywood show people I never found out, but there wasn't one he didn't know. Anyhow, he brought me over to Capone's table and introduced me. I felt flattered when Capone asked me to join his party.

I got to know Al quite well; in fact, our friendship lasted a long time, even after Bulger's death. I never had any business relationship with him, of course, but I attended many of his parties and always found him to be a good host. On several occasions, I was a guest at his winter home on Hibiscus Island on the Miami Beach causeway.

I met his wife and son. May Capone was a lovely Irish lady with a fine sense of humor. The boy was a nice-looking, well-mannered lad of twelve when I first met him.

Capone never took advantage of our friendship by asking me to throw a fight. He did ask me for a favor once. I did it for him.

(Incidentally, I never fought a crooked fight in my life—knowingly, that is. There were several, however, in which I may have carried an opponent, or refrained from knocking him out, or made sure he didn't look too bad or get hurt much.)

Capone asked for the favor before a fight with Sailor Friedman in Chicago in 1925. The Sailor was a tough boy, and he was very popular in Chicago. The Arena was filled for the fight, and I was sitting in the dressing room waiting for the call when Capone and one of his lieutenants sauntered in. As we shook hands, Al said, "Mickey, the Sailor is a friend of mine. Don't hurt him." He said it quietly; it was no threat. But I knew what he meant. "Don't worry, Al," I assured him, "I won't."

I won the decision easily. Capone had a ringside seat. He never once looked toward my corner. He just sat there chewing an unlit cigar. I could have knocked the Sailor into his lap any time I wished.

Capone and I had words only once. It was in the early 1930's, a few years before he pleaded guilty to income tax evasion and was given a prison term. Capone had a big party going at the Metropole Hotel in Chicago. Jack Kearns, who was my manager then, and I were invited. Actually, it was more of a convention than a party. Gunmen from all over the country showed up; the Purple gang from Detroit, the Mayfield gang from Cleveland, and others from Chicago, New Orleans, Los Angeles,

71

Miami, Philadelphia and New York. The amount of iron carried in inside pockets was impressive. Everybody was drinking, including Capone. Al could handle his liquor; you could hardly ever tell when he was drunk, but this time he showed it. It was obvious to me, even though I was stiff, too.

Somehow, I got into an argument with Capone's lawyer. I don't even remember why except that I just didn't like his looks. The legal beagle and I were going at it when Capone butted in. The next thing I knew he's backing up this lawyer. I knew he had no idea of what we were arguing about, so I told him to butt out of it. He didn't like that, and began calling me names. Capone or no Capone, I cocked my left hand and was just about to let it go when Swifty Morgan stepped in and grabbed me.

While Kearns was pacifying Capone, Morgan hustled me out of the hotel. They told me later that while the argument between me and Capone was going on, the air in the suite was electrifying, with every hood watching, tense and nervous. I was unaware of this and I guess it would have made no difference even if I had been. The way I felt I was ready to take on Capone and his whole gang.

But that was not the way I felt the next day, especially after Kearns told me what had happened. I don't mind admitting I was scared. We decided that the best thing to do was to go right over to Capone's hotel and apologize to Al. He just laughed when I tried to explain and told me to forget it. It was largely on account of that lawyer's testimony that Capone was convicted. He turned state's evidence and was rewarded with a good government job. Several years later, he died of lead poisoning.

I corresponded with Capone when he was serving time

in Alcatraz. He was a very sick man when he came out. I tried to see him in Florida. When I arrived at his home, his wife met me at the door.

"I think you'd better not see him, Mickey," she said. "It wouldn't do either of you any good. It's better for you to remember him as he was, not as he is."

Al Capone's mind was gone and his body was wasting away. He died shortly afterward.

My friendship with Capone was typical of the times. It was an era of high living and low morals. A heedless, high-rolling hysteria held the country in a whirl. Gangsters and gunmen were glorified, accepted socially and given homage by a ginned-up public. It was an honor to know a racketeer. The hoods ruled baronial empires in the underworld and normally decent citizens fawned on bootleggers, mobsters and even killers.

The country was headline-happy. Anyone who made the front pages—for reasons good or bad—was a character. There came to be little difference between the famous and infamous; a nod or handshake from a murderer was more prized than the autograph of a Hollywood star. The mobster was on the same celebrity scale as the matinee idol or the heavyweight champion of the world, and mingled with the socially prominent set.

I fell into the general pattern of those unbelievable times.

CHAPTER EIGHT

I knew sorrow for the first time in 1924. Deep sorrow. In fact, double sorrow. I lost two of the most important people in my life: my dad, Mike, and my best friend, Jack Bulger.

I had a fight in Virginia on February 15th. Pop was anxious to find out how I'd done. Usually he learned the same night. When I fought in more distant places, such as Chicago, Detroit or Cleveland, he'd have to wait until the next day.

The morning after the Virginia fight, he took his customary walk to Bill Turley's saloon, where he'd get his daily morning snort before going to work. The bartender, as was his custom after each one of my fights, handed him the newspaper. Mike sat down on the bar stool and began unfolding the paper to the sports pages. Suddenly, he let out a long sigh. He reached out to grasp the bar rail, missed and fell to the floor. The newspaper floated down on top of him.

By the time the bartender reached him, Mike was dead. His heart had gone out on him. He was only forty-eight and had never been sick a day in his life. I wonder if before he fell off the stool he saw the headline in the paper: "Walker Kayoes Wildcat Nelson in 4." I hope Mike died happy.

My grief for Pop was deep, but you can't bring back the dead. I plunged into my work harder than ever and that helped me forget. I fought eight times that year, a lot for a champion. I outpointed Jock Malone twice, making up for the licking he had given me early in my career.

The toughest men I met that year were Lew Tendler and Bobby Barrett. Barrett was not a great fighter, but he was the hardest hitter in the welterweight division. Tendler, a southpaw, was a different proposition. Smart, a good boxer and a hard hitter, he was far more dangerous than Barrett.

We drew nearly eighteen thousand people to the Phillies' old ball park. It was a good battle all the way with the referee giving me eight of ten rounds.

Dave Shade, a fighter whom I had licked a few years before, was coming on strong and the New York Boxing Commission was after me to fight him for the title. Bulger wasn't interested in such a fight because he felt it wouldn't draw. The guy Jack wanted was Benny Leonard. Benny was then at the peak of his career—the incomparable lightweight champion of the world. Pound-for-pound the greatest fighter in the business, the experts said of him.

According to all the dope, a Leonard-Walker match figured to draw the second million-dollar gate in boxing history. Tex Rickard, the top promoter of the time and maybe tops of all times, was interested. But it took a lot of dickering. Benny had loads of money and wasn't in a hurry. He was appearing in vaudeville in Cleveland. He said he could lick me without any trouble at all, and I guess he had a right to be cocky. Except for losing on a foul to Jack Britton, he hadn't been beaten in ten years. No one had come close to taking away the title he won from Freddie Welsh back in 1917.

While negotiations were going on, Bulger figured I'd better keep in shape by fighting some tune-ups. He matched me with a fellow called Johnny Gill, in Philadelphia. A couple of days before the Gill fight, we were at a party in the Cumberland Hotel in New York. Jack complained of a stomach ache. That was the first time I had ever heard him complain of being sick. He didn't feel any better the next day.

"You go down to Philly by yourself," he said. "I don't feel just right. But I'll see you the day of the fight."

On the afternoon of the fight, I got a telephone call from Newark. Jack was in the hospital. He was seriously ill. His appendix had burst. I didn't wait to hear any more, but grabbed a cab to the Thirtieth Street Station. I forgot all about the fight; I didn't even think of calling it off. Later on, I learned that Muggsy Taylor, the promoter, had to refund the money.

Somehow, I knew that Jack Bulger was dying. I knew it even before I got to St. Michael's Hospital in Newark. He knew it, too. Only two persons were in his room when I walked in . . . his wife and his brother. Nobody else was allowed to see him. He was so shriveled up, his face looked like a death mask. They had given him a couple of blood transfusions, but he needed more. My blood didn't match.

I was sitting next to his bed when he motioned me to lean closer. When he spoke, his voice was hardly more than a whisper. I had trouble making out his words.

"Mick," he croaked, "always be on the level. That's the only way. Don't pay any attention to the con guys. They'll only get you in trouble.

"Don't dissipate. God has given you a wonderful body. Don't mistreat it. If you take care of yourself, your future is assured. Some day you'll get the chance to be the heavyweight champion of the world. Be ready for it. Don't let yourself down. Don't let me down."

Those were Jack Bulger's dying words. They didn't sink in right away. Not even minutes later when Jack was gone. I was too stunned to give them much thought. All I could think of was that my great friend was dead. A chill went through me. It seemed like a part of me had died.

CHAPTER NINE

I felt the effects of Bulger's death for a long time. Nothing could make me forget . . . nothing could make up for my loss. No friendship in life had meant so much to me. For months I was constantly depressed, no longer happy-go-lucky. Gone was the grin which had been my trade-mark in and out of the ring.

For more than a year after Bulger's death, I was on my own. I just wouldn't think of tying up with anybody else. Every manager was after me. I didn't want to have any-thing to do with anybody. Most of them were all right, I guess, but I kept comparing them to Jack Bulger. And they didn't stack up. Bulger had not only been my man-ager; he had been my pal. Many of the top managers, in-cluding Leo P. Flynn, who later was to manage Jack Dempsey, offered me big money to sign contracts with them. But I refused. I had no personal feeling for them. They were too cold, too businesslike. They were strangers.

I knew I needed somebody to handle the business end for me so I appointed Joe Diegnan, who had been Bulger's secretary, as my front man. I figured Diegnan would do as well as anybody. It made no difference. I was really my own manager.

Bulger and I had made a wad of dough together, but when he died, we were both broke. It was up to me to get a new stake. I picked up where he left off, trying to land the Leonard match.

Tex Rickard had wanted for a long time to arrange a match between Leonard and me. He knew it was a bout that could set a receipts record, outside of the heavyweight class. Benny had cleaned up in his division. He was a master boxer; I was a slugger. He was a New Yorker and I was practically one, too. The setup was perfect. The public wanted the match. Nobody wanted it more than me. Man, I needed it.

The match was finally arranged. It was set for Boyle's Thirty Acres in Jersey City. Rickard guaranteed me $140,000 with a privilege of accepting 35 percent of the gate. Leonard was to get $100,000 or 30 percent. I was then twenty-four; Benny was twenty-nine.

The reason the fight was slated for Jersey City instead of New York was that the New York Boxing Commission refused to sanction the bout until I defended my welterweight title against Shade. I was always in trouble with the Commission. Bill Muldoon, who had trained John L. Sullivan and had been a friend of my father, was head of the Commission then. He was a perfect gentleman and the squarest shooter in the world, but we just never saw eye-to-eye. It was the same even later, when General Phelan, and then Jim Farley, headed the Commission.

The fight got tremendous ballyhoo. It looked like it was going to make a lot of money. Then the New York Commission had a change of heart and let Rickard convince them the fight should be held at the Polo Grounds.

But I got Bill Muldoon mad at me all over again by insisting on a neutral referee and judges. I was suspicious of the New York sharpshooters. Billy Gibson, who managed Leonard, was in with the smart set and I figured Benny would get the best of it from New York officials. We wrangled for weeks, and got nowhere.

I was already in training at Johnny Collins' place in Summit, New Jersey, and it was costing me a lot of money. Also, commuting to New York every day or two didn't do my training any good. Being my own manager, I had to battle for my rights in person.

We were making no headway with the officials. Muldoon became so infuriated that he threatened to throw the fight right back to Boyle's Thirty Acres. I refused to budge from my position.

"You can put the fight in Boyle's basement for all I care," I told him. "I'll flatten Leonard no matter where I fight him. As for the New York Commission, you can all go to hell."

Muldoon's face turned red as a beet. He wasn't accustomed to being talked to that way. "Walker," he roared, "you can't dictate to the Boxing Commission."

He was still pounding the table when I walked out of his office.

Though I was almost broke, I was always thinking big-money thoughts. I had my eye on a large yacht, about 75 feet long. It was a thing of beauty and I had my heart set on owning it. It had once been the property of a big-time bootlegger but it had been confiscated by the federal government. Now it was up for auction. The original price was a quarter of a million dollars. I got it on a bid of fifty thousand, five thousand down and the rest to be paid in thirty days. I intended to pay for it out of my purse.

The yacht was the main topic of conversation in my training camp. Every evening after we knocked off work, my sparring partners and I discussed the yacht. We even planned our first trip. We were going to sail down the Atlantic coast to Florida and become beachcombers. I was automatically the commander even though I had no idea how to operate a boat. Abie Bain, the heavyweight, elected himself my first mate. He was challenged by Jack McVey, the light-heavyweight. Eddie Whalen and Cy Shindell, my two other sparring mates, challenged both of them. This went on every night.

By now, I was already in the hole for a good chunk of dough. Bulger would never have let me get in that deep if he had been alive. But I had no one to guide me. And when it comes to money, I still don't know how to handle it. I wasn't worried though, for I was sure the fight with Leonard would fix me up. That hundred-forty grand would take care of my expenses, buy the yacht, pay off my debts and I'd still have money left.

Leonard took a warm-up fight with Pal Moran in Cleveland and came out of it with a busted thumb. My fight was postponed. A couple of weeks later, Benny called it off altogether. I was left holding the bag. I was hooked for some forty thousand dollars in expenses and loans. Then there was the yacht. I could forget that now—and the five-grand down payment. Five thousand dollars' worth of dreams. That's all I had. In cold cash, I didn't have a nickel.

I had never been in a tougher spot. I was over my head in debt. I had to grab a fight and grab it quick. The debtors were pressing. Then came a break. Herman Taylor in Philadelphia offered me twenty-five thousand to defend my title against Bobby Barrett. Ordinarily, I never would have accepted such a murderous puncher at that price, but I needed dough badly.

80

It was a bitter cold October night in the Philly ball park. There weren't enough people to keep themselves warm. A half hour before the fight, Taylor came into my dressing room and told me he couldn't meet the purse. Would I accept $23,500?

Any other time I probably would have packed up and left. But not now. Tonight I needed the money. I had to fight.

I agreed.

I'll never forget that fight. I almost froze before it was over. I was first in the ring, wearing only my tights and the purple sweater my mother had knitted for me. I had to wait ten minutes until Barrett came into the ring. As angry as I was, I had to laugh. When he finally showed up, he came all wrapped up in a blanket. He looked like the Sultan of Turkey sitting in his corner.

I could hardly wait for the bell to ring. My teeth were chattering and my flesh was all goose pimples. But the time always comes. The bell rang. I tore across the ring and let Barrett have one in the kisser before he had hardly unraveled himself from the blanket. He went down but he was far from out.

I put him to sleep in the sixth round.

It took several months and three more fights to clean up my debts. One of those fights was with Mike McTigue, the light-heavyweight champ. I gave him a thrashing in twelve rounds in Newark, but I didn't get the title. McTigue wouldn't sign for the fight until I agreed to a no-decision match. The only way I could win the title was to knock him out. I didn't, but I always felt I was entitled to the light-heavyweight crown.

I even have a silver cup to prove it. It was presented to me after the fight. The inscription on it reads: "Mickey

Walker wins light-heavyweight title by defeating Mike McTigue in Newark. Date . . . January 7, 1925."

A cup meant just as much as the title—nothing. That's because nobody paid any attention to it. At that time, it was a dead title. The light-heavyweight championship didn't become important until such men as Paul Berlenbach, Jack Delaney, Tommy Loughran and Jimmy Slattery won the title. Know what I weighed when I licked McTigue? One hundred forty-seven. Mike weighed one seventy.

The McTigue fight was a lifesaver for me. It not only cleaned up the last of my debts, it gave me a modest bank roll to boot.

Things were going good again but there was one thing I had my heart set on. More than anything else, I wanted a match with Harry Greb, the middleweight champion of the world.

Greb was one of the best, but I felt I could take him. If I could get a fight with him and whip him, I'd be sitting on top of the world. Not only would there be plenty of money in it for me, but I'd have two titles: welterweight and middleweight.

I finally succeeded in making the match. The New York Boxing Commission agreed to lift their ban on me if we held the fight in New York. They didn't want the big gate and glamour to go to another state. It was set for the Polo Grounds in July of 1925—for the title. As my own manager, I agreed to take a flat $25,000.

It was early in February and I had to plan some tune-up fights during the next few months in preparation for Greb. I got an idea. Maude, who was pregnant, was after me to take her to California. She had a sister in San Diego whom she hadn't seen in years. I thought it would be a good thing for her since I hadn't been giving her much of my time and a woman in that condition tends to become depressed when left alone.

Besides, tune-up bouts were as easy to get on the West Coast as in the East and I felt like seeing California. I had never been west of Davenport, Iowa.

So I lined up a fight with Bert Colima, a leading California middleweight, for February, in Los Angeles.

Before that, I had another engagement to keep—with the President of the United States. As honorary chairman of a committee working on behalf of needy children, I was to make a personal appearance at a fund-raising affair in Washington, D. C. President Coolidge asked me to have lunch with him at the White House when I visited the capital.

Nat Fleischer, editor of *Ring Magazine*, gave me a pair of miniature gold boxing gloves to present to the President. At that time, Coolidge was feuding with Congress. When I gave him the gloves, the serious look left his face for a moment and he broke into a smile.

"These are just fine," he remarked. "They're just what I need to use on Congress."

And they said Calvin Coolidge had no sense of humor.

Maude and I spent a couple of days in Washington enjoying the sights before taking a train to California.

I was looking forward to Hollywood. Broadway was my street and I loved it. But the guys and gals who had been on the West Coast told me Hollywood was even greater, the gayest place in America. A world in itself . . . where people lived high, dreamed big and put on the dog. That's for the Mick, I told myself.

In Hollywood, we stayed at the Barbara Hotel, which was owned by Jack Dempsey and Jack Kearns. The pair of Jacks had broken up their partnership by then, and were in the midst of their tight-lipped feud which was to last twenty-five years. Doc and Dempsey's wife, movie beauty Estelle Taylor, didn't get along. Kearns didn't want him to marry Estelle and, after the wedding, criticized her for interfering too much in the champ's professional life. She might know the picture business, he contended, but she knew nothing about the boxing racket.

After spending a few days in Hollywood with me, Maude went to San Diego to be with her sister. This was a good arrangement for both of us. Maude wanted her sister with her when the baby was born. It was due in June. I was straining at the leash to taste the life and lights of Hollywood. I wanted to be free to move around.

Of course, I had to prepare for the fight with Colima, too. Since I didn't have a manager, Dempsey appointed himself as my acting manager for the fight. I trained at his gym in Los Angeles and he supervised my workouts during the day. I was left on my own at night because Jack and Estelle had their own life to live.

At first, Hollywood proved a disappointment. I had hoped to crash it with a bang, but I didn't even make a dent. Nobody seemed to know me, and worse, nobody seemed to care.

Out of necessity, I concentrated on the fight. A week before it was scheduled, Colima suffered a badly cut eye in training. A postponement seemed certain and that worried me. Dempsey felt the same way. As my self-appointed manager, he was afraid a delay would hurt the gate. So he made a deal with Colima's manager: if Colima went through with the fight, Jack promised I would lay off the damaged eye.

I didn't know anything about the deal until Dempsey told me just before the fight, but it was okay with me. I lived up to Dempsey's promise. I knocked out Colima in the seventh but not once did I hit the bad eye.

I had made up my mind to return East right after the Colima fight. I was satisfied to leave Maude with her sister and get back to Broadway where I felt at home. I had looked forward to knowing the movie stars and tasting the glamour and excitement of their world. Instead of a friendly town, it turned out to be cold and distant.

I got the brushoff. The people were snooty and stuck-up. I may have been a big shot and a world champion back East, but in Hollywood I was just another pug. They acted as though they had never heard of Mickey Walker.

I was cooling off in the dressing room after a shower, when Dempsey came in. He didn't have to introduce the fellow with him. Along with every other kid in America, I knew Douglas Fairbanks. It felt good to be congratulated by him. It felt even better when he invited me to have dinner with him the next night.

While we were talking, I had another visitor, Charlie Chaplin. He, Doug and I sat there and talked for half an hour and I felt like a little boy in dreamland. Both knew boxing because they had boxed in their younger days.

Doug and Charlie opened the gates of Hollywood to me.

Fairbanks and I had dinner at Henri's, a swanky restaurant loaded with celebrities. But none was bigger than Doug and as his guest I was accepted. Suddenly, I was a somebody.

Gone was my desire to pack up and run home.

85

A few days later, returning to the hotel, I found a message from Kearns. He asked me to drop up to his suite. We didn't know each other well, but I had heard a great deal about him. He had watched me in training occasionally but had never offered any professional advice because Dempsey was handling me and he didn't want to interfere.

Kearns didn't waste any time making his pitch. I had just gotten seated when he said, "Walker, I can make you heavyweight champion of the world."

I looked at him, startled.

"Are you kidding?"

"No. And I can get you purses you never dreamed of getting."

Before I could answer, he quickly added, "What are you getting for the Greb fight?"

"Twenty-five grand," I answered, telling the truth.

"They took you for a sucker," he sneered. "You should get a hundred thousand for that fight."

I was interested. We talked some more. The more he talked, the more I liked the idea of teaming up with him. He sold me, which wasn't hard.

He didn't have to convince me that he was a smart manager. I knew that. His fast talk and charm didn't do it—I'd met that kind before. I felt mainly that here was a man who would look out for me . . . be more than a manager or a partner. More like a friend.

We shook hands. That was the only contract we ever had.

The next day, I told Dempsey what I had done. It was a delicate subject. Jack himself wanted to be my manager and felt that he was in line for it after guiding my training for the win over Colima. But he still was active in the ring as heavyweight champion. I felt it wasn't good for one fighter to be managed by another. I turned him down. He took it like a champ.

"Mickey," Dempsey said, "you'll make millions with Kearns—but you'll die broke. He's the fastest man with a buck I've ever known. Money to him is just something to spend for a good time. I have no love for Doc, but in all honesty I've got to say he's a great manager. The best in the business.

"I'll tell you something else about Jack Kearns," Dempsey added. "He's the kind of guy who'll take your eye out if you don't watch him, but should you lose one, he'll give you one of his."

Doc was already a legend in the fight game. Of course, I knew how he had maneuvered Dempsey into the heavyweight title and the million-dollar gates with Carpentier and Firpo.

I had also heard the fabulous stories of his earlier life. As a teen-ager, he was in Alaska with Jack London and dealt cards in Tex Rickard's saloon during the gold-rush days in the Klondike. About the time of the Spanish-American War, he was touring Australia with a string of fighters.

He had been a millionaire and a hobo. At various times, to eat and stay alive, he had hustled cemetery lots in Los Angeles, run a saloon in Chicago, and even—unlikely as it seems—had operated a dairy farm in Michigan.

Nobody had a more fabulous career. He broke two banks promoting the Dempsey-Gibbons fight in Shelby, Montana. The fight proved a flop, drawing only eight thousand people. Doc had received half of the $200,000 guarantee when he signed. He demanded the other half before Dempsey got into the ring. The merchants, who had underwritten the fight, had to empty the banks to get the dough. The fight broke the town. Doc and Dempsey had to hightail it out of town by hitching a ride on the caboose of a freight train.

I had heard that he was cold, selfish and hard, that he thought only of himself and to hell with everybody else . . . But nobody ever accused him of conniving at anything but victory. If he schemed and manipulated, he did it for one reason: to win.

Doc, who must be eighty-five now, looked old even then. He was tall and spare, with a bony face which constantly was drawn into a preoccupied pucker. He was a flashy dresser as well as a quick talker. The doctor sported a four-carat diamond ring and had a wardrobe of a hundred suits which cost $250 apiece and up. He'd buy a dozen suits at a time and three or four topcoats and overcoats and sometimes gave half of them away before he ever wore them. He changed his clothes three times a day from the skin out.

Kearns even breathed with a flourish.

I admired the job he had done with Dempsey and had often thought I'd like to have a man like Doc handling me. I never wanted to bring it up myself because of my friendship with Dempsey. Doc beat me to the punch.

Now that he was my manager, I wondered how we would hit it off, how well we could work together as partners.

It turned out to be a fabulous relationship. In our time—a span of eight years—we earned close to eight million dollars. He handled all the dough and always gave me a fair shake.

CHAPTER TEN

Shrewd as he was, I don't think Kearns knew the kind of a character he had teamed up with. I went Hollywood. The glamour, the flash, the freewheeling and spending, this was what I wanted.

Golf with movie stars such as Fairbanks or Lloyd Hamilton, dancing with movie queens, race tracks, parties, movie sets—this kind of living was intoxicating. There was no stopping me. I hit all the places, went to all the big parties. I became infatuated with one of Hollywood's most beautiful women, Lilyan Tashman. Since we were both married, our friendship never went beyond mutual liking and respect. Had it been different, I could easily have fallen in love with her.

She was a wonderful woman, full of life and love. She was like me, she lived every minute of her life. Unfortunately, she was stricken with appendicitis while visiting her folks in Brooklyn a few years later, and died.

I became fat and lazy. I did no training at all, paid no attention to my condition. I did my road work in a ten-thousand-dollar sports car. I had bought it from a guy who was down on his gambling luck. It was worth sixteen grand.

It was a party and a different doll each night. Even when my money ran out, I didn't stop. There were always guys around to pick up the tab and my credit was good. I had friends.

Kearns, a pretty good night-lifer himself, tried to get

me to ease up. I paid no attention. I went Hollywood even in my clothes, having them made to order by Tartagli, a tailor for many movie stars. I wore two-hundred-dollar suits. I was Hollywood's new glamour boy.

Kearns, figuring the only way to get me off this Hollywood binge, made a match for me. He picked Lefty Cooper, a hard-hitting middleweight from San Francisco. Kearns knew he wouldn't be easy but felt I could handle him if I got into shape. I began training in a Los Angeles gymnasium but my heart wasn't in it. It was tiresome. I had lost my enthusiasm for training. I just couldn't get the glitter of Hollywood out of my brain. I was bored stiff.

I began looking for excuses to dodge training. I was to do road work every morning, but cut it to twice a week. My trainer, Bill Bloxham, begged me to take it seriously, but I knew I could handle him and didn't listen.

I was in my hotel room one morning when I was supposed to be out doing some running. I had a doll. She had spent the night with me. The telephone rang.

"It's me, Jimmy, the bellhop," the voice said. "Kearns is coming up."

I quickly got the doll out of my bed and shoved her, naked, into the closet. Then I flung her clothes in after her. She didn't raise any objections, probably thinking my wife was coming up. By the time Kearns came into the room, I had my excuse all ready.

"Gee, Doc, I overslept and didn't do my road work. I'm sorry."

Kearns paid no attention. His eyes wandered around the room. He reached under the side of the bed and came up with a pair of silk stockings.

"You're mistaken, Mickey," he said sarcastically, "you've

done plenty of road work today. No wonder you look so worn out."

Without another word, Doc spun toward the closet and yanked the door wide open. There stood my blushing beauty, naked as Venus de Milo, but with arms which were vainly trying to cover too many things at once.

After hustling the dame out of the room, Kearns turned to me.

"Mickey," he said, "I'm getting you out of here before it kills you. From now on, you'll do your training in San Francisco. I'll come up to keep an eye on you and make sure you don't do any more of this kind of road work. You got time for dames after a fight, not before.

"Also, you've got a new trainer. Don't try any tricks with him. He knows all the answers."

That's how Teddy Hayes became my trainer.

Hayes and I remained together a long time. He proved to be a good companion as well as a fine trainer. If anybody loved life more than Kearns or me, it was Teddy Hayes. He had been a fighter himself and, after quitting the ring, he became Jack Dempsey's trainer. When the two Jacks split up, Hayes went with Kearns.

Hayes was a tough taskmaster and he saw to it that I trained hard for the Cooper fight. He was on my tail all the time. I couldn't sneak out of the camp. Girls were out. I couldn't even look cross-eyed at a dame. I regretted that I had hooked up with Doc Kearns.

I was mad, but pretty soon I was also in great condition. And brother, it was a lucky thing I was. The fight was hardly a minute old when Cooper hit me a crunching left hook to the solar plexus. It was one of the hardest blows I ever took. It paralyzed me from the waist down. All the wind was knocked out of me.

91

I was practically out on my feet. I would have fallen if my feet hadn't been frozen to the canvas. Naturally, I couldn't move, so I just stood there waiting for him to come to me. Cooper didn't realize how much he had hurt me with that punch. He moved in warily. When he got within reach, I let go with a right that had everything behind it. I gave it all I had because I knew if he hit me again, I'd be in dreamland.

That punch caught him flush on the button. Cooper dropped as if he'd been hit by a fast freight. The referee counted ten, but he could have counted ten times ten. Cooper never moved a muscle until long after he had been dragged to his corner. The ref came over to raise my hand. I just stood there. I had to; I still couldn't move my legs. It must have been a strange sight, the referee holding up my arm with one hand and clutching me around the waist with the other so I wouldn't fall down.

Hayes and Kearns dragged me back to our corner. I was grateful that Kearns had forced me to train. That one punch might have changed my whole career. I made up my mind then and there I was going to listen to Doc all the way.

Kearns never deprived any fighter he ever handled of the things he himself enjoyed most, and my life changed drastically after he became my manager. Under Bulger I had lived a comparatively restricted life. No drinking, no women, no night life. Doc didn't bother with such rules. Doc saw nothing wrong with wine, women and song, just as long as they didn't interfere with fighting.

Kearns, in fact, goaded me into it the night I took my first drink at the Silver Slipper.

I was twenty-four at the time. We were with Van and Schenck, the vaudeville team. Bill Duffy, the owner of the place, was sitting with us. Doc began ribbing me about being afraid to take a drink. Doc was a great one for ribbing. My curiosity finally got me. Maybe it was the late hour, maybe it was the soft music. I thought about all the parties I had attended where the people drank and got gay. I had often wondered how it would feel to get that way. I decided to find out.

I ordered champagne. The first sip tasted bitter, the second a little better. After I had finished half a bottle, I began to float on air. Before I realized it, I was on the floor doing a mean Charleston. Everybody joined in. Schenck sang some of his famous songs. We had a wonderful time.

At first I drank only beer, wine and champagne. I never drank enough to get really drunk. I'd get high but always knew what I was doing. I didn't consider a guy drunk unless he was unable to move.

Why did I suddenly begin to drink? Why does anyone drink? I guess it's an outlet or a release. For me, it was the effect of liquor, not the taste. It was an excuse for acting up. The booze stimulated me and made me bubbling and gay. Under the influence of liquor, I'd think nothing of doing crazy things I wouldn't dream of doing when sober. Such as getting out to the center of the dance floor at Texas Guinan's and doing the Charleston, or climbing up on the stage to act as master of ceremonies at a night club, or reciting poetry to an unappreciative whore in Polly's joint, or riding a horse on a busy highway in New Jersey, or racing in a hansom cab on the Champs Elysées.

I drank because I wanted to have fun and there was more fun when I drank. The glow one gets from a few drinks brings a wonderful feeling about life and people.

Of course, drinking to excess is downright stupidity. Liquor can make you happy but too much of it can make you sad. It's like a drug to some people. They can't stop. Those are the ones who shouldn't drink at all. That, it turned out, was my trouble. I had to go to extremes in everything I did.

We returned East late in May. Maude, who certainly must have learned of my running around, decided it was time to get out of California. Mickey, Jr., was born in Newark in June. He was a wonderfully healthy little guy and I was a proud father. He looked like his mother—which was a break. He didn't inherit my Irish mug.

I was training at the time for the Greb fight, at Harry McCormick's place in Red Bank, but for a week, I must have spent more time at the hospital than I did in the training camp. Maude was even happier than I was. I guess that was the most wonderful time in our life together. I promised her that we'd have a party for the family after the Greb fight. I didn't dare break training even then, for this figured to be the toughest fight of my life.

CHAPTER ELEVEN

On July 2, 1925, I fought Greb at the Polo Grounds for the middleweight title. Humbert Fugazy promoted the fight, which was for the benefit of the Italian Hospital Fund. That was a night of nights. My old fighting pal,

Dave Shade, beat another very good middleweight, Jimmy Slattery, in one of the preliminaries. Harry Wills, who sought in vain for years to fight Dempsey for the heavyweight championship, flattened Charlie Weinert in two heats in the semi-final.

Thirty-five years ago sports events were backed with a little more sincerity than they are today. Especially prize fights. But both times have one thing in common. The "sure thing" gamblers are on hand, looking to win sucker money.

Arnold Rothstein made the gambling odds on sporting events in New York in those days. He could be seen almost any night of the week at Lindy's on Broadway. Lindy's, just as it is today, was then the gathering spot for show folks and sportsmen from all over the country, especially the night before and on the day of any big boxing match.

My fight with Greb naturally was all smoked up. We came down the training home stretch with tremendous ballyhoo. Greb, a shrewd gambler, sometimes deliberately gave the impression that he was the worst-conditioned fighter in the world. And he went out of his way to prove it.

The night before the fight, Harry hustled a couple of his girl friends into a cab and made the rounds. After displaying himself in several night clubs, Harry headed for Lindy's where he knew Rothstein and the other betting boys would be.

With an eye to business, Greb climbed out of the hack first, stumbled and almost fell into the gutter, missing his footing purposely. His girl friends quickly grabbed him under the arms and helped him back into the cab. It was

Harry's intention to have the gambling mob think he had been drinking heavily.

The ruse worked. Overnight, the odds on Greb changed. The gamblers made me the favorite. They knew I was in good shape. The gamblers figured not even a great fighter like Greb could climb into the ring with me less than twenty-four hours after a spree, and fight fifteen hard rounds.

The next day, at the weigh-in ceremonies, Greb walked jauntily into the New York Boxing Commission's offices. He was nattily dressed. He was clear-eyed.

At the examination, the doctor gave him a clean bill of health. He weighed 160 to my 148. A reporter, who had been tipped off that Greb had been drinking heavily the night before, asked him how he felt.

"I feel fine," Greb grinned. "How do you feel?"

The Polo Grounds was jammed that night. As we stood waiting in our corners for the bell, I bent down to bless myself as I did in all my fights. Greb, watching me, grinned and did the same. I got the idea he was making fun of me. When the bell rang, I tore from my corner in a wild fury. Greb met me in the center of the ring, and one of the greatest fights in history was under way.

We fought hammer and tongs all the way. Round after round we slugged each other all over the ring. Neither of us took time out to step back from a punch. With our heads down and our arms swinging, each of us tried for a knockout from the opening gong. We were each called on fouls repeatedly. The referee, Ed Purdy, was having a hard time. Once Greb hit him by accident and almost knocked him out of the ring.

The break came in the seventh round. Purdy sprained his ankle and that was that. He'd had trouble before. Now he couldn't handle us at all. Until then, it was one of those even-Stephen things—anybody's guess who would win.

Greb, who would use a razor in the ring if he thought he could get away with it, kept bulling me. He slammed, slapped, backhanded, and ground his glove into my face. My Little Lord Fauntleroy days had been over a long time ago and I did some street fighting of my own.

For thirteen rounds the battle continued this way. Neither one tried to be smart. All we wanted to do was punch it out. We just stood there under those lights, pounding away and ducking every now and then, with 65,000 fight fans screaming their heads off.

In the fourteenth, Greb jabbed his thumb in my eye, partially blinding me. The water coming out of it blurred my vision and I backed up against the ropes. I tried to clear the eye by wiping away the blur with the thumb-tip of my right glove.

I saw his right hand coming. I can still see it. It looked as big as a balloon shooting toward me. I raised my left shoulder to protect my chin, confident I could block the blow. But somehow, it slipped past and landed high on my jaw. I was knocked ragtime, not off my feet, but I was silly. You know, like a man walking in a dream. It nearly tore off my roof.

For the next two and a half minutes, Greb crawled all over me, firing punches from all angles. He hit me with everything. I was reeling from one side of the ring to the other. When the bell rang, ending the round, I was draped over the top rope.

Hayes dragged me back to my corner. He doused cold water over me. The smelling salts under my nose cleared my head. But my left eye was completely closed and the right eye wasn't much better. Hayes was in my corner alone that night, because Kearns was still under suspension by the State Athletic Commission for ignoring their order for Dempsey to fight Harry Wills for the title. Doc wasn't even allowed to attend the fight. He listened to it on the radio in LaHiff's Tavern.

It was a wild fifteenth. As we were shaking hands, I made up my mind that if I had to be knocked out, I'd go down swinging. I was lucky. My first punch caught Harry flush on the chin. That put him in the same condition I was in the previous round. It just about knocked him loose from his brains. I couldn't finish him, though. I was too far gone from the belt he handed me in the fourteenth. Greb managed to last out that final round and the decision went to him.

The clip on the chin he fed me had me on queer street for a half hour after the fight.

The fight over, I returned to the Park Central Hotel (now Park Sheraton) where Kearns and I were staying. Hayes had fixed me up as best he could but my left eye was still closed and the other was just a slit. Anyway, I was able to maneuver down the street to LaHiff's.

Kearns was still at the Tavern when I arrived there. He was sitting in our usual corner. Mae Clarke, my date of the evening, was with him. Mae, one of Tex Guinan's gals, later became a fine actress in Hollywood.

It was about one o'clock in the morning, but LaHiff's was crowded. I had little difficulty making my way to Doc, and I was almost there when I heard someone calling my name. Though I couldn't see too well, there was nothing wrong with my hearing. I could recognize that voice anywhere. I had been listening to it, drumming into my ears, all night. It belonged to Greb.

"Mickey," Greb called out. "Have a drink with some friends of mine, will you?"

He reached out his hand in welcome and smiled.

Always the gentleman, always polite. That was Harry Greb, outside the ring.

Seated with him were two gorgeous dolls. I was young, too, and when Greb invited me to join the party and relax over a few drinks, I thought why not? Especially since I'd had a busy night at my work. Greb said he'd had a busy night, too, and he would appreciate and enjoy the company of so willing a workman.

I was drinking prohibition ale in those days and in a very short time, I was in a mellow mood. So was Greb. We sat there and talked and talked about everything but the fight we had just finished. The girls became bored stiff and went home. We didn't even notice when they left.

Greb had a reputation as a drinker, but he really couldn't drink. Two stiff slugs knocked him for a loop. He was worse than I was.

I would have been okay had I stuck to ale, but I switched to wine and that got me. Greb, who began with straight whiskey, also switched to wine, probably not wanting to be outdone by me.

Gradually everyone left, including Kearns, who took my date with him. Greb and I were the only customers left. The waiters, looking on impatiently, started putting the chairs on the tables. When Harry and I made no move to get up, they began dimming the lights. We finally got the idea we weren't wanted.

It was now three A.M., but I didn't feel like going back to the hotel. Taking Greb by the arm, I said, "Let's go to the Silver Slipper. Duffy is not like LaHiff. He appreciates good customers like us."

Harry had no objections to anything by this time. We were feeling no pain as we made our way, arm in arm, up Forty-eighth Street. Suddenly, I remembered I had something to ask Greb.

"Say, Harry, why did you make fun of me when I was blessing myself?"

He looked at me out of the corner of his good eye.

"What the hell are you talking about?"

"The time I blessed myself just before the bell at the start of the fight?"

"Made fun of you, hell," Greb growled. "You think you got a monopoly on help from up there? I knew what a tough fight it was going to be and I wanted all the help I could get."

I had been mistaken. Harry Greb had not ridiculed me.

As we neared the Silver Slipper, I began to feel very good. Finally, just outside the door, I stopped Greb.

"You know, Harry," I said, "you never would have licked me if it wasn't for your heeling and if you hadn't stuck your thumb in my eye. That was one of your downright Dutch tricks."

Greb turned red.

"Why, you Irish lug," he burst out, "I can whip you any time of the day. You ought to know that. I can lick you with one arm tied behind my back."

He turned to go inside, but changed his mind.

"In fact," he said grimly, "I'll do it now."

Greb made one mistake. He began to peel off his coat, and that was too good a chance for a roughneck who'd been raised on street fighting. When the coat was halfway off, I bounced one off his chin. The punch would have kayoed any other man—but not Greb. You might have killed him with an ax, but I don't know of any other way.

He fell back against a taxicab waiting at the curb and dented the fender. The cab driver charged out and began punching Harry, but Greb paid no attention to him. He was bent on murdering me.

We slugged away and people came running over to see what it was all about.

Can you imagine two guys who had just fought for $75,000 between them before 65,000 people, brawling for nothing in the gutter? It's unbelievable, I guess. Hundreds of people have sworn they saw that fight, the one outside the night club after three in the morning. Actually, when it began, there were only a newsboy, the cab driver and the doorman. When it was over, there may have been a few dozen people watching us.

They had never seen anything like it before. Two champions going at it with bare fists. No rounds, no ducking, nothing but punching. We'd probably be fighting yet if a giant Irish cop on the beat named Pat Casey had not pulled us apart and heaved us into separate taxicabs. Casey knew both of us well.

"If you bums won't stop," he threatened, "there will be a double champion on the police force tonight."

I lost the first fight to Greb, but I always thought I won the second one.

It was not until I got back to my hotel that I remembered something—my date. I knew Doc as a ladies' man and I could just picture him making time with Mae. I didn't like that. I grabbed the phone and began making calls. Nobody had seen Kearns. I finally called Duffy's place.

"Doc just left," the bartender's voice came over the telephone. "He's been here for hours."

I was thinking about Kearns enjoying himself in Duffy's,

never knowing that his fighter was involved in a street brawl just outside, when the barkeeper's voice came back on.

"Hey, Mickey, there's a friend of yours here who wants to talk to you."

Who was the friend? You guessed it. Harry Greb!

"What I said before still goes," he yelled into the mouthpiece. "I can lick you any time, any place; you and your whole family."

"Why, you . . ."

"And furthermore, Walker, I've got your girl."

I was shouting curses so fast and so loud, I didn't hear Kearns unlock the door and come into the room.

"Who are you talking to like that?" he wanted to know.

"That no good, rotten, yellow-livered Dutchman," I said.

"Give me the phone," Doc roared and grabbed the thing out of my hand.

"Listen, Greb," he shouted, "you were lucky tonight. You won't be so lucky the next time. Only you'll both get real dough out of it this time. A return match between you and Mickey will bring a million-dollar gate."

We were down at Tex Rickard's office the next day, Kearns and I, to pick up my check for the fight. Greb and his manager, Harry Mason, were already there when we arrived.

Rickard, who never missed a trick, had the contracts for a return bout in his hands. He handed one to me and the other to Greb.

"There's a $100,000 guarantee to each of you for a return bout," he said. "All you have to do is sign these papers."

Greb let his eyes wander over the contract. He looked

at Rickard, then at me. His face was all marked up. I wasn't exactly fit to pose for a cigarette ad, either.

"Mickey," he said slowly, "there are too many other guys around for us to keep on fighting each other."

"That suits me exactly, Harry," I said. "Let's step out and have a drink."

We formed a sincere friendship, but it didn't last long. Less than sixteen months later he was dead.

On the night of August 20, 1926, Greb was driving through the Allegheny Mountains in the rain.

He topped a hill, saw two cars parked side by side on the road ahead, and slammed on his brakes. The tires wouldn't hold on the wet pavement and the car turned over twice. Harry wound up in the hospital with a broken nose. Later he went to Atlantic City for an operation on a bone near the base of his skull. He failed to recover from the anesthetic.

One of the few times I ever cried in my life was when he died.

Greb was the greatest fighter I ever saw. I've heard that Dempsey refused an offer of $100,000 to fight him after they had boxed a few rounds together in a gym and Jack knew how good he was.

Greb was only a middleweight but he could fight any man, of any size. They called him the Pittsburgh windmill. He had over three hundred fights through thirteen battle-scarred years and was the only man ever to lick Gene Tunney. Tunney, as you know, retired as the undefeated heavyweight champion in the early thirties.

I never saw anybody faster than Greb, either with his hands or his feet. He won two titles, the middleweight and light-heavyweight, yet seldom scaled over 160 pounds. Greb licked headliners in the three top weight classes while totally blind in his right eye. Kid Norfolk blinded him early in his career with a terrific left hook.

Greb was one of the strangest guys I've ever known. He was a big better himself, but he hated the Broadway gamblers and sharks. He had a reputation for being cheap because he never paid for others' drinks. But he wasn't cheap. He just preferred to pay his own way. He wouldn't allow anyone to buy him a drink; he always insisted on paying for his own and his girl's.

Harry was a sucker for girls. He would meet a waitress, fall for her, and the next day she'd have a Cadillac or a mink coat. A lot of people thought he was broke when he died. Few knew that he left his daughter a quarter of a million dollars.

CHAPTER TWELVE

On September 21, 1925, I defended my welterweight title against Dave Shade in the first really big-money fight under Kearns's management. We received a $100,000 guarantee. It was a tough fight all the way. I had knocked Dave out back in 1921 in Newark, but he was just a young fighter then, coming up. Four years later he was in his prime.

Leo P. Flynn, who later managed Dempsey, was his manager, and a good one, even though he didn't like me. I had refused to let Leo manage me after Bulger's death. Maybe because of that rejection, he had a burning desire to manage a fighter who could lick me. He tried several times, without success. When he couldn't beat me with his own fighters, he'd bet on others to beat me, but I don't think he ever collected one of those bets. And maybe I fought a little harder when I saw Flynn in the other man's corner.

Fortunately, I was in the best condition of my life for the title bout with Shade, also held at the Polo Grounds.

Kearns was the best corner man in the business. He could sense, before anyone else, when the other guy was beginning to weaken. He knew how to figure out styles. I always listened to him. Which was why I needed a guy in my corner I could trust.

When I got back to my corner after the fourteenth round, I felt I had the fight in the bag. But Kearns shook his head. "No," he said. "Mickey, you've got to knock him out in this round. If not, you'll blow your title."

Doc never believed in taking chances.

I won the fifteenth big and took the decision. Shade managed to stay on his feet but he was so badly beaten he had to be taken to a hospital.

I took a long layoff after the Shade fight. Kearns had a big mansion on Kingsley Drive in Hollywood, and he took me out there for a rest. His mother and sister lived there. My wife, Maude, went with me. So did Teddy Hayes, my trainer.

I was no longer a stranger in Hollywood. I knew who to call and where to go. Besides, I had Doc with me now. I hardly missed doing the town a single night of the six months I was there.

I had a lot of freedom. Maude and the baby stayed with Doc's mother and sister while we moved to a hotel. Being a new mother, Maude was kept busy with the baby and I was left pretty much on my own to do as I pleased.

Maude knew I was running wild but she couldn't do anything about it.

I put on weight from the soft living. My only exercise consisted of light boxing with Charlie Chaplin and Doug Fairbanks and some golf with Walter Hagen. I used to visit Charlie in his private quarters at the Chaplin Studios. He'd stop work and we'd go into his private gymnasium and put on the gloves. We'd spend an hour or so at a time, and I'd show him how to get more steam and speed into his punches.

Hagen was the Professional Golf Association champion. Kearns introduced us. Doc was a real golf enthusiast, and Haig loved the night spots as much as Doc and I. He was playing in a big tournament in Los Angeles. The night before the final round, Walter, Doc and I really had a dinger. After drinking up the town, we ended up in Haig's apartment. I don't think he slept a wink. In the morning, he showered and shaved, went out to the links and won the tournament.

One day, Doc and I decided to go to the horse races. We couldn't simply go to a track in Los Angeles, or even in California. No, not us. We had to go down to Tijuana in Mexico.

We stayed up drinking the night before. The next morning, driving down in Kearns's Lincoln, we were feeling no pain. We had a couple of girls along and enjoyed ourselves at the track, where we picked up a few pesos. Then we all went to a Mexican saloon in Caliente for the evening.

How it began, I don't know, but not long after we arrived at the saloon, Doc and I inherited a friend. He said he was a Mexican Army officer and had ridden with Pancho Villa as his top lieutenant. Before long we had become such warm friends that Alfredo Juarez, as he called himself, confided that he was planning to overthrow the Mexican government. All he lacked was a group of followers.

The idea sounded exciting. It promised lots of action. The only trouble was . . . who would be the general? Alfredo claimed the honor rightfully belonged to him since it was he who proposed the idea in the first place. Doc wasn't going to let any Mexican rank over him. No, said Doc, *he* was going to be the general.

Doc has always had one peculiarity when drinking. If he's with a group of actors, he fancies himself an actor— but the best damn actor of them all! If he's with fighters, he feels he could lick them all. If he's with racketeers, he becomes public enemy Number One. Now, of course, he was the top revolutionist in Mexico.

Kearns, therefore, proceeded to nominate himself as the general and appointed this character a colonel.

"Mickey is too small for anything but a major," he announced.

"Major, hell," I squawked, "either I'm a general, or you can take this entire army and shove it."

My mention of army did something to Alfredo.

"Si, señores," he said, "we have to have an army. You can't overthrow a government without one."

Doc and I paid no attention to our amigo. We were still arguing over rank. During the argument, Colonel Juarez disappeared. We never missed him. Some thirty minutes later, he was back. This time he had twenty compañeros with him, and five horses. Since the horses were for the officers, Kearns got one and I got one.

Now we had an army. We were ready to overthrow the government.

"Follow me, señores," Alfredo said, mounting his horse. "We must gather more sympaticos for our cause. When we have enough men, we go on our first raid."

Kearns was all for it although he hadn't the slightest idea where we were going. The way I felt, I wouldn't have cared if we raided Mexico City.

Just when we were about to start, we heard a lot of noise. Before we knew what had happened, we were surrounded by a horde of Mexican Police on horseback. They had been summoned by the owner of the saloon.

"Conspirators are plotting to overthrow the government," he had warned them. "Come quickly."

So instead of going on a raid, we found ourselves cooling our heels in the hoosegow. We were jailed as dangerous revolutionaries.

Drunk as we were, we had sense enough to realize we were in serious trouble. What made it even worse was our inability to understand Spanish. We couldn't rely on Pancho Villa's lieutenant because he was kept in isolation.

Lucky for us, Kearns remembered he had a good friend in Tijuana, the owner of the Tijuana track, Jim Crawford. The police got in touch with Crawford and, after an hour and a half behind bars, we were freed in custody of Crawford.

When Doc and I got back to Hollywood, we jumped right on the merry-go-round again. The term rock 'n roll hadn't been coined in our day, but that's what we were doing. We caroused in speak-easies, night clubs and house parties. The doors were open to us and we never said no to an invitation.

We went to a party one night in 1926 and got high, which was par for the course. Lloyd Hamilton, the deadpan comedian of silent pictures, was there. Maybe you remember him, the fat guy in the black-and-white checked cap. Hamilton was near the end of his career. He had lived high, had blown millions and needed money. He owned a large tract of land in Laurel Canyon, in the hills above Hollywood.

Ham wanted to leave Hollywood. He was sick of the place and was washed up in pictures, too. Anyway, he wanted some quick dough, hoping to go to New York and make a fresh start.

Doc and I were feeling no pain and it didn't take much salesmanship on Ham's part to sell us his real estate. We bought it for $55,000, sight unseen. It was a rather unbusinesslike transaction. Lloyd was as looped as we were.

When I got up the next morning, wearing a head like a rhino, I vaguely remembered, through the fumes, that we had made a deal. I tried to phone Hamilton and call it off, but he had left for New York.

"Hello, Sucker," I said to Kearns on the phone. "What do we do now with these hills we own?"

We agreed we were stuck with the property, but Doc, as usual, knew the way out. "We'll find another sucker," said the good doctor.

We did, and in a hurry. We put it on the market at once, and considered we had pulled a fast one when we sold it for $58,000 a couple of days later. The rest you can guess. Our "sucker" developed the land and sold it for several million bucks. Many of the biggest names in Hollywood live there now on palatial estates. I'll say one thing for Doc and me—we did everything big, including the mistakes.

I was so in love with Hollywood and the life I was living, that Doc became disgusted with me and decided I had better get back into shape and into the ring—before the Toy Bulldog grew up to be a waddling midget mastiff.

He insisted we return to New York and get back in the ring. My wife thought it was a good idea for me to get back East, too. She sure didn't see much of me in Hollywood.

But New York didn't change my way of living much. This was 1926, the year which saw the nation's gravy train really rolling, with more and more passengers climbing aboard. The gangsters had taken over the night life in the big city, and the spoiled, thrill-seeking socialites were their best customers. The girls especially went for gangsters. A hard-hitting young columnist, Walter Winchell, coined a name for these society broads. He called them "debutramps."

Their fathers and mothers had found their pleasure in such elegant spots as Rector's, Delmonico's and Tony Pastor's, but these kids dumped their good money and drank their bad liquor in such clip joints as the Hotsy Totsy Club (owned by Jack "Legs" Diamond), Dutch Schultz's Embassy, Larry Fay's El Fay Club, Owney Madden's Cotton Club and, of course, Guinan's saloon.

There never had been anyone like Texas Guinan, who owned the 300 Club. Few could forget Texas raising her jewel-covered arms and shouting, "Hello, Sucker!" The customers ate it up, knowing they were being taken— and loving it. Guinan was a smart dame. She was all business, a magnetic showman with a lightning mind. She knew how to pick her girls, too. Several of them became stars. There were Ruby Keeler, who married Al Jolson, and Ruby Stevens, who changed her name to Barbara Stanwyck. Guinan never drank, which made her smarter than her customers.

The night Guinan opened, New Year's Eve of 1926, I

was part of the floor show. I did an impromptu Charleston and also an imitation of Joe Frisco, the stuttering comedian.

"Come on, Mickey," Tex egged me on. "Show these suckers how it should be done." The audience applauded and I bounced out on the floor, with a cigar and a derby on the tilt, and danced.

Then there was Belle Livingston, who ran The Mansion on Fifty-eighth Street, where you paid plenty for the privilege of drinking while seated on the floor, Japanese-style. She used to say that her booze would put you on the floor, anyway, so you might as well start there.

Another famous place was the House of Morgan, where blues singer Helen Morgan would bring tears to the eyes of sentimentalists and drunks when she sang: "Can't Help Lovin' That Man." Lucky Luciano owned that joint.

At five o'clock in the morning, when I should have been home asleep, I would be in one of the spots putting on a floor show.

Another famous lady of the day—or should it be lady of the evening?—was Polly Adler, who ran the plushiest whorehouse in town. Polly's was actually an apartment rather than a house. But it was large, beautifully furnished—and men came there for uninterrupted drinking and gambling as well as sex. Polly supplied the food, drinks, cards and girls and, more important, privacy. She didn't care what a person's tastes in entertainment were, as long as he could pay for them. She catered to the richest people and she took great pains to have available both the youngest girls and the oldest whiskey. In some establishments similar to hers, this order was reversed.

Polly's customers included bankers, politicians, show-world celebrities, and members of the social register as

111

well as racketeers and mobsters. She also catered to college men from the Ivy schools. Indeed, some of her affluent customers sent their collegiate sons to her—and even brought them in person.

As I say, the customers didn't always come for sex. Polly's place was used by rich men to meet friends, play cards and hold dinner parties. Some men just killed time there.

Of course, she was famous and she had to have "protection" to stay in business. Even so, during her career, she was raided often by reform administrations. She simply set up shop in different locations, all in the Central Park area in the vicinity of the Fifties and Sixties. The cops would close her up and then look the other way while she settled in a new location.

Dutch Schultz, who later was assassinated in Joe Regan's brother's café in Newark, made Adler's house a hangout—or a hideout when the gang wars were raging. When he was there, nobody else was permitted in the place. Polly was scared to death of him.

She might have been the Queen Madam, but to me, she was always a stand-up guy. In my book, she is a real champ. She was a sharp businesswoman, a financial brain. You had to be somebody to go there, and you had to pay plenty—no matter who you were or how well you knew her.

If you wanted to, you could bring your own doll. It mattered to her only that you paid the bill. She ran an honest store and expected her customers to play the game, too.

The largest amount of money I ever blew in one spree was at Polly's.

When I was rolling high, I wouldn't let anyone pick

up a tab, except maybe Kearns. It made me feel important to grab the check in the company of big shots. In those days, if it got around that a guy blew fifty thousand in a floating crap game, the next day he could get credit almost anywhere. Today, if you blow twenty-five bucks, you're a sucker.

Everybody wanted to be around the "live" guys in my time.

Anyway, Doc and I went up to Polly's one evening and found the place full of brokers, politicians, Broadway characters and big-time mobsters.

I was pretty well loaded with a package I had picked up at Guinan's. When I saw all these money men, I decided I was going to be the biggest shot of them all. I insisted on picking up the tab for everybody for the whole night's entertainment.

They took me up on it pretty quick. Kearns didn't stop me. Polly didn't care. The "entertainment" lasted two nights and a day. It ended only when Polly's girls complained they needed some sleep. The bill came to about twenty thousand dollars. I paid it without batting an eye.

Later, when I had my own saloon on Eighth Avenue just opposite Madison Square Garden, I overheard my uncle, Daniel Higgins, say that Mayor LaGuardia was going to chase Polly out of town. As an architect, Uncle Dan had designed many buildings in New York. He knew some of the top politicians and got the word from them.

Dan didn't know I was a friend of Polly's. I figured I had to warn her that a raid was planned. I left the saloon, pretending I had to attend to some business, and took a cab to Central Park South.

Polly appeared grateful for the information and quickly grabbed the phone to call her connections.

Since I was there, I decided to enjoy myself. It was a quiet night, with only a few customers, and I had the place pretty much to myself.

I had four hundred dollars in my pocket when I came in. I must have spent about a hundred on girls and drinks. After a couple of hours, I knew I was in no condition to return to my saloon, so decided to spend the night at Polly's place. The last thing I remember that night was Polly leading me into her private quarters and putting me to bed.

When I woke up the next morning, Polly was gone. So were the girls. In fact, the joint was empty, save for the maid. I dressed and automatically reached into my pocket to feel my money. It was gone. I was cleaned out! Didn't have a dime. I had to borrow five bucks from the maid for carfare back to my saloon. I just couldn't believe that Polly had rolled me. That night, she came into my joint.

"Hey, Polly," I whispered to her. "I had three hundred dollars in my pocket when I fell asleep. You were the only one in the room besides me."

She made no attempt to deny that she had taken the roll.

"What the hell do you think I'm running, a free lunch counter?" she asked.

"But I was there to do you a good turn," I said. "I'm your friend."

"What's friendship got to do with business?" she asked.

I had to laugh. What could I do? That was Polly.

I did most of my gambling at a place in New Jersey called The Farm which was about twelve miles from the Holland Tunnel on Route One.

The Farm was a big converted residence in the suburbs and did a tremendous business . . . as much, I'm sure, as the gambling places in Las Vegas do today. Craps, poker and twenty-one were the main games, although faro, chemin de fer, roulette and the other games got a big play, too. They had different tables for different stakes. There were one-hundred-dollar-limit tables and there were no-limit tables. I never bothered with any but the no-limit tables.

Everything was done in elegant style. They had regular limousine service—customers were picked up in New York in chauffeur-driven Cadillacs. All meals were on the house, including drinks and smokes. When you were through, there would be a car waiting for you to take you back to your hotel or wherever you wanted to go. Yes, everything was first class.

I visited The Farm two or three times a week.

I was also a regular at the race track. I was known as a plunger, I suppose. I was friendly with the horse owners and the jockeys and received good information. As a result, I was a big depositor in the Second National Bank of Red Bank. The bank president kept urging me to invest my money, and I finally agreed. As it turned out, I proved pretty lucky in real estate and in the stock market, too.

I had first-mortgage bonds in one of the biggest bonding companies in New York, which were paying me 4 percent; I had property in Rumson, on the Shrewsbury River; I had five hundred shares of Ford Ltd. of England; I had a thousand shares of American Telephone and Telegraph.

I owned an expensive house in Rumson and had five cars, in addition to the Locomobile, which I kept in California. I had a cream-colored Duesenberg, a specially built La Salle, a dark-blue Cadillac sedan, a Lincoln and a Ford. The Duesenberg was my "flash" car which I used for trips to New York. The La Salle was my country car

—for driving around Rumson. The Cadillac was for my wife. The Lincoln was for Jimmy Duryea, my chauffeur, and the Ford was for use by my house guests. The Ford always stood outside my house and any of my pals were free to use it.

CHAPTER THIRTEEN

Fame and fortune at the age of twenty-five. I wasn't equipped mentally for it and I made mistakes.

I ran around so much I had practically no home life. I had even less time for Maude and Mickey, Jr., than I'd had for them in Hollywood.

I never carried less than a thousand dollars in my pocket. I was too young to realize the value of money. Well-meaning friends deplored my extravagance and pleaded with me to sink some of my dough in annuities.

"If you start putting some money away in annuities now," a friend advised me, "you'll get a hundred dollars a week, for life, starting at the age of forty."

I had to laugh.

"A hundred a week?" I snorted. "Why, that's my usual tip to waiters!"

I didn't mind investing in the stock market or real estate, because there was the opportunity for huge profits in a hurry. It appealed to my gambling instinct. But that slow, steady buildup for an annuity wasn't for me. It was too dull.

I was a sucker but I didn't care. I guess I was out to prove that Texas Guinan was right, for I really talked myself into another terrific tab in her joint one night. I always celebrated after a big victory and on this particular night there was good reason to celebrate. Doc and I had just returned from Chicago where I had taken the middleweight title away from Tiger Flowers. We hit Guinan's at a late hour after having been on the town for most of the night.

Among the customers at Guinan's was a Broadway regular, Fred Perry, who commuted regularly between New York and Cuba. He was entertaining a large and noisy party. Corks were popping at a merry pace. The phony champagne at twenty-five bucks a copy was flowing like water. As the night wore on, Perry invited us to join his table.

Finally, it was daylight and time to go home. I asked for Perry's check as well as my own, and I offered to lick anyone else who tried to pay. The more Perry objected, the more I insisted. Perry finally shrugged his shoulders.

"Okay, give it to the sucker," he told the headwaiter.

When the waiter arrived with the itemized account, which looked like a railroad ticket to Johannesburg, I glanced carelessly at the total and tossed out a five-hundred-dollar bill.

"Keep the change," I said gaily.

The waiter fidgeted a moment, then coughed apologetically. "I'm sorry, Mr. Walker," he stammered, "it's not four hundred twenty; it's four thousand, two hundred."

The Perry party had been in the Club for three days. I shuddered, but I paid it. After all, how would it have looked if I'd backed down then?

Texas Guinan and her girls occasionally used to come down and spend a weekend at my home in Rumson. It was a big five-bedroom house and we had lots of space.

Morton Downey attended several of my parties. So did Dan Healy and his vivacious wife, Helen Kane, the Boop-Boop-a-Doop girl, and Fanny Brice, and Billy DeBeck and actress Nancy Carroll, Billy LaHiff's niece. DeBeck was the famous cartoonist who drew Barney Google.

My guests also usually included friends in the sports world and such famous writers as Damon Runyon, Bill Farnsworth, Joe Williams, Hype Igoe, Paul Gallico, Jackie Farrell, Sid Mercer, Jim Jennings, Ed Van Avery and Mark Hellinger.

I have been asked many times why my brother, Joe, who is nine years younger than I, never tried to be a professional boxer. There's quite a story behind that and as so many things in my life seemed to, it began with a party.

Joe, then sixteen, was an altar boy at Sacred Heart Church. At St. Benedict's Prep in Newark, he was an outstanding all-around athlete. He was a husky youngster, taller than I, and pretty handy with his fists. He had a friend, Johnny MacGuire, who encouraged him to become a fighter. There was soft money in the prize ring, MacGuire convinced him, and besides, his brother was a champion and that would save him a lot of time and work in gaining a reputation.

Joe was in fine physical condition and when vacation time rolled around he had made up his mind to become a fighter. MacGuire was to be his manager. There was just one obstacle—me. Joe knew I was opposed to having another prize fighter in the family.

However, he was determined to become a fighter. But how was he going to break the news to his brother? That was a problem. Joe and Johnny put their heads together and came up with a plan. Why not have a party, get me in a mellow mood, and then spring it on me?

118

Having made up their minds, they approached Harry McCormick, who owned a golf course in Shrewsbury, and sold him the idea of staging a "Mickey Walker Night" at his country club and bringing down from New York some of my show business friends to entertain. Such a stunt, they guaranteed, would bring a great deal of publicity to his place.

Harry went for it. And it turned out to be a great night. Morton Downey sang beautiful Irish ballads. Joe Frisco danced. Van and Schenck sang. So did Fanny Brice. Texas Guinan brought her Broadway show. We had a marvelous time. All evening, MacGuire kept assuring me that he and Joe had been responsible for the party.

When we arrived home about three o'clock in the morning, I was happy from hooch. Joe and Johnny were going to stay at my house and Joe decided this was the appropriate time to tell me.

"Mickey," Joe announced boldly, "I've got a good offer to become a fighter. I want to become one very much. I know you're opposed to it. But with or without your consent, I'm going to become a prize fighter."

After all the trouble he'd gone through to arrange the fine party, I just couldn't give him a flat refusal. I tried to reason with him, but got nowhere. Finally, I had an idea.

"Joe," I said, "I don't want you to become a fighter for good reasons. It's a tough game. Now, listen. I'll make you a sporting proposition. I'll let you fight on one condition. We'll go out to the gym right now and we'll put on the gloves. We'll box three rounds. If you last those three rounds, I'll let you be a fighter . . ."

MacGuire interrupted: "That's not fair. You're a champion. He can't last three rounds with you. You'll knock him out with one punch."

"Let me finish," I said. "I promise not to throw a punch. You, MacGuire, will be the referee and the timekeeper. If I as much as lay a glove on Joe, I lose. If Joe hits me once in three rounds, he wins."

Joe laughed. "You mean you won't hit me?" he asked.

"That's right. But if you don't hit me, I'll have your word that you'll forget all about fighting."

That was the agreement when we went to the gym above the garage. Although it was a small room, it was equipped with all the boxing paraphernalia. MacGuire, tying a last knot on Joe's soft sixteen-ounce gloves (I didn't want to use regular eight-ounce gloves), turned and said:

"Hey, what happens if Joe hurts you?"

"That's the idea," I assured him. "He's supposed to tag me."

This may sound silly, but it's true. When one is sparring just for exercise, boxing is a pleasure. On the other hand, when one starts throwing punches with everything behind his blows, boxing takes on a different turn. An athlete, no matter how well conditioned, unless he had practiced boxing, would find it difficult to last three rounds in a hard fight with an experienced boxer.

Round One: Joe feinted with his left, trying for an opening. He let go his right . . . and missed. It was a real haymaker. He had nothing to lose. He knew he wasn't going to get hit in return. He tried again and missed. Again he missed. Every time he swung, I either turned my head or ducked. In the meantime, I kept talking to him, encouraging him to throw his best punch. I kept ducking, bobbing and weaving, forcing Joe to do all the chasing. Finally, MacGuire called time. End of round one.

Round Two: This was a duplicate of the first. I kept Joe off balance, making him miss. He never laid a glove on me. He was in good shape, but not in boxing condition, and pretty soon he began to breathe hard. Before the round ended, he was gasping for breath. His own wild swinging was tiring him out.

Round Three: Joe's swings were slower and his breathing was faster. Before the round was two minutes old, I knew he was all in. Joe was doing twice as much work as I was. He was gamely staggering around, though, and I knew that in another minute, I would have to keep my promise. I had to think fast. I held out my unprotected chin and invited Joe to swing at it. MacGuire yelled: "Let it go, Joe!"

Joe saw his opportunity. He wound up from the floor and took his last shot. I turned my head and the punch missed. Joe spun around and fell flat on his face. His chin hit the hard floor and he lay there, stunned. MacGuire stood staring at Joe's quiet form. Then, bending over his friend, he said, "That's all, pal. We retire from prize fighting."

Joe never lost his interest in boxing, however. He was a middleweight on the boxing team at Fordham University. Years later he became a referee, and in 1954 he was appointed Boxing Commissioner of New Jersey, a position he still holds. He was an all-around athlete and at one time was badminton champion of the State. He still is a low-handicap golfer.

Unlike the Walkers, MacGuire didn't have the fighting blood in his veins but he loved athletics and he settled on golf. It's a good thing for him he took up law, too. After these years of playing, I'm still about the only man he can beat on the links. He's had much better success in the courts, however. Johnny MacGuire is Judge John J. MacGuire now. He tied the knot at my last marriage. I wonder if the Judge, when he's sitting in the governor's chair in New Jersey, as he's sure to some day, will think back and wonder what might have happened had he and my brother not arranged a certain party for Mickey Walker one night in 1926?

That brief impromptu match with brother Joe was the only boxing I did for six months. I was getting ring-rusty. Kearns was getting worried. He knew I needed action, and there was still another reason Kearns thought it was time I fought again. The Boxing Commission was on his back, screaming for me to defend my welterweight title.

Kearns looked over the field and decided on my old rival, Pete Latzo. Pete, from the coal regions of Pennsylvania, was knocking them dead around his home town of Scranton and had become the idol of the miners. There aren't any more enthusiastic fight fans anywhere in the world than those Pennsylvania coal miners and we were offered thirty thousand dollars to defend my title in a ten-rounder against their favorite son in Latzo's home town. Kearns was cool to the idea at first. He didn't think thirty grand was enough of an inducement for me to risk my title. When he told me what was on his mind, I laughed.

"You have nothing to worry about, Doc," I told him. "Latzo will be just a warm-up for me. If there's any man in the world I can lick, it's that guy. Didn't I kick him around like a rag doll in Newark back in 1923? There'll be nothing to it. Thirty grand for trimming Pete? Why, it's the easiest money I'll ever earn."

(I'll always remember that first fight with Pete Latzo.

That was when they hung the nickname Toy Bulldog on me. It was given to me by Francis Albertanti, a New Jersey boxing writer. He wrote that I reminded him of bulldogs he used to watch tear each other to pieces in fights.)

"Doc," I insisted, "I'm sure I can lick Latzo. Get him for me."

"But he's been going good," Kearns hesitated. "He's beaten Schlaifer, Italian Joe Gans and a lot of other pretty smart coots. And there's always a chance of us being jobbed. We don't want to be caught with a home-town decision against us."

"Don't worry. I'm going to give up the night clubs for the gym. No more Broadway, no more bright lights. I'm going to get in shape and I don't care if the fight is in Latzo's back yard. It won't even be close."

Kearns gave in and the match was made. My only concern was my weight. I hadn't stepped on the scales for weeks. Frankly, I was afraid to. I knew I had ballooned into the middleweight, or even light-heavyweight class. I was getting bigger all the time and that meant I would have to take off more than just fat.

I weighed 170 pounds when I began training at Harry McCormick's camp in Red Bank for the fight. I had to take off 23 pounds in four weeks. I trained harder for this fight than for any of my others but ten days before the fight, I was still 14 pounds over the welterweight limit of 147 pounds. The weight came off agonizingly slow so Doc and I decided to double my program. During the final days I boxed wearing heavy sweat clothes. I spent as much time in the steam room as I did in the ring. I did a lot of extra running, too. The weight really came off then.

The day before the fight, I tipped the scales at 144, three pounds under the welterweight limit.

Doc was alarmed.

"You're too light now," he warned. "You look drawn. You've sweated off good weight. Mickey, you've grown into a natural middleweight but you're still fighting as a welter. Damn it, Mick, you've sweated off more than just extra weight—you've sweated off blood and muscle."

CHAPTER FOURTEEN

But if Kearns had any real worries about the outcome of my fight with Pete Latzo, he didn't show it. On the surface, he was still the same gay, light-hearted doctor. The night before the fight, Doc threw a party and invited a number of our friends. The next morning, we left for Scranton in a special Pullman car reserved by Doc. Our group included trainers, handlers, a dozen or so newspapermen from New Jersey and New York, and some friends.

I had plenty of supporters that night in Scranton. Special trains from New Jersey ran into the coal town every hour loaded with my friends and neighbors. Latzo had his own following, of course, and the lobbies of the Casey and Jermyn hotels, where the fight folks gathered, were swarming with miners and Broadway sports. The town was mad with excitement.

When I entered the ring to face Latzo, I was all dried out. I felt listless, as though my strength was sapped. I started off pretty well but my punches were not packing steam. Also, after the second round, I was breathing un-usually hard. Pete, himself, was a different fighter than the one I had whipped so handily three years before. I could feel it in the first round.

From the fourth round on, Latzo fought with more assurance. I was punching less and clinching more with every round. When the tenth finally came, I knew I had to win it big to pull out the fight. I made the effort, all right, but I was too weary and just couldn't get those fists up. I didn't have to wait for the referee's decision. Before he raised Latzo's arm, I knew I had lost the fight and the title. I suppose I should have been dejected but I really wasn't. Oh, I felt bad about dropping the title but I knew that if I hadn't been forced to take off all that weight, I would have put Latzo away for keeps even though he was an improved fighter.

There's an old saying in the fight game: There's never a defeat when you don't learn something. I learned some-thing from the Latzo defeat. For the first time, I came face to face with one of life's bitter lessons. We had set out for Scranton to fight Latzo, surrounded by friends. Now we were going back. Latzo had licked me. I was no longer champion of the world. How big was our party? Well, besides my handlers and the Doctor, there was Jim Corbett, the old heavyweight champion, and a writer. Yes, just one newspaperman—Hype Igoe. A dozen or so had left with me; only one came back.

"Look around you now, Mickey," said Corbett, the man who knocked out John L. Sullivan, "and see who your real friends are. You're now the ex-champ."

Corbett put an arm around my shoulders and smiled. "Don't feel too bad," he said. "That's the way life is. I went through the same thing."

I didn't brood long. That isn't my nature. Unpleasant things never stay long with me. When Jack Bulger died, I felt I had lost my best friend. It was a great shock and I grieved, but I knew life had to go on. I couldn't afford to live in the yesterdays.

So, after the Latzo fight, Kearns was more depressed than I was. He had his own reasons. He felt his reputation for shrewdness had been damaged. A championship gone and only thirty thousand dollars to show for it. That didn't sound like good business. I had my own reputation to consider. After a couple of weeks' rest, I was eager to fight again.

"Doc," I said, "get me another fight. I'm far from washed up. I just laid off too long. All I need is more action. Get me somebody, Doc—anybody. I don't care who he is."

So Doc signed me for a ten-round match with Joe Dundee at Madison Square Garden. Dundee was not a flashy performer but he had a sound, conservative style; his right uppercut to the heart carried a quart of chloroform.

I should never have fought Dundee. I hadn't really learned my lesson from the Latzo fight. As Doc had said then, I wasn't a welterweight any more—but I still didn't realize it. I had outgrown the class. For every pound I took off I lost that much in strength and stamina. In the fight with Dundee, I was sluggish and tired. My reflexes wouldn't respond. I knew what I had to do, but my body wouldn't do it. It was only my stubbornness that kept me going. I never had a chance.

The fight with Latzo had been close, but the one with Dundee was a massacre. The referee finally had to stop it. Dundee opened a cut over my left eye that bled

126

through the whole fight. When it became clear that I couldn't see any more, the fight was stopped. My face was a bloody smear. My head felt like someone had split it open with an ax. My legs were so rubbery I had to grab the referee to keep from falling on my face. But I squawked like the dickens—hell, I wasn't quitting to no-body. Hot tears of anger rolled down my cheeks.

Here is the *New York Post*'s story of the fight, in part: ". . . It was a burned out, slow, directionless fighter who came into the ring to face Dundee; a man who lacked the speed and punch he had shown only a short time ago. Whether the rumor was true that he sacrificed those qualities on the dance floor of Broadway, or lost them in the torturing effort to make weight, doesn't matter greatly . . ."

This was the most bitter blow I ever suffered. Nothing else compared to it during my entire career, not even the licking I later took from Max Schmeling. My heart was dead. How could I face anyone now?

This question pounded in my mind as they took me to Polyclinic Hospital and wheeled me into the emergency ward. But Mark Hellinger, then a writer with the *New York News*, told it better than I can:

"One of the sweetest characters I have ever known," the article began, "is Mickey Walker. The boy is highly intelligent, reads a good deal, and never boasts of his accomplishments. In some respects he is like Gene Tunney, but so far as character goes, he is a better man than Tunney can ever hope to be.

"The Mickey Walker who fought Joe Dundee was young. Wherever he went, admiration was his. He enjoyed living, and craved excitement. He had a $10,000 car. He had been a world's champion and most people believed

127

he could win that title back again. He loved the night clubs because he thought there was fun to be found in them. He didn't know how sad they really are. Maybe he still does not. But he will someday.

"At any rate, this was the fighter who crawled through the ropes to meet Joe Dundee. He held Dundee very lightly, so lightly, in fact, that he insisted on fighting even though one hand was injured. He rode to the Garden that night in his $10,000 car. A big party had been arranged for him at the Guinan Club as soon as Dundee had been knocked out.

"Joe Dundee gave Mickey Walker the worst beating of the latter's career. The fight was stopped in the eighth round, with that sweet guy hanging on the ropes, a battered, bruised, bloody, beaten man.

"Ten minutes later, Mickey was in his dressing room. From the constant swallowing of blood he was as sick as could be. Above his eye was a cut that was going to require some fifteen stitches. Except for his trainer, Teddy Hayes, he was alone in that room. There were no cheers, no phony hand-clasps, no double-crossing backslaps for Mickey at that stage of the game. The stick-with-the-winner boys were in Dundee's room.

"Some thirty minutes later Mickey Walker was in the emergency ward of a hospital near the Garden. A doctor was stitching that cut. The pain was terrific. How that man felt at that moment you can readily understand. He thought he was through. Where were his pals? Where were the friends who had fought to ride in his $10,000 car? Over at the Guinan Club, no doubt, dancing.

"A drunk staggered into the emergency ward. Another doctor looked after him. The drunk pointed to his bloody head and explained that he had been crowned with a bottle during a fight in a speak-easy.

"While the doctor was fixing the needle, this fellow looked over and recognized Walker.

" 'Lo, Champ,' he hiccoughed.

"Mickey didn't answer. He was too sick. Every time the doctor took another stitch, he groaned. It was like fire running through his brain. The drunk gazed at him for a few moments, and then shook his head.

" 'Shay, Champ,' he muttered. 'What are you squawking about? You at least got paid for it!' "

Paid for it!

Sure I got paid for it. Twenty grand. But I'd have cheerfully given it back to reverse that knockout. That money couldn't come near to compensating for the defeat and the loss of my pride. Paid for it? Half a million dollars couldn't even up for what had happened to me.

Most of the New York sports writers reported that I was through as a first-class fighter. Night life had taken its toll, they wrote. I was burned out—finished—at the age of twenty-five.

I thought so, too. I was worn to a frazzle. I suffered more from the training grind than from the fights themselves. The writers were sure I would never be in physical shape to fight again.

The wolves were on Kearns, too. One boxing writer wrote:

". . . Ever since Jack Dempsey became champion of the world, we've been hearing stories of how smart Kearns is. 'It was Kearns who made the champ.' That's how the stories always started or ended and a lot of people believed it. But these same people have begun to change their opinion of Kearns since the quick downfall of a once great boxing champion, Mickey Walker, has spread a tragic chapter of the world's boxing history.

"Kearns, in an incredibly short time, has changed Walker from a powerful champion to a prize weakling. The decline of Walker was swift and sure. His defeats in the last months by Latzo and Dundee were no surprise to those in Hollywood and Broadway who saw Walker greasing the pugilistic skids as he played the night life role . . . The gay life knocked Walker from his lofty perch and transformed him from a sturdy fighting man into an easy victim for the first good man who confronted him. Kearns was Mickey's manager all the time Mickey was hitting the high spots."

That's the way it was. And those fair-weather friends had begun making themselves scarce the night I lost my title. Now they were avoiding me like the plague. I was a great guy when I was laying 'em out like stiffs and wearing the crown. When I was champ, they swarmed around me like flies—all wanting a little of the honey. Now they didn't give a hoot what happened to me; they were buzzing around looking for another queen bee.

It hurt, too. I tried to shrug it off, but it wasn't that easy. Sure, sure, it's that way with all ex-champs . . . isn't that what Jim Corbett told me? And hadn't it happened to me once before in Elizabeth? But it still was a shock to go through it again.

I suppose the undertakers did feel a right to stomp on my grave. It looked as though I was all washed up. A great career knocked for a loop before it had even gathered full steam. The experts were disappointed. They had predicted such wonderful things for me and now they felt

I had let them down. It was no use explaining that the night life and the dissipation hadn't shoved me downhill. No use telling them that my body was still strong and my reflexes still good. They'd only laugh if I tried to tell them the reason for my supposed downfall was the fact that I had outgrown the division I was fighting in—making the weight had taken its toll more than the carousing and the drinking.

Okay, so I was a bum. I wasn't looking for sympathy and I gave no excuses. But what really griped me was the way they hammered at Kearns for not looking out for me, for letting me lead the kind of life I had led. It wasn't his fault; he could no more have kept me from having my fun than he could have stopped breathing. If he was to be criticized for anything, it should have been for letting me fight as a welterweight and against the best in the business. He should have realized that the Toy Bulldog had ballooned into a pretty big pup. Twice he had let me trim down from 170 to 147. That's torture to any athlete, especially a fighter. Anyone who has had to work 23 pounds off a lean, athletic body in a couple of weeks knows what an ordeal that can be.

Anyhow, I had reached the crossroads of my career.

What would I do now? Twenty-five years old—and on the bargain counter with the odd-lots. An ex-champion. A has-been who the experts agreed was through. Start all over? No, sir. Not me. I didn't have to fight. I had twenty times as much money as most guys my age. And my name was still an asset even after those lickings. Why keep on taking punches? I had seen what that could do to a person.

Having made up my mind to quit, I decided I had to get into some kind of business. I had no financial worries but wanted to work, to keep myself occupied. I had to be busy doing something; I'd go nuts being idle.

A friend tipped me off about a lease that was available for a proposed theater and amusement place in Asbury Park, about ten miles south of Rumson. Walter Reade, who owned several movie houses, including the Carleton Theater in Red Bank, was after the property too, but for some reason, the city officials were opposed to him.

I figured I'd get the property under my name and go into partnership with Reade. I had money, but no experience in the business. Reade was a theatrical impresario, so I decided he was my man.

I had never met Reade but knew his partner, Morris Jacks. Through him, I arranged to have a talk with Reade. We met in his Red Bank office. Reade was a big man. He must have weighed 210 to 220 pounds. I explained my proposition.

"What makes you think the municipality of Asbury Park would lease the property to you?" he asked scornfully.

"Why not me?"

"You're a prize fighter," he said. He made it sound like a dope peddler.

"What's wrong with being a prize fighter?" I demanded.

"Why, you washed-up bum," he blurted. "You're trying to get back to being a big shot and you think you can use me for that purpose."

I saw red.

"You a big shot?" I exploded. "You're nothing but a no-good punk. In my estimation, Reade, you stink."

He became livid with rage. He got up from his chair and wound up for a right-hand punch. I wasn't about to wait for it, and hit him with a left hook. He dropped like a sack of potatoes. Poor Morris Jacks, scared to death, dashed out screaming for help. Somebody telephoned the police.

Reade refused to press charges. But he got even with me. He gave out a story to the newspapers that I had become abusive in his office and he was forced to flatten me.

Anyway, that was the end of the theater idea.

It was summer and I decided to take a vacation. During July and August, I was going to take it easy, do nothing but swim and play golf. My face was still all plastered up from the Dundee fight.

I went swimming every day, at either Seabright or the Highlands. The salt water and sun did wonders. I felt more fit each day.

I had lots of time to think. There's something about the sand in your toes, the soft lapping of the waves, which makes you think straight. I thought about it all—this full, frantic and so often foolish life I had led. In five years I'd risen from a Keighry Head "punk" to a world championship.

I was lucky. This I knew. I told myself that whatever the future held, I had to thank the Lord for what he'd given me—or let me earn with my fists—so far.

Still, there were so many empty hours . . . so much time to feel despair . . . a revulsion toward people. It is hard to face the world as a failure.

No one can realize the sorrow of an ex-champ unless he has experienced it himself. I missed the applause and admiration. I missed the excitement and the congratulations of my friends and neighbors. That was nothing, however, compared to the hurt that came to me when I caught the "townies" smirking and making remarks behind my back. I could hear them when I went to the post office opposite the town park, for my mail.

"There goes the *champ*," they taunted as I pulled away in my convertible. I didn't let on but I felt rotten.

The neighborhood kids, however, remained faithful. When I walked along the river and watched them diving off the dock or fishing off the pier, they'd see me and come over.

"It's okay, Mickey," they'd say. "You'll be champ again."

Although I had no thought of returning to the ring, the kids made me feel better. One day I got them all together and asked if they'd like to form a baseball team. They were all for it. We formed the Mickey Walker Athletic Club. I bought them baseball uniforms at Eisner's and Gordon Parmalee, the vegetable king, was kind enough to let us set up a baseball diamond in his corn field. We had games all summer. Occasionally, I even played with them. I was the right fielder.

About the end of summer I began thinking of my future. I was tired of doing nothing. I still wanted to go into some sort of business, but couldn't make up my mind what I wanted to do. I took my chauffeur into my confidence, for by then Jimmy was like a member of the family.

He came up with the bright idea that I enter politics. A new mayor of Rumson was due to be elected in November. Why didn't I run for mayor? Jimmy assured me that with him as my campaign manager, my winning would be a cinch. He swore that he had enough relatives alone to give me a majority. The entire voting population of Rumson was not more than 1500 to 2000.

Well, Jimmy sold me on the idea, and I became a "politician." I ran on the Democratic ticket. My opponent was a man named W. Warren Barbour. He was a member of Rumson's social set, but he was a swell guy. His father, Colonel Williams Barbour, was a wealthy thread merchant.

Barbour, Jr., was a very good boxer. In fact, he was the amateur heavyweight champion of New Jersey. As intercollegiate champion at Princeton, they wanted to match him with Jack Johnson, then heavyweight champion of the world, but he refused. Professional promoters begged him to turn pro. They thought he could eventually win the heavyweight title.

CHAPTER FIFTEEN

During the height of my campaign for mayor of Rumson, I received a visit from Doc Kearns. He was pleased at how well I looked. I was brown from the sun and all the disfiguring marks had disappeared.

"Mick," he marveled, "you look in great shape. I've never seen you any better."

"I feel good," I admitted.

Kearns wasted no time explaining the reason for his visit.

"Mickey," he began, "I want you to return to the ring. I deliberately stayed away from you all summer because I wanted you to have a good rest and regain your health."

"No, Doc," I said. "I'm through. I'm finished. No more fighting. I'm retired and am going to stay retired. I'm in politics now. I'm going to be the next mayor of Rumson."

Doc didn't believe me.

"Mickey, you're a fighter, not a politician," he insisted.

"Politics is not your racket. Besides, you'll have plenty of time for that when you're old. You're still a young man. And you can still fight. Hell, Mick, you were cut out to make a living with your fists, not with your mouth."

We argued for a long time. I held out as long as I could.

"Mickey," Kearns said, "I'm leveling. I've always leveled with you. I wouldn't want to see you hurt for anything in the world. Not only do I think you can still fight, but I honestly believe you can become a champion again. Only one thing. You're not going to fight welterweight again. You're going to be the next middleweight champion of the world."

I knew Kearns's reputation for ribbing, so I looked at him long and hard before I spoke.

"If you really believe so, Doc," I finally said, "I'll make a deal with you. Let's find out quick whether or not you're right. I'll fight again, provided you match me with the toughest fighter you can get in the 160-pound division. If I win, I'll forget about politics and go after the middleweight title. If I lose, you forget all about me fighting again."

Doc was satisfied. We shook hands.

True to his word, Doc got me one of the toughest middleweights around in those days. His name was Shuffles Callahan. Shuffles drove a truck when not fighting. He was a great favorite in Chicago, where he was knocking everybody stiff. He had a murderous punch. He had caught the imagination of the fans by his habit of parking his truck outside the arena where he was fighting and driving away in it after he had knocked his opponent cold.

Now that I had made up my mind to return to the ring, I looked forward to it with pleasure. The old battle thrill came back to me. I was rarin' to go.

Through a friend in the paper-manufacturing business, I got a job with the Murray Bay Lumber Company in Cape Breton, Nova Scotia. Kearns's new heavyweight hope, a fellow called Jack Dorval, came along with me. We signed as lumberjacks and worked ten hours a day, six days a week, cutting down trees and lugging logs. This was a new experience for me, a city boy all my life. Yet I thrived on it. At the end of a day's work, I'd find time to shadowbox and punch a bag I'd brought along.

This hard-labor conditioning lasted a month. The clean air and heavy manual work made my body sound and healthy. Although the fight with Callahan wasn't until early October, I came back home in September. I wanted to see the fight between Dempsey and Gene Tunney in Philadelphia's Municipal Stadium on September 23, 1926.

Even though Kearns and Dempsey had broken up, Doc had never lost his admiration for Jack as a fighter. He was sure Dempsey would win and he and I bet $25,000 on Jack against Bernard Gimbel, the department store magnate. Gimbel is a great friend of Tunney's and he had as much faith in Gene as we did in Jack. In fact, we offered Gimbel 6 to 1 odds but he insisted on an even bet. We figured we had a sucker's money.

The odds on Dempsey ranged from 4 to 1 to 7 to 1. The only knowledgeable fight man I knew who was smart enough to take the short end was Harry Greb, who put ten thousand dollars on Tunney and won sixty grand. Greb had inside knowledge of their styles. He had worked out with Jack in gyms and had fought Gene five times, beating him only once.

Harry came to me before the fight.

"Mickey," he said, "bet on Tunney. He's going to beat Dempsey. He has real boxing ability . . . he has the tools . . . He's classy—a much better fighter than any-body imagines."

Like almost everybody else, I didn't believe it.

Kearns and I were at ringside, along with Gene Fowler, the author, and Mark Kelly, a Los Angeles newspaperman who later became an executive with Twentieth-Century Fox. We had seats in the first press row and were drenched because it rained hard throughout the fight. Tunney was giving Dempsey a boxing lesson.

I felt sorry watching Dempsey blow his title. Kearns sat next to me and didn't utter a word as he watched, stone-faced. He gritted his teeth and winced whenever Tunney landed a solid blow. I knew that in his heart, Doc was sorry for Jack, too. I grew more and more nervous as the fight went on. I could see that Jack was not fighting Tunney right.

I couldn't stand it any longer. Between the sixth and seventh rounds, I jumped up and rushed over to Jack's corner. Grabbing Gus Wilson, Dempsey's trainer, by the seat of his pants, I yelled: "Hey, Gus! Tell Jack to keep throwing the left hook. Tell him to throw a thousand of 'em. One is bound to land. Don't forget. Tell him to keep throwing left hooks until he's down."

Then I beat it back to my seat. Doc had seen and heard what I'd done but he didn't say a word. I could sense that he approved and I was sure that he would have done the same had he not had that damned pride. Why did I do it? I really don't know, except that I liked Jack and felt he would have done the same for me.

Later, Mark Kelly told me that while I was shouting at Wilson, he had poked Kearns, "Get up in his corner and help him. Those guys in his corner are no damned good to him."

138

"No," Kearns said. "Let him take it."

Kelly looked at him again. "Why, you're crying," he said.

"I'm not crying," Doc answered. "It's the rain in my eyes."

"You're not kidding me, Doc. You're crying, you bum. Get up there and help him."

But Doc couldn't do it. He wanted to, but pride tied him to his chair.

After watching that classic, I resumed training in my private gym. I weighed 158 pounds. Not an ounce of fat. I was a full-fledged middleweight.

I felt more nervous than usual when I climbed into the ring in Chicago on October 4, 1926.

A fighter dies a thousand deaths in his dressing room. That's why I was always so late for my fights. I used to worry my manager and handlers to death. I'd arrive at the arena or ball park maybe twenty minutes before I was due in the ring.

I'd get very irritable sitting around waiting to go on. Tension would build up in me. Dempsey was the same way. Jack was like a wild man in the dressing room before a fight.

I don't think there was ever a fighter who did not know fear on entering the ring. And don't let anyone tell you differently. If he does, he's a liar.

By fear, I don't mean that I actually was afraid of my opponent. My great fear was of losing. I was afraid that I wouldn't please. I wanted to be accepted by the crowd. The whole thing scared me. The lights, the crowd, the noise. The excitement gets you.

But once the bell rings and you rush into action, your fear disappears. Until you hear the bell, however, all kinds

139

of crazy thoughts enter your head. Many a time I'd climb into the ring, my head would pound and I'd think to myself, "This is awful."

But I loved it. Every fight gave me a new thrill. You have to have desire and enthusiasm for fighting to be good in the ring. Sure, you fight for money, but you've got to like it, too.

That's the difference between fighters. Some are in it strictly for the dough. Others are kids who grew up in corner gangs and had to fight to prove themselves. That's how fighters develop. You seldom get them out of college. You can't take a football player, just because he has a set of muscles, and make him a champion. A fighter has to be born in a tough atmosphere and he has to condition himself, mentally. He has to learn to love to mix it and keep punching, no matter how badly he's hurt.

Prize fighting teaches you to conquer your fears. A man without fear is a dumb, unemotional man. He is a foolish man.

So, that night of my first comeback fight, I was scared but determined to win and show I wasn't washed up. What concerned me most was that I hadn't fought for four months, and Callahan was a dangerous puncher.

It turned out to be one of my best fights. I knocked him out in the eighth round. I had proven to myself that I could still fight.

The publicity which followed helped my campaign for mayor of Rumson. A day or two after I returned home, I had a visitor . . . W. Warren Barbour. After congratulating me, he asked whether I was serious about running for mayor. If I was, he said he was ready to step out, since it would be useless to run against me.

Frankly, I had given up the idea of politics after whipping Callahan. I could see Barbour wanted very much to get the office. It was a non-paying job which meant a lot to him, nothing to me.

"Mr. Barbour," I said, "it's me who's pulling out, not you. Now, not only are you going to run, but I'm going to turn over my entire support to you. I think you are going to make a fine mayor."

Warren Barbour not only did make a fine mayor but he went on to represent New Jersey in the U. S. Senate. We formed a sincere friendship which lasted until his death in 1955.

Kearns was determined now, more than ever, to make me middleweight champion of the world and I was beginning to believe it possible myself. I had a couple of tune-up bouts (Joe Simonich in Philadelphia, November 1st, and Jock Malone in Boston on the 22nd) and won both by decisions.

Doc then matched me with Tiger Flowers, a Georgia Negro who had beaten Harry Greb for the middleweight crown. It might seem strange that the Doc was able to get me a title bout after only three comeback fights, not one of them against a really top contender. But it must be remembered that I had been a world champion, even though in a lighter division, and I still had a reputation and a following. Besides, Doc was unbeatable when it came to landing big and important matches for his fighter.

The fight was held on December 3, 1926, in Chicago. It was a ten-rounder and at the conclusion I was awarded the decision. It was very close. There were a lot of people who thought I didn't win the fight. In fact, Walk Miller, the Tiger's manager, screamed that his fighter had been done out of the title and threatened to go to the Boxing Commission.

The fact remained that it was I who had Flowers on the floor, even though I couldn't kayo him. The Tiger was a good fighter, but he didn't win that fight. The fellow who squawked the loudest—even more than the Tiger's manager—was Leo Flynn, who apparently still remembered and resented my refusal of his offer to manage me. I knew that he bet against me whenever he thought I could be licked, and there were rumors at the time that he lost a wad of dough on Flowers.

Flowers, himself, never complained. He was a tiger in the ring, but outside of it he was a kindly, good-hearted man, a reader of the Bible and a church deacon. I liked him personally and promised his manager a return match but I never got to keep my promise. In less than a year, Flowers was dead, following what was considered a routine bit of surgery in a New York hospital for scar tissue removal.

He died on November 16, 1927, a little over a year following the death of Harry Greb. It was a ghastly parallel. Two successive middleweight champions, both 32 years old—both dead after supposedly routine operations. But I wasn't the sensitive, neurotic type. I attributed both deaths to coincidence, which I'm sure they were.

I didn't let the criticism of my victory over Flowers bother me. I was champion of the world again. That was all that mattered. Looking back now, I don't think copping the middleweight championship gave me as much of a thrill as winning my first title, the welterweight crown, four years before.

It should have, I suppose. The middleweight crown is more important since it is only two divisions removed from the heavyweight class. It usually brings more prestige and more money. But there's nothing that matches the thrill of winning your first world's championship, no matter what the division.

Now I was a seasoned campaigner who already had tasted the first flush of success. I felt I was a man of the world, having lived through events at the age of twenty-five that most people don't experience in a lifetime.

Just seven months after I had hit rock bottom, I was back on the pedestal. A has-been one night, world champion the next. Now I was older—and should have been wiser. I should have learned how to accept the responsibility that goes with being a champion—in any field. But I hadn't learned a thing.

If anything, I became even less responsible. Maybe it was the association with Kearns; maybe it was my own light-headedness—a way for my pent-up emotions to break loose. Whatever the reason, I was bent on enjoying life to the full. I was naturally restless, always looking for something, always seeking something I really couldn't put my finger on.

I never was much for staying home and that didn't lead to a very happy marital life. I was criticized for the kind of life I led, and rightly so . . . but looking back now I doubt if I would have done anything differently. I was no angel.

Shortly after I won the middleweight title from Flowers, the Boxing Writers Association of New York decided to present me with the championship belt at their annual dinner in the Waldorf-Astoria. It was quite an honor and I got all swelled up for my trip to New York. I dressed in a sports outfit: light trousers and a blue blazer. I had the Duesenberg washed and polished so that it shone like diamonds. I was feeling pretty good as I drove along with the top down and the red leather seats gleaming in the sun.

About twelve miles out of Rumson, it suddenly turned cloudy. Before I had a chance to turn the top up, it began to rain. Looking around for a garage where I could pull the car in and get the top up, I failed to see a truck turning a corner. We hit almost head-on. Luckily, neither of us was going fast—but the grill of my car was smashed in.

The truck driver barged out of his cab and began to abuse me. He was a short, stocky guy, built much like myself. Being a world champion and headed for the Waldorf, I couldn't afford to get into a street brawl. So I kept myself under control and patiently tried to reason with him. We were standing in the rain getting wetter by the minute. This guy paid no attention to what I was saying. He kept swearing at me. Finally, I exploded.

"You're a fresh punk," I told him. "A punch in the jaw might do you some good."

He didn't wait. Instead, he hauled off and hit me in the eye. I closed in and grabbed him by the arms. But he got one of them loose and belted me in the mouth, bringing blood. I was just going to let him have my Sunday punch when somebody in the crowd that had gathered recognized me and hollered:

"Hey, you're Mickey Walker! What ya tryin' to do, kill the poor guy?"

There I was, with my right eye closed, my lips cut and bleeding, and this nut was asking if I was trying to kill the other guy—who hadn't a mark on him. When the

144

truckman heard who I was, he turned white, stammered some kind of an apology, leaped back into his truck and slammed the door. Once inside, his courage returned as quickly as it had left him.

"Whaddya know? Wait till I tell the gang who I licked. They'll never believe it," he crowed.

Then, with a loud, derisive guffaw he banged his foot down on the pedal and roared away. I just stood there, blood-stained and rain-soaked.

When I finally reached New York, I went directly to LaHiff's to meet Kearns. Doc was seated at a table with an old friend of ours, Jimmy Durante. Schnozzola was going to the boxing writers' dinner, too. He was a rabid fight fan then and one of my biggest rooters.

I was a bedraggled figure when I came in, hardly recognizable. Durante looked at me over that nose of his and barked: "What the hell happened to you? You run into a locomotive or sumpthin'?"

I had a hard time making Jimmy and Doc believe my story.

"You're in no condition to be seen at the Waldorf," Doc snapped. "Go upstairs, clean up and take a nap. I'll accept your belt and think up some excuse why you didn't show up. We'll meet you at Guinan's at midnight."

After they had gone, I went upstairs to our apartment above the tavern, cleaned up and tried to get some sleep.

Doc accepted the belt, a beautiful diamond-and-ruby-studded belt with my name, the date of the title fight, and the name of my opponent inscribed on it. But as it turned out, I didn't see the belt until months later.

Here's what happened. Kearns and Durante left the Waldorf at about eleven-thirty. They had had a few drinks each and were feeling pretty gay. Doc had the championship belt with him as they took a cab to Guinan's at Broadway and West Forty-ninth Street, where Jimmy was appearing with his partners, Eddie Jackson and Lou Clayton. Their first show was scheduled at midnight.

Forty-ninth Street is a one-way street. Instead of having the cabbie take them full around the block, Doc and Jimmy decided to get off at Fiftieth Street and walk the one block.

They began walking none too steadily toward Guinan's. Doc, who knew that Durante once had ambitions to become a fighter, suddenly whipped out the championship belt and said to Jimmy:

"I'm Doc Kearns, the maker of champs. Stand still, Schnozz. I'm going to make you a champion, too."

With that, he wrapped the belt around Durante's stomach, raised Jimmy's right arm and pronounced him "the new middleweight champion of the world."

Durante went right along with the gag. Unmindful of the people who had recognized him and stopped to see what was going on, he began to jig as if he were shadow-boxing. He ducked and weaved and threw punches at an imaginary opponent, giving out with his favorite "Hot-cha-cha" expression every time he let go with a punch.

"Hey, lookit the new middleweight champeen of the woild," Schnozz shouted, as he tried to imitate a fighter by rubbing his thumb across his nose while dancing down the street. "Left, right, left, right. Here comes the Durante haymaker."

Jimmy doesn't drink now and he didn't drink much even in those days. But everything went by the board when you were with Doc.

By the time they had reached the night club, a fair-sized crowd had gathered to watch the great comedian's impromptu act. During the height of this front-door show, a drunk emerged from the crowd. He stopped directly before the dancing Durante. After watching Jimmy huff and puff for a minute or so, he suddenly hauled off and belted Durante right on the nose. Jimmy went down on all fours. While he was trying to get up, the drunk reached down, ripped the belt off Jimmy and beat it before anyone could lay a hand on him. That was one of the few times Kearns was left actionless—as well as speechless.

I was already inside Guinan's when all this happened. Durante had quickly sobered up and was full of apologies.

"Chee, kid, it's all my fault," he said. "We'll find out how much it costs and I'll give you the dough for it."

"Forget it, Jimmy," I laughed. "The only thing I'm sorry about is that I didn't see you out there doing your stuff. You must have made a hell of a champion."

"Yeah," Durante grinned, "but I sure had the shortest reign of any champeen in history."

Durante felt a lot better later when I told him that Nat Fleischer, editor of *Ring Magazine*, after learning what had happened, had a duplicate belt made and presented to me.

CHAPTER SIXTEEN

Now that I had the middleweight crown, Kearns began looking for a big-money match. We didn't get much more than play-money out of the Flowers bout. As champ, Flowers got 50 percent and, as challenger, I had to take

10 percent to get the match. The gate was ninety thousand dollars and my end came to only about ten thousand.

Doc figured that the best pairing, for dough, would be with Tommy Milligan, the British Empire middleweight champ. Doc was hot for the match to be held in Europe. He felt I would draw better in London than Milligan would in New York. When Charles B. Cochran, the theatrical producer who also promoted fights in England offered us a guarantee of $120,000, Doc grabbed it. That was a lot of money in those days before the television revenue ballooned purses for championship fights to where they are today. And the dollar was worth 100 cents, then.

We were due to sail in May to set up a training camp in England for the bout on June 30th. The fight was still six months off. Doc was afraid I'd get rusty if I laid off all that time. So he arranged a tune-up scrap . . . and what better place than California? It gave us a chance to whoop it up again in Hollywood.

Doc and I took a train from New York for California on New Year's Day, 1927. Maude stayed home. Kearns had matched me with a kid named Mickey Wallace, a great favorite around Fresno and a good drawing card there. It figured to bring us a few thousand bucks to throw away in Hollywood and it looked like a pretty easy fight.

It was the night of February 1st. While the preliminary bouts were on, Wallace came to my dressing room. He introduced himself. He was a clean-cut youngster and I liked his looks right away.

He told me I was his idol. He had even adopted a ring-name which came about as close as it could to sounding like mine. I'd wondered about the similarity of names.

"I'm not looking for sympathy and I don't want you to go easy on me," the kid said. "I'm proud to be fighting

148

you, but I hope I lick you tonight. I'm going to try awfully hard. But win or lose, this is the biggest thing that ever happened to me."

He told me his parents and brothers were at the fight and I saw him wave to them at ringside when he climbed through the ropes. They were fine-looking people. I made up my mind that I wasn't going to make him look bad in front of them.

As I waited for the opening bell, I said to Kearns, "He looks like a nice kid, Doc. His folks are proud of him. I'll let him live."

It didn't take me long to find out he was not much more than a preliminary boy, but he did have a good left hand. I relaxed more than I should have, I suppose, because in the middle of the second round he threw a wild left hook that opened up a gash over my right eye. The blood streamed down my face.

While Kearns worked on the eye between rounds, he warned me, "Better take him before the fool referee stops it. Wouldn't it be fine, before the big fight in London, to have this ham-'n-egger score a technical knockout over the great Mickey Walker?"

I had no choice. As we came together in the third round, I let ride a punch, giving it everything I had. It was a left hook and the kid went out like a light. That was the meanest thing I ever had to do in a ring. I think I felt almost as bad as if I had lost.

I went into Wallace's dressing room later. The kid was sitting on the rubbing table without a worry in the world. He had a smile on his face. He wasn't the least bit downhearted.

"Mickey," he said, "I tried, but I wasn't up to it. Yet it was an honor to fight you and be knocked out by you."

We shook hands and I turned to go.

"Would you do me a favor?" he asked. "Do you think I have a chance in the fight game?"

I saw he was sincere.

"Kid," I told him, "if you were my brother, I'd make you quit. You're young, good-looking and you have a future, but not in the ring. If I were you, I'd start in some other business."

He took my advice and hung up his gloves. Years later, when I was fighting in San Diego, I received a long distance call from Fresno. It was Wallace. He had gone into politics and had become a prominent state official.

After the Wallace fight in Fresno, I took it easy for a couple of months. I didn't go on the wagon. I couldn't, with those Hollywood night lights dazzling Doc's eyes— and mine. But I did keep in shape. I managed to have a helluva time, without getting cockeyed every night. I drank, but for once I used some sense about it.

We returned East and spent most of April—and many thousands of dollars—enjoying spring in New York. The spring nights, that is. We didn't let daylight interfere with us much. It was a good time to sleep. Maude couldn't keep up with me. She went out with me less and less and finally stopped altogether. Soon I had other women for company.

Early in May, the night before we sailed, Texas Guinan arranged a real Broadway send-off. Nobody went to bed. The next morning the whole gang—most everyone pretty well oiled by then—went with us to the dock. Tex got a dozen open touring cars, big four-door jobs with tops which folded all the way back. They used to call them phaetons or sports sedans.

Her girls filled a couple of the cars. Texas, Doc and I

were in another car—waving to people on the street who stared popeyed at the weirdest and wildest parade they probably ever saw. The other cars were filled with a crazy mixture—entertainers, gamblers, sports writers, fighters, Broadway hustlers.

Tex had loaded up another car with a jazz band which led that zany parade down Broadway. With each block, the line got longer. Those who couldn't scramble into the cars walked. Every car had tubs of iced champagne and we handed out bottles to the new paraders. We turned west on Forty-second Street toward the Hudson River.

Among those invited in the official party were columnists Bugs Baer, Floyd Gibbons and Ed Sullivan, who at the time was sports editor of the *New York Graphic*. Sullivan didn't make the trip to Europe, but Baer and Gibbons did. They were assigned to cover the fight for the Hearst newspapers.

At the Cunard Line Pier, we found another large but quite different group. It had gathered to bid bon voyage to Sir Ramsay MacDonald, the British Prime Minister. He was returning on our ship, the *Berengaria,* after a good-will tour of the United States. Among those in this party was a political group headed by Al Smith, then Governor of New York. Our crowd thought he was down there to see me off and they gave him a big cheer.

We continued the party in our staterooms. Most of our uninvited paraders came on board and joined in. Many were too crocked to get off by the time the ship sailed— and others, I'm sure, stayed aboard by design.

When the *Berengaria* was about ten miles out to sea, stowaways from the parade began to come out from their hiding places. It was like a scene from a Marx Brothers picture. One of the officers wanted the ship turned back to get rid of its unexpected guests, but it was decided, instead, to make these characters work their passage. That would have been a novelty; some of them had never done an honest day's work in their lives.

Kearns saved a sticky situation by agreeing to pick up the tab for the odd-lot, and there must have been a dozen of them. The free-spending Doc wasn't going to be played for a sucker, though. He knew that many of our "added starters" had special talents, and he saw a chance to clean up.

Some were professional gamblers. They moved in on the tourists, and Doc dealt himself in on 50 percent of the profits. He had cleaned up by the time the ship arrived in Europe.

Our reception in England was quite different from our send-off in the States. Only two people were on the dock at Southampton to greet us: Charles Cochran, the promoter, and Sir Harry Preston, the bookmaker.

Bookmaking is legal in England and the bookie, unlike one in this country, is a respected citizen and business-man. Kearns, always quick to get to the point, immediately asked Preston what the odds on the fight were.

"Sir, we are placing our chap at two to one over your lad," Sir Harry answered.

Kearns, who could dead-pan a possum into a nervous breakdown, blinked his eyes and said, "Sounds like a tough price, since we're fighting on your grounds."

Kearns, naturally, played it big in London. We moved into a huge suite in the ultra-rich Savoy Hotel. It was big enough for a ball . . . or a brawl . . . and we got around to both. We had three bedrooms, a parlor, a dining room and a bar, as well as a kitchen and bathrooms.

One of the first things I noticed in London was that

No, this is not a picture of my sister. This was me at the age of five, in 1906. Get a load of those long curls. They were my Mom's pride and joy—and the target of all the kids in the neighborhood.

These are the Walkers. I was twenty-one then and had just taken the welterweight title away from Jack Britton. See the different expressions on the faces of Dad and Mom? Pop was opposed to my fighting even though in his youth he boxed with the great John L. Sullivan. Mom was all for it. That's brother Joe getting ready to sing.

In 1925, I made my first visit to Hollywood, where I met the incredible Doc Kearns for the first time. Doc and I were partners for nine years, without ever signing a contract. During that time we must have made and spent eight million dollars.

I met Chaplin in 1925. I was boxing in Los Angeles and Charlie was a surprise visitor in my dressing room after the fight. We disagreed on a lot of things but, along with Doug Fairbanks, he was the first to befriend me in Hollywood.

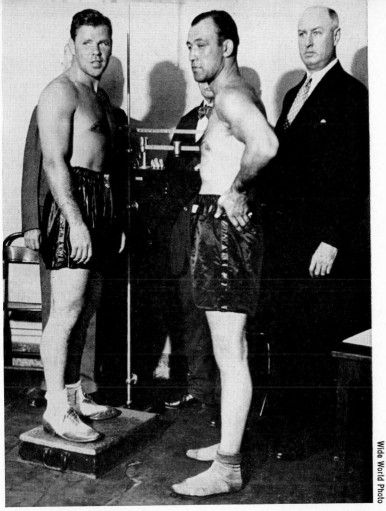

My fight with Jack Sharkey for New York's version of the world's heavyweight championship in Ebbets Field in 1931 was probably the high point of my boxing career. I won that fight—referee Arthur Donovan gave me 11 of the 15 rounds—but they ruled it a draw when the two judges disagreed. I felt embarrassed because Jack towered over me so I insisted on wearing my shoes when I weighed in. James Farley, who years later was appointed postmaster general, was then New York State Boxing Commissioner.

This is one fight I'd rather forget. Max Schmeling, the guy who's belting me, smashed all my dreams of ever becoming the heavy-weight king of the world by handing me a technical kayo in the Long Island Bowl in 1932. The German simply murdered me. They tell me Doc Kearns threw in the towel in the eighth round. I never knew it. It was the worst beating I ever took in the ring, but I continued to fight for another three years.

Doc Kearns knew practically nothing about golf but that didn't prevent him from trying to give me a few pointers. He always insisted he could do everything better than me—even fight. This was in 1933 when we were still living it up in Hollywood.

Whenever I boxed in Los Angeles, there were always a number of movie celebrities at ringside. Lupe Velez, shown here leaping up and waving her arms after I knocked out Artjur DeKuh, the 220-pound Belgian champ in 1932, was one of my favorites. She was one of the most dynamic persons I have ever known. John Boles, the actor-singer, and Johnny Weissmuller, the swimmer-actor, are sitting beside Lupe.

I usually celebrated my victories in the ring with a party in a night club right after the fight. Like most Irishmen, I have a little bit of ham in me and often I put on an impromptu act. Later I tried it professionally for a while. Jackie Gleason was a bartender in one of the night clubs where I entertained. Here I am putting on my act at the Club Cavalier in New York City in 1937.

Boxing, acting, singing, radio announcing, refereeing and painting weren't enough for me so I tried punching a typewriter for a while. From 1948 through 1955 I had a regular sports column for the Police Gazette, *a weekly tabloid.*

My daughter Pat's a dead ringer for me—same build, same disposition, and same temper. She resembles her old man but is much prettier. If she were a boy, there would have been another champ in the Walker family. I painted this portrait of her in 1949, when she was eighteen.

*After five marriages, I felt I had had enough matrimonial bliss
and I vowed no more women in my life. I forgot all about these
good intentions the first moment I laid eyes on Marci. That was
in 1955 when she visited my cabaret, The Glove and Palette on
Broadway. I think it was that wonderful smile of hers that did it.
If I'd only met her thirty years before, my married life would
have been a lot less complicated.*

virtually every man wore a topper, or a high hat, regardless of the time of day. Back in Rumson and the other Jersey watering places, the high hat was a sign of class and social standing and I'd always had a secret yen to own one. But I'd been afraid to wear one because my Broadway friends would have called me a "swell" and slammed it down over my ears.

In London, I didn't have to worry about that. I decided to buy one.

On Bond Street, where the fine men's clothing shops are located, I bought the topper—then decided to go whole hog. I bought a wardrobe. I got three golf suits with knickers, a flannel suit, a couple of lounge suits, a dinner jacket, a dress suit, and a tail coat with striped trousers. And of course, I had to have a dicky and an ascot tie, too. I also bought a cane. I tried to get a monocle to complete the "veddy British" look, but my eyes are small and they didn't have a monocle to fit me.

I trained on Tagg's Island in the Thames. About half a mile long and four hundred feet wide, the Island was an amusement center and was owned and managed by Fred Karno, who had been Charlie Chaplin's first manager and who had brought the comedian to the States.

Wealthy Britishers docked their boats in the Island's yacht basin and there were many houseboats anchored offshore. We lived in a kind of hotel which was really a houseboat, docked but floating in the water. The only means of transportation from the Island to the mainland was by way of punts. Directly across from Tagg's Island was Hampton Court Palace, where English monarchs once lived.

Shortly after I started to train, Cochran, the Ziegfeld of London, invited me to attend his hit musical, *One*

Damn Thing After Another. When I got to the theater, I found that the star of the show was Edie Baker, a Broadway cabaret entertainer. After the show I went backstage to see her. She already had a visitor, the Prince of Wales. Through his influence, she had gotten the leading role.

Edie introduced us. The Prince loved Americans and American ways, so we hit it off immediately. He was a genuine sports fan and loved horseback riding. When I told him of my interest in horses, he invited me to ride with him. But Doc ruled that out. Kearns didn't want me to fall off a horse and have the fight called off. However, he had no objection to my playing golf with the Prince. When we were on the course alone, I called him Prince and he called me Mickey. The Earl of Westmoreland, the Prince and I, played a threesome on the Coomlie Golf Course twice a week.

The Prince was an occasional visitor at my camp. He liked boxing and enjoyed watching me train. This was a fight for which I truly trained. I kept my nose clean—no drinking, no dames and no late hours. Strict conditioning . . . Doc had laid the law down to me on the boat when we were coming across.

I invited the Prince to be my guest at the fight. He refused.

"I shan't be seeing the fight," he said, "because I'll be out of London inspecting coal mines." Then he added, "Mickey, I can't honestly wish you luck because I want the middleweight title to come to England. But may the best man win."

We shook hands on that.

Other celebrities came to watch my workouts. Georges Carpentier was still the idol of France, even though Dempsey had knocked him out when he tried to win the heavyweight crown. Another well-known Frenchman who visited us was Maurice Chevalier. For the benefit of newsreel cameramen and newspaper photographers, he climbed into the ring and put on the gloves with me and you know, for an actor, he wasn't too bad a boxer. This ring stunt was Kearns's idea and it got us a lot of publicity.

Doc was a wonder at milking publicity out of almost any incident. I loved to paddle a canoe on the Thames when I could get a breather from actual work in the ring. Canoeing helped my conditioning. One day, Doc challenged me to a race on the Thames, just like those college boys from Oxford and Cambridge. We had gone about a mile and I had a slight lead when I suddenly looked up and saw a boatload of women and children directly in front of me. In the excitement, I hadn't seen them. I tried to change course to veer away from them, but my paddle slipped and I plunged headlong into the water as the canoe overturned. Luckily, I was a strong swimmer and made shore easily.

Kearns, seeing a chance for publicity, lost no time in capitalizing on my accident. He gave out a story to the press which made a hero of me. According to Doc, I deliberately capsized my craft in order to avoid a collision, risking my own life. This quick thinking on my part, he said, no doubt prevented certain disaster. I don't think there was another soul who saw the accident; but according to Kearns, a huge crowd on a nearby dock cheered me wildly. As he told it, the people lifted me, wet clothes and all, and carried me on their shoulders.

Doc's mind was always working. Not a day went by that he wasn't dreaming up some scheme that would either add interest to the fight or money to his pocket.

He'd invite celebrities and groups for whom he'd hold special days. One day it would be the bookmakers of London; another, the actors and actresses in the leading shows. He'd bring other athletes, boxers and soccer-football players to my camp. Even cricket players.

One day, our guests were a group of jockeys. Kearns invited all the riders who were to be in the Derby at Epsom Downs, which was scheduled to run two weeks before the fight.

The Epsom Derby is to the English what the Kentucky Derby is to us. It is even older, with more color, pageantry and pomp. It is a social as well as an athletic event.

Doc really put on a jamboree for those jockeys. An excellent host, he gave them a spread such as those little men had probably never seen before. Champagne flowed like water and you'd have thought caviar was going out of style.

At the end of the day, Doc and I went down to the dock with the jocks. As each got into the punt to go back to London, Kearns shook his hand and left in it a roll of money—American bills. I wondered about this. After all, half of it was my dough. I knew that Doc had a reason for everything he did and I usually didn't inquire about things. But on the way back, I asked him about this.

"Listen, you lug," he said sharply. "You'd like to know who's going to win the race, wouldn't you? Well, who knows more about horses than the jockeys? I just slipped each one of those kids a hundred bucks, American. In return, they'll give me all the dope I want about the race. I'm just buying security, that's all."

That's the way Doc operated. He was always looking for a sure thing or the closest thing to it. On the day of the race, we wore our best sporting clothes, toppers and all, and sat in the Prince of Wales' Royal box. We wound up with the winner all right, collecting a bundle of about thirty thousand dollars.

Kearns had a hard time getting suitable sparring partners for me. Doc didn't believe in bums as sparmates. He wanted guys who'd test me. He felt that if one of them could hurt me, I'd work out a way to defend myself against him and therefore have a sounder defense when I met Milligan. Certainly Milligan figured to be better than any of the guys hired to work with me.

As a result, each workout was a real fight. No wonder. After weeks of searching, Doc had finally rounded up a group of sparmates that included four European champions, a former titleholder and a tough British light-heavy named Johnny Smarks. The champs were: Person of Sweden, Presach of Norway, Bolenski of Belgium and Tiermonti of Italy. The ex-champ was Georgie West, who had lost the British middleweight crown to Milligan fourteen months before.

Training at Tagg's Island was expensive. It must have cost us at least three thousand dollars a week for salaries. Doc paid fifty dollars a day to each of the seven sparring partners, in addition to my two trainers, two rubbers and a masseur. And there were plenty of other expenses. I never did learn exactly how much it cost us. I didn't care. I never could be bothered with bookkeeping. I figured that was Doc's end and that we'd wind up in the black, as usual.

CHAPTER SEVENTEEN

The London newspapers, of course, played up the fight in big headlines . . . top billing on the front pages. It was the hottest fight in Europe in years.

I remember one story by a London *Star* reporter named Durrant. "He never drinks," wrote Durrant, "never smokes and, like his opponent, is a Catholic. He is probably the most devout boxer living. He is a regular church-goer and nothing induces him to eat anything but fish on Fridays."

I must have made a good impression on Mr. Durrant.

At that time, someone was always coming out with a blast against boxing. The London *Daily Express* quoted Sir Hall Caine, an English novelist, in a tirade against the fight game. He denounced prize fighting as a "prevailing and preposterous passion for triumphs of brawn over brain." Sir Hall called for a halt to "orgies of corrupt, degrading humanity, these gross exhibitions of merciless savagery and loathsome trafficking in human suffering."

Kearns's reply to this was: "Sheer piffle . . . early Victorian flapdoodle . . . balderdash."

Two days before the fight, I took my final heavy workout. While sparring with Georgie West, I was clipped with a hard left hand and the old cut over my right eye reopened. That was a souvenir from the Wallace fight, when I was playing the kindhearted big brother and got walloped for my good intentions.

The cut was deep and mean, and required four stitches.

Kearns was so upset he wanted to put off the fight. He shrieked at me for being so dumb as to get hit like that. And he raised hell with West, who was only doing his job.

I didn't want the fight postponed. Aside from the cut, I was in the best shape of my career and wanted to go through with the bout. I was razor-sharp and felt I might lose that edge if I had to lay off while the cut healed and then go through that training ordeal again. Besides, I was tired of training and looked forward to the fight as the end of a dull grind. I wanted to get it over with, kick the hell out of Milligan, and then kick up my heels in London and on the Continent. I was a hungry fighter—hungry for something else besides fighting.

Kearns finally saw my point and decided not to ask for a delay. He could tell when his bulldog was really fed up—and I think I'd have busted him in the nose if he'd gone to the promoter for a postponement.

We didn't try to hide the news of the cut. We couldn't have, anyway. At that stage of my training, the London press was with us twenty-four hours a day. All the London papers carried stories and pictures of the busted eye.

Naturally, that was the end of my training, except for a few jogs around the island. Fortunately, the fight was only forty-eight hours away.

The night before the fight, we were sitting in the grill of the Savoy. Besides Doc, myself and Hayes, my trainer, there were a half-dozen others: Charlie Cochran, the promoter; Tom Webster, fight writer with the London *Daily Mail*; Bugs Baer and Floyd Gibbons; Lord Westmoreland, and Sir Harry Preston, the big betting commissioner.

Preston turned to Kearns and asked, "Mr. Kearns, how do you fancy?"

The way Preston said it, the word came out 'fawncy."

Doc blinked. "Fawncy? I fawncy fine."

Preston smiled, "I'm afraid, Mr. Kearns, you don't understand. I mean how much do you like your boy's chances in the fight?"

Before Doc could answer, Preston said, "I fancy Milligan. Are you willing to wager a few ponies on your boy?"

"Ponies?" Doc repeated. "Why not make it a whole horse-and-wagon?"

This brought a laugh and the suddenly red-faced bookmaker explained that he was talking about a sporting bet.

Doc, always spoiling for a bet, put on a real act. The con-man in him came out and he said, slowly, "I'm not much of a better. But when I do make one, it's got to be real good."

He smoothed his impeccable trousers, adjusted the cuffs of his white silk shirt and toyed with his monocle.

"Bet your limit," Preston snapped. "I'll cover any amount you put up. The odds are two to one, but I'll give you a point over because your boy's eye is so badly cut."

"Is that your word as a gentleman?" Kearns asked.

Preston nodded.

Kearns turned to me. "Want to shoot the works, Mickey?"

"You mean, bet the entire purse? The whole hundred-twenty-thousand dollars?"

Doc nodded—a bit slyly, I thought.

"All right, go ahead," I said, knowing he'd do it anyway. "Just make sure there's enough money left so we don't have to swim home."

The bet was made, $360,000 to $120,000. No ponies, no horse-and-wagon. Just good American money. It turned out that a "pony" actually is a one-hundred-pound note, worth $420 at the time. A handshake sealed the wager. Then Doc and I went up to our suite to get some sleep. He slept a lot better than I did.

The fight was held on June 30, 1927, at London's Olympic Stadium, which had been built for the 1908 Olympic Games. The crowd was only about ten thousand people, due to the high prices. The promoter charged fifty dollars for ringside seats. Only the wealthy and titled could get those seats and most of the ringsiders were elegantly gowned ladies, with their escorts in evening clothes. They included members of the peerage, of Parliament and other figures prominent in diplomatic and government life.

The fight was bloody and brutal. Milligan, a good, game boy, started off too fast. I paced myself, figuring I could get to him in the late rounds. He was ahead on points until I nailed him in the seventh round. I won the eighth and had him close to a knockout in the ninth but the bell saved him. When he came out for the tenth, he was helpless. He'd already been down six times.

I turned to the referee, a Frenchman named Eugene Corri, who had been a featherweight champ. "You'd better stop it," I advised. "He's nearly dead. I don't want to hit him any more."

He refused. "Fight on," he said. "You fight on."

Milligan was swaying, his hands down, his face battered and bloody. Disgusted and determined to end it as quickly and painlessly as possible, I let go with a punch which carried all I had. When it landed, he crashed to the canvas with blood spurting from his ears and mouth.

I felt like the meanest man in the stadium. Like the time with Mickey Wallace, that was one punch I hadn't wanted to throw. The man was helpless and the punch was unnecessary. It could have killed him. Thank the Lord it didn't.

Milligan was unconscious for nearly five minutes after they dragged him to his corner and he hemorrhaged so badly that he had to be rushed to a hospital.

Preston paid off right after the fight, handing Doc $360,000 in cash, American money. We now had over half a million dollars, counting the bet, the purse and the money we'd won at the race track.

We had a victory party that night after the fight. This one was wilder and wetter than any we'd ever had before. The champagne never stopped flowing. It didn't take the bubbles long to lift me up into the clouds. But, high as I was, I remembered a promise I'd made Kearns give me.

On the *Berengaria*, I'd got Doc to promise he'd take me to Ireland—win or lose. Being Irish, I had a yearning to see the land of my forefathers. My father's side of the family came from Roscommon and my mother's people were from Keighry. I wanted to greet all the people who had been writing me letters, claiming they were cousins. They were warm, friendly letters from gay Irish hearts and I was very anxious to see these lads and colleens.

At the party, before I got so drunk I didn't care, I made him promise again that we'd sail for Ireland the next morning.

The party was in our suite at the Savoy and every guy had a dame. Good-time Charley Friedman, a Damon Runyon character who used to tag along with Kearns, was in love with a French actress who was at the party with him and was leaving for Paris the next day. The wing-ding lasted all night and nobody went to sleep unless they passed out.

By morning, we were still in a fog from the champagne. Kearns sent Friedman to make reservations for the trip to Ireland. But Good-time Charley, still thinking of his cherie from Paree, said to himself "to hell with Ireland" and bought us all tickets for France instead. Friedman definitely had no ties with anything Hibernian.

When Charley came back with the tickets, Doc saw at once what he'd done, but Doc didn't care. He wanted no part of Ireland, either. And his real name is John Patrick McKernan.

"Don't tell Mickey," he cautioned Friedman. "He'll kill both of us."

Soon we were all on a boat crossing the channel, nine of us, including Baer and Gibbons.

Kearns, of course, didn't tell me we were headed for France. I thought we were on the way to Ireland. I still felt like a big bubble that just wouldn't burst. It was a wonderful sensation. I didn't want to be sober ever again.

A crowd was waiting for us on shore. Somehow, word of our coming had gone on ahead. News of the fight had made all of the European papers and I was a celebrity. As I stepped off the boat and heard all these people cheering me, I figured they must be my relatives. I was sure of it when some of them grabbed me and kissed and hugged me. They were jabbering away in a strange language which I took to be Gaelic. Feeling like a conquering hero in the ould country, I started handing out dollar bills which I got from Doc, who had a big roll on him.

It wasn't until two days later, when I sobered up in Paris, that I learned for the first time we were not in Ireland at all. The place where I greeted my "relatives" was not Shannon but Cherbourg and the language not Gaelic but French. By that time I didn't care. I was having too good a time.

To this day, I've never seen Ireland!

That stay in Paris proved to be one of the wildest times of my wild life. Just picture us: a bunch of reckless, irresponsible zanies, full of spirits, merry as a bunch of sailors on leave, with more money than the whole French Navy, and you may begin to get an idea of the fun we had.

We stayed at the Ambassador Hotel. It's a wonder the building was still standing by the time we left—at the request of the management. Champagne flowed over my tonsils like Niagara Falls—endlessly. One night we were at a night club. I had a couple dozen people as my guests, though I don't think I knew half of them. Somebody remarked, "The Yanks were a bit late getting into the war. They waited until everybody else was weary and worn."

I took it as an insult to my country and started swinging. The brawl which followed was a beaut. They finally threw us out and we had to pay 10,000 francs (about $2,500) in damages. We ruined furniture, dishes, glassware—and somebody threw a bottle which broke an expensive crystal chandelier.

Commander Richard E. Byrd was in Paris at the time, just prior to his first expedition to the South Pole. Someone tossed a party for him and his companions at a cabaret in Montmartre and, as an American celebrity, I was invited.

Kearns really promoted himself with the dolls in Paris. A couple of American vaudeville actors, Lester Allen and Bill Halligan, had come over on the *Berengaria* with us, and Kearns got Allen booking as master of ceremonies at the Ambassaaor. As a pay-off, everytime Allen opened the show, he gave Doc a special introduction as "the handsome millionaire fight manager."

During our first month in Paris, I don't think I was sober a single night.

Friedman had his French bonbon, Doc his Countess and I—just kind of foraged. The territory was fertile.

One night I had a date with a chorus girl in a show at a Montmartre café. Doc was with me. We watched the show and I was waiting for it to end—somewhat impatiently. At the other end of the café I noticed the Prince of Wales with a group. I was going to say hello after the show.

Just before the final number, the head waiter brought me a note. It was from my girl in the chorus, a stunning brunette. The Prince of Wales had asked her for a date, she wrote. She regretted having to break our appointment.

"Tell her it's okay with me," I told the waiter. "The Prince is a pal of mine."

I was being stood up and Doc couldn't resist the opportunity to jab the needle into me.

"Who does that Limey think he is?" Doc asked aloud. "Imagine taking Mickey's girl away from him. We won't let him get away with it, will we, Mick? Imagine the nerve of the guy—pretending to be a friend and then stealing your girl!"

Kearns kept working on me, trying to stir me up so that I would tell off the Prince. And he was succeeding. Finally, I got so worked up, I leaped from my chair and started toward the Prince, determined to punch him in the nose. Kearns, realizing he had gone too far, grabbed me by the arm. "Cool off," he said, laughing. "I was only ribbing you, Mick."

Lucky for me he stopped me. How would it have looked if the middleweight champion of the world and the future

King of England got into a brawl over an undressed Parisian chorine?

I met Norma Talmadge, the American movie queen, in Paris. Fanny Brice introduced us. Norma and I formed a friendship that lasted for many years.

We were having a party one evening at the Ambassador. Norma was my date and we were having a ball. I got drunk as usual, and came up with the romantic notion that I had to buy flowers for Norma. There were none available at the hotel, so I stumbled out into the street in search of a florist. There wasn't one open, of course, this being the wee hours of the morning. I couldn't even find one of those old ladies who usually are on the street corners of Paris begging you to "buy a posey for the lady."

Finally, I wandered into an alley and found a beat-up old bouquet of roses which somebody had dumped into an ash can. I grabbed them and barreled back into our suite where, with an exaggerated bow, I presented the flowers to Norma.

"This beautiful bouquet is for you, milady," I said with a courtly swagger, almost falling on my face.

Norma, high and happy, herself, returned the bow and accepted the flowers.

Fanny Brice leaped from her chair and grabbed Norma by the shoulders. "Hear, hear," she shouted, making a mock introduction, "I want you all to meet Broadway Rose!"

That broke everybody up, and for the rest of our stay in Paris we all called Norma "Broadway Rose." "Rose" was a panhandler who used to hang out at Broadway and Fiftieth Street in New York and ask for handouts under the guise of "selling" a withered bouquet of roses to escorts "for the lady."

166

The owner of the Ritz gave us a dinner at the American Bar one evening. Norma and Fanny were late and the rest of our party were seated, drinking. Kearns was with his Countess; Teddy Hayes was with his girl, Pauline Mason. She was an American movie actress who later married comedian Skeets Gallagher. Friedman had his Parisian patootie, as usual. Also along for the fun were Floyd Gibbons and Bugs Baer as well as Dan McKetrick, one of Kearns's fight-racket cronies. There was one other guest at our party . . . the Countess' dog, a Russian wolf-hound.

We were drinking champagne and Doc, as usual, was sitting at the head of the table playing host.

I occupied myself by composing a romantic poem to Norma. In those days, I wasn't yet interested in art, but I was on a poetry kick.

Kearns pulled the sheet of paper from my hand—I was writing on the back of the menu—and read the few lines I'd scribbled. I can't remember them now, but they probably were silly and trite, like a greeting card verse.

"Hey, look at our Mick. Writing poetry," he roared. Then, with a big wink which was intended for the whole table, he jibed: "Hell, Teddy Hayes can write better poetry than that, Mickey."

"You need inspiration to write a love poem," I snapped. "How can Teddy become inspired with the tomatoes he goes around with?"

Hayes's girl got sore and Teddy insisted that I apologize. "Don't call my girl a tomato," he warned.

I was mad at Doc for embarrassing me and took it out on Hayes. For no good reason, I reached across and popped him on the chin.

As I hit Hayes, the wolfhound let out a bleat and

167

jumped, knocking over the table and spilling the drinks in our laps. Hayes charged me and we spun out onto the dance floor. Doc jumped in, trying to separate us and the waiters joined in. Pretty quickly, it was a melee, with everybody swinging. Somebody hit Gibbons on his good eye—he had no sight in the other one and was famous for the patch over it—and he crawled around on the floor, unable to see.

It's funny what you think of during a fight. There I was belting Frenchmen and piling them up all over the joint. Yet I thought of Bugs Baer, my little friend.

The French fight with their feet and one of them knocked me down with a kick. I got up and clobbered him. Then I looked around for Bugs. I saw him scooting under a table, trying to keep out of the way of flying feet, fists and furniture. I grabbed little Bugs by the coat collar and hung him upon a coat rack to keep him out of danger. Bugs still loves to tell the story, impossible as it may sound today.

After making sure Bugs was out of harm's way I resumed the battle, and all through it Bugs hung up there hollering, "Get 'em Mickey! Hey, watch behind you, Mick!"

The gendarmes were called, of course. After the fighting ended, I got into an argument with the manager and the cops over the damages. I lost. It cost me five hundred bucks.

Out on the street, we counted the casualties. I had a bruised cheek and jaw, Hayes was bloodied up, Doc had lost his Countess and her wolfhound, and Gibbons had two bad eyes.

The next day, Kearns decided we better get out of

Paris. If we'd stayed much longer, we'd have started the Second World War sooner than Hitler did.

The hotel bill for our stay in Paris came to about sixty thousand dollars. Doc had taken the whole floor for our party, he and I in the same suite and the others in the remaining rooms.

When we finally boarded the *Homeric* for home, Kearns decided to split the money we had left. He emptied his pockets and his money belt. He always dealt in cash—no banks were going to go bust on him. We counted $120,000 —all that was left. Doc and I split it, taking sixty grand apiece.

CHAPTER EIGHTEEN

Doc and I were sitting on top of the world after we returned from Europe. We picked up where we left off . . . right on the dance floors of the leading night clubs in New York.

I paid practically no attention to my home life. I took my wife for granted. Maude stayed home most of the time while I was out gallivanting, drinking, carousing and generally raising hell. I spent little time at home and whenever I did, I usually wound up in an argument with Maude. The next day, I'd be sorry and would call her and promise I'd settle down and be a better husband and father. I'd reform for a few days but it never lasted. I just couldn't stay away from parties.

I did plenty of fighting, too. I had three fights during the remainder of 1927, all against light-heavyweights.

Fighting heavier men was my idea. I had more trouble with light nimble-footed opponents than with the heavier, cumbersome type. Besides, the big fellows made a bigger target for my left hook.

I fought Mike McTigue again and this time I knocked him out in two minutes and fifteen seconds of the first round. (Mike was no longer the light-heavyweight king; he had lost the title to Paul Berlenbach two years before.) McTigue was unconscious for five minutes after this fight and it scared me. Dave Barry, of the famous "long count," was back as referee for the first time since the second Dempsey-Tunney fight. He was as much the center of interest as McTigue and I were. The minute he was introduced, the crowd went into a slow count which ended at fourteen. This was repeated between each round of the preliminary fights. I think Barry was happier over my first-round knockout of McTigue than I was.

The record book shows that I had fifty-two knockouts. I should have had sixty. The books don't include the ones I had the night after I fought Paul Berlenbach in Chicago, November 25th.

Kearns, Hayes and I were guests of Knute Rockne, the great Notre Dame coach, for the Notre Dame-Army game at Soldier's Field. Hayes was a friend of Rockne's and that's why we were invited. We stayed at the Morrison Hotel, which also was headquarters for the Notre Dame team.

The Friday night before the game, I won a ten-round decision over Paul Berlenbach. Paul was no longer light-heavyweight champ. He had lost the title to Jack Delaney.

That night Doc held open house for the newspapermen in our hotel suite. Because of the double weekend attraction there were many out-of-town writers in Chicago.

Kearns hired Bee Palmer, a famous shimmy dancer in Chicago night clubs of that era, to entertain for the boys.

I didn't attend. It had been a tough fight and I was tired. I got a separate room for myself and went to bed. I didn't feel like drinking and I didn't want to get mixed up with Doc.

While things were rolling along and Bee was doing her act, three strangers crashed the party. Doc, ever the gracious host, treated them cordially. There was always room for more at any party Doc was running.

But one of the outsiders got stiff pretty quickly—they hadn't been sober when they busted in—and made a pass at Bee. Kearns tried to stop him, but the guy took a punch at him. Doc, helped by Teddy Hayes and Billy McCarney, Luis Firpo's manager and a good friend, tossed the three intruders out into the corridor.

Next day, we went to the game. Notre Dame lost to Army, 18-0, its only loss that season. Hayes and McCarney hadn't gone to the game. They were in Doc's suite, with Jackie Farrell, a boxing writer with the *New York Daily News*. While they were waiting for us, the same three guys who had barged in the night before, came in. This time, they had two more fellows with them.

They started to shove Hayes and McCarney around. Hayes, tough and fearless, was jumped by four of them. One of them grabbed Farrell, who stands four feet, ten inches and weighs less than most jockeys—under 110 pounds.

"Hey, I'm gonna throw this little son-of-a-bitch out a window," he roared.

Farrell squirmed loose, dashed out of the suite and into the hall looking for the house detective. When he finally returned with the house dick, the troublemakers had vamoosed, leaving Hayes and McCarney battered and bloody.

When Doc and I arrived, there was a crowd in the suite. Among those I recognized were Lee Moore, a Chicago gangster, and Machine Gun Jack McGurn, one of the most vicious gunmen of the prohibition era. Doc and I knew both. McGurn, a Capone torpedo, had led the St. Valentine's Day massacre the year before. He was also the guy who slit the throat of comedian Joe E. Lewis—all but severing the entertainer's vocal chords—merely because Lewis had given up star billing at a Capone-controlled night club to work for a rival mobster.

Hayes, through swollen lips, told us what had happened. Moore grinned savagely, "Where are those sons-of-bitches?"

Farrell thought he recognized them as Notre Dame football players and he had an idea where they were because he had seen them disappear down the other end of the corridor.

Moore wanted to follow them and give them a good going over.

"Now wait a minute," I butted in. "Let's not start any trouble with those Notre Dame boys. They're just kids. Besides, Rockne treated us real well. Why don't we just find them, shake hands and tell them there are no hard feelings?"

Moore and Farrell went along with Doc and me. We had no trouble finding the room they were in. There were about a dozen of them there, drinking and singing. When they saw us, they thought we were looking for trouble and were ready for another fight. I shouted them down.

"Wait a minute, you guys," I called out. "Take it easy.

We just came in to shake hands and tell you there are no hard feelings."

All were willing, except one big red-headed kid who insisted on fighting. Moore whipped out a .38 and would have blown the kid's belly apart. I grabbed the gun, slipped it to Farrell and told him to get rid of it. Poor Jackie turned gray. He didn't know what to do with the gun and tried to hand it to Doc. I shoved Jackie out of the room and watched him run down the hall to Doc's suite where he hid the gun in the dresser drawer.

I heard a crash and hurried back. Moore and Kearns were in a battle royal with the football kids. I waded in and started swinging. I was sober; they were drunk, and it was easy for me to pick them off. I flattened seven or eight. I maneuvered them one by one to the doorway, knocked them through it, and piled them up in the hall-way.

Farrell came running back then, but when he saw the shambles, he ran down for help again. The assistant manager called the city cops. Three policemen and the hotel detective rushed up, but by that time the fight was over. We were willing to drop the whole thing, but one of the kids who was still on his feet, shouted:

"Let's round up the rest of the squad and clean up these guys!"

Hayes and McCarney had arrived on the scene by that time. McGurn was staggering along behind. They heard the kid's threat. McGurn, who was drunk, beat it back to his room and returned with a machine gun. He yelled he was going to mow them all down.

I pleaded with the crazed gunman and finally got him to go back to his room. I called down to Harry Moore, the hotel manager and a good friend of mine.

"Harry, you gotta clear those Notre Dame kids out of here before they get into real trouble," I told him. "That McGurn is drunk and he's liable to kill some of them."

Harry rushed up and advised the kids to pack and check out.

Rockne heard about the fight after he got back to South Bend. That week, before we returned East, the coach invited Doc and me down to the school to meet his team on a friendly basis.

A couple of weeks later, when I was back in Rumson, Moore forwarded a letter which he had received from the fighting men of Notre Dame. They apologized for the trouble they had caused and added: "We had no idea who we were mixed up with. Our chief regret is that we fought Mickey Walker and didn't get paid for it."

Most of the Rumson population of that day were old-line blue bloods, proud of their family backgrounds—not the nouveau riche of the sports and entertainment worlds.

I was tremendously impressed with their way of life. I listened to their stories of game-fishing in the Florida Keys, big-game hunting in India and Africa, their trips to the South Sea Islands. I envied their manner and talk. I wanted to be one of them. It wasn't enough to wear white tie and tails and buy champagne. I wanted to be socially prominent, to live and play with the blue bloods. Me, the Mick from Keighry Head, wanted to be accepted as one of them. Edward Michael Walker, gentleman, not Mickey Walker, prize fighter.

To crash Society became a mania with me.

In grasping for position in Society, I continued to neglect a part of real society—my family. I didn't know that a man who desires to win the respect of others, first must establish it in his own home. This I had never done. I had drifted steadily away from Maude, first along the glittering road of Broadway, then Hollywood, then Europe. Now I was off on a new kind of binge.

One of the wealthiest of my new friends was General Arthur Borden, who was known as the "Cotton King." He owned a textile firm on Worth Street, in downtown New York. He had a string of polo ponies and played polo with Cecil Smith, Pete Bostwick and Rube Williams, all ten-goal men. I used to practice with them, and though I turned out to be a pretty good horseman, I never could get the knack of hitting a polo ball.

I played golf and tennis at the Rumson Country Club, where I was always welcome as a guest; but that's where they drew the line. I was never invited to their private parties. Most of them had a sporting interest in boxing and tolerated me because I was a champion. But they never offered me a membership.

They came to my camp to see me train for a fight but they never cared to have me as a guest in their own homes. They treated me as a celebrity, when I wanted to be treated as an equal.

The social barrier between the country-club set and an ordinary guy like myself was something I just didn't understand. They were established society; I was a pug. I belonged to the other country clubs, in Deal and Red Bank, but not to this one in Rumson. One day I decided to make a pitch for membership at Rumson Country Club. I didn't think I'd have much trouble.

General John Reed Kilpatrick, former head of Madison Square Garden, was my sponsor. He was then a colonel. Even his sponsorship didn't carry enough weight to get me in, however.

I couldn't understand why. I was bitterly disappointed. I felt that I'd had a rotten deal. I was as good as any of them, I figured, except that I wasn't a millionaire. Yes, that must be it, I decided. I didn't have a financial rating like theirs.

All my life, when I wanted something badly enough, I'd fight for it. Now I had a different sort of fight—to become a millionaire. I made up my mind to get a million dollars and crack that exclusive club. I was sure that money would open the doors of Society.

With my million, they'd be forced to accept me. I'd bring a million dollars in cash to General Borden and the others and then there'd be no excuse.

Besides a few thousand bucks in "walking-around money," I had $300,000 in my checking account. I turned it all into cash, getting the bank teller to give it to me in one-thousand-dollar bills. I bought a safety box and stacked those three hundred big ones in it. I built the million around that. I made nearly half a million dollars in purses in 1928 and '29. I was doing fine in the market and my real estate was thriving. I turned some of those stocks and properties into cash. Still, I was short the million.

So I went out and finished the job in my own way. I went on a gambling spree, hit it big with hot horses and hot dice, and made up the difference. It took me a year and a half of feverish financial operations, as well as a dozen fights, but I made it.

The income tax bite then wasn't anything like it is now. You could keep ninety cents out of every dollar you made.

Finally, the great day came—M-Day. I walked into the vault, got out the box and counted up the money, which I had been accumulating week by week. It was stacked up neatly in ten little piles, one thousand bills with "$1,000, United States of America" printed on each one. It looked good. I smiled. I touched it. It felt good. It added up to a million dollars exactly. I was rich. I was "in."

I'll never forget that moment . . . the thrill of having a million dollars in your own two hands at one time. Then I thought how little it looked, stacked up there. It took so little room. Why, it wouldn't cover half the kitchen table in Mom's house.

As I looked at it, the glow began to fade and I realized suddenly that I wasn't really any different. All right, I was a millionaire. But I was still Mickey Walker. My blood was still red, not blue.

So what was all this for? What did I need these people to do for me? To make me a snob like themselves? I began to feel sorry for them, that they were so haughty and selfish. Let them keep their noses turned up. If they thought a million dollars made you a better person, to hell with them and their false values. I wanted no part of them.

Funny what can go on in a young man's mind. Looking back now, I can see that I was all wrong. You need more than money to be Society. I had the money but I didn't have what goes with it—background, tradition, class. And I suppose I was jealous of those who had. I think I yearned for Society because to me it stood for wealth. When I became wealthy, there was no longer any need to crash Society. I just didn't belong.

CHAPTER NINETEEN

During the time I was trying to crash Society, Kearns
and I were embroiled with the New York State Athletic
Commission and were under suspension for various real
or fancied infractions of their rules. I seemed to be forever in hot water with the Boxing Lords, mostly because
I didn't defend my title within the stipulated six-month
period after my knockout victory over Tommy Milligan
in June of 1927.

I saw no good reason for defending my middleweight
title. I was looking for big purses and there wasn't a
middleweight contender around with whom I could draw
at the box office. I fared much better financially fighting
bigger men in other places. Since I was suspended in
New York, I did all my fighting elsewhere. It's a matter
of record that I didn't have a single fight in New York
from June of 1926 until July of 1931.

The big moguls in New York may not have liked me
back in the late twenties, but I was very popular in
Chicago, where I had fought seven times and had never
been beaten. The fight fans there loved me as though
I were a home-town boy. They had practically adopted
me.

Jim Farley, who was then Boxing Commissioner in
New York, promised to lift my suspension if I signed
to defend my title in his city. But that meant fighting
under the promotion of Tex Rickard, who was then the
Madison Square Garden promoter. Kearns didn't like

Rickard. The two had been cool toward each other ever since Kearns's break-up with Dempsey. Doc always felt that Rickard could have straightened out the trouble between him and Dempsey if he had wanted to. He never forgot that.

Early in 1928, Kearns signed me with Ace Hudkins, for a ten-round middleweight title defense in Chicago. Hudkins, who was called the Nebraska Wildcat, had come into prominence as the logical middleweight contender. He had lost only once in his last twenty-one fights.

Farley objected to the fight being held outside New York, but we didn't care. Kearns figured the fight would draw better in Chicago, because Hudkins had a midwest following. So we said to hell with New York—and of course, Farley didn't lift my suspension, even though I was finally defending the middleweight title.

I worked myself into top shape for Hudkins. I had four tune-up fights in the five months before our meeting, which was scheduled for June 21, 1928, at Comiskey Park, home of the White Sox. I did my preliminary training in New Jersey, as usual, and finished up at Hawthorne Race Track on Chicago's Southwest Side.

When I arrived in Chicago, there was a mob headed by an official delegation from the city, at the station. Big Bill Thompson, the Mayor, greeted me and made a speech. It was the largest ovation given a boxer in the Windy City since Tunney went there to defend his title against Dempsey. I was paraded from Union Station to City Hall, where the Mayor presented me with the key to the city.

There was a press luncheon at the Morrison Hotel. About fifteen of us, including the Mayor, Kearns, and several newspapermen crowded into one elevator. The overload caused it to drop as we started to go up. No wonder. The Mayor, himself, weighed 300 pounds; he wasn't called Big Bill for nothing. The cables became jammed and we were held prisoners for a hot and scary half hour. It was hard to breathe and a couple of the guys got sick.

They had to call an emergency crew to pull some of us out through the escape hatch in the roof.

I caught cold just before the fight. The day of the bout, I had a 104-degree temperature. Kearns called a doctor, who advised us to ask for a postponement. Not me. I was in no mood to call it off. I knew that once I broke training, I would have a tough time getting back into condition. A big city had too many other interests to take my mind off my work . . . fillies with four legs—and two. That's one reason I never trained in a big city. Too many distractions, too little will power.

To make everything just dandy, it began to rain right after the opening bell, and I mean it rained. It came down in sheets, lashing everybody. The spectators were drenched. The ring soon became a watery mess and Ace and I splashed around it, hardly able to keep our feet. There were times when we looked more like swimmers than fighters.

Hudkins was tough. He was as hard to get rid of as a leech. He was in close all the time, crowding me and punching from bell to bell. I had no trouble hitting him, but he absorbed the punches like a sponge. I couldn't knock him out. He punished me considerably in the body and it was close all the way. Despite the terrible conditions, it was an exciting fight and I was lucky to win.

Hudkins was handled by his two brothers and when the referee lifted my arm at the end of the last round,

180

they both jumped into the ring raising howls of protest. One of the brothers, Clyde, was officially listed as Ace's manager.

The brothers claimed they were "jobbed," and later in interviews with fight writers, clamored for a return bout. Doc promised we'd give Hudkins another crack at the title but he didn't say when.

The Chicago fight was a good payday, one of the best purses I ever earned. Eighty thousand bucks.

The next day, I headed back to New York, but Doc and Teddy Hayes had to go to Los Angeles on personal business. We took a cab to Union Station.

In the taxi, Doc counted out forty thousand dollars in cash, my half, and gave it to me. Actually, he had just ten grand for himself because he had gotten only fifty thousand dollars on account, from Jim Mullins. For some reason, the promoter didn't have all the cash available and Doc took an I.O.U. for the rest.

I boarded the Twentieth Century for New York and went right to the lounge car. I was alone but had a bottle with me and poured myself a snort. A young lady sat across from me. I offered her a drink and we got talking. Her name was Josephine. After pleasant talk over several drinks, I suggest we continue drinking in my compartment. She needed no urging and we finished the bottle in private. We were both mellow by the time we were ready for bed.

Somehow, we managed to get undressed. She crawled into the lower berth and immediately corked off. I tried to get in with her, but not tonight with this Josephine. She was too bulky, so I said to heck with it and struggled into the upper berth.

Suddenly, even in my vague condition, I thought of

181

my forty grand. I took the roll of greenbacks out of my pocket and stuffed it into the toe of one of my patent-leather shoes.

I fell asleep almost immediately. When I awoke in the morning, still woozy, I looked down on Josie who was dead to the world. I looked for my shoes. The dough was uppermost in my mind. The shoes were gone. Boy, did I sober up in a hurry. I searched all over the compartment, but no shoes. There was only one answer. Josephine had taken the money and hidden the shoes.

I shook her awake.

"Where are my shoes?" I screamed.

The sleep was still in her eyes and the whiskey still in her head. She didn't understand. I shook her again, roughly.

"Give me my shoes," I demanded.

"Shoes? What shoes?" she asked blearily. "And who are you?"

That's all I needed. Now she was rubbing it in.

"Don't play innocent with me," I blazed. "You stole my shoes. I want 'em back."

"What would I want with your shoes? I've got my own."

Now I thought she was really playing with me.

"Look, you lying witch," I said. "I know you hid my shoes someplace. No one else could have taken them. The door is locked. I'm not going to let you out of here until you give me my shoes."

She was frightened now and began to cry. "I didn't take your shoes. I swear I didn't," she whimpered. "I have no idea what happened to your shoes, but I swear I didn't touch them."

I didn't believe her, of course, and I rang for the porter. I was still giving her hell when the buzzer sounded.

I opened the door.

"Good morning, boss. Heah's yo' shoes, boss," sang out the porter. "Nice and shiny like the ace of spades."

I grabbed the shoes and quickly stuck my hand into the toe of the right one. Sure enough, there was the roll, soft and bulky.

I sagged in relief, the perspiration running down my face. I looked at Josephine who by now was almost dressed. I had some explaining to do.

"I'm sorry, baby," I said lamely. "I lost my head."

She was still sniffling and I could see that all she was thinking of was getting on her clothes and scramming out of the compartment.

I pulled out a hundred-dollar bill and stuck it in her hand. "Thanks, Josephine, for being such a good guy about it," I said.

She took the money without a word and reached for her purse.

"Mister," she said dryly as she turned to go, "you must wear real expensive shoes."

I never felt any guilt about these hit-and-run affairs. Even when I got back East, I continued to run around with girls. By this time, it had reached the point where I went my way and Maude went hers. But I still had to be careful about being too brazen about it; my face was familiar along the whole Jersey shore and I didn't want to become front-page news. I had to find a hide-out and I hit on a small night club in Asbury Park, the Bluebird Inn. Rose, the girl I was squiring around at the time, and I became steady customers.

One night, I got a good load on and decided I wanted

to own the place. The owner tried to talk me out of it, but I insisted.

"Look, Mickey," he said, "you don't wanna buy this joint. It ain't makin' a quarter. You'd be throwing away your money. The only reason I'm keeping open is that it's a front for my real business."

He was a bootlegger, of course, and he stored the hooch in the cellar.

That didn't stop me. I insisted he name his price.

"Okay, Mickey," he shrugged. "If you insist on being a chump, you got a half interest for twenty-grand."

The next night Rose told me what I had done and I felt like a sucker who had been clipped, but good. But, drunk or sober, a deal was a deal.

Then I got an idea and decided I could make it pay. I brought in entertainment from New York, top Negro acts who were friends of mine: Bojangles Bill Robinson, Cab Calloway, Buck and Bubbles. The place was soon jumping—and jammed every night until dawn.

There was only one thing wrong—it still didn't make any money. I was too good a host. As soon as I got loaded, everything was on the house. Nobody could pay a tab.

My partner, being a businessman, couldn't understand how we could do so much business and take in so little money. After a month or so, he called me into the office.

"You're not cut out for the café business," he said. "If we keep this up, you'll have us both broke. Now, I like you, so here's what I'll do: I'll give you double what you put in—but from now on, you're out."

From the tone of his voice, I knew he meant it. I took the forty grand and walked out with 100-percent profit on my investment.

All my running around didn't affect my fighting ability

or slow me up in the ring. After I made the comeback against Shuffles Callahan, I was unbeaten for more than two years, winning sixteen fights in a row. I didn't bar anyone, any weight. Most of those fights were against light-heavyweights who outweighed me by 15 or sometimes as much as 20 pounds.

Kearns encouraged me to fight the big ones. He had never given up the idea that I could become heavyweight champion of the world.

He even signed me with Dempsey. That was about six months after Jack had failed to regain the heavyweight title from Tunney in September, 1927. Our fight was set for Los Angeles. Kearns agreed to let Dempsey have $250,000 or a percentage of the gate (whichever was more). Doc would have given anything to see me lick Dempsey. The contracts actually were signed but Dempsey decided to retire and there was no fight.

Had Kearns been his manager in the second Tunney fight, Dempsey might have retired with the title. Doc and I didn't see that fight. We had just returned from our European trip and were too travel-weary to continue on to Chicago.

This was the famous "long-count" fight in which Dempsey decked Tunney, and referee Dave Barry didn't pick up the timekeeper's count until it had reached five. This was in the seventh round and Barry was too busy trying to get Jack to go to a neutral corner. When he did pick up the count, Barry started at one. Tunney struggled to his feet at Barry's count of nine but actually had been on the floor for fourteen seconds.

As soon as ten seconds were gone, Doc would have jumped into the ring and gotten Dempsey out of there before anybody knew what was happening. His quick mind would have taken advantage of the mix-up immediately. There would have been a big stink, but Dempsey would have been champ again.

Dempsey was the greatest fighter I ever saw. But he was lost without Kearns. Dempsey admitted that when he was at his peak, denied it after he and Doc had split and were bitter enemies, then admitted it again when they made up twenty-five years later. In a public hatchet-burying scene in 1950, Dempsey said, "If it wasn't for Kearns, I'd still be a bum."

I can't say that because I had the welterweight title even before I met Kearns. But Doc did steer me to title bouts in the middleweight, light-heavyweight and heavy-weight divisions.

I fought Tommy Loughran, the light-heavy champ, in Chicago on March 28, 1929. Tommy Harmon promoted the fight, which opened the new Chicago Stadium.

The financial arrangements were peculiar. Loughran was the champ and he figured the title was worth a lot of money. So he offered a strange deal, which we had to accept—or no fight. If I lost the decision, I would get fifty thousand dollars; if I won, I'd only get ten thousand dollars, with the title. Loughran's end was 55 percent of the gate. The rest of the receipts went to the promoter.

People grew suspicious when they learned about the unusual method of splitting the purse. Who ever heard of a guy getting five times as much for losing as for winning? But there was no funny business, believe me. I'd have been a fool to lay down for Loughran. A victory would have made me one of those rarities: a champ in three divisions. That's an opportunity which comes to few fighters.

The fight was close. Until the decision was announced, I thought I'd won. Most of the spectators agreed with me because they booed for ten minutes. Nearly all of the writers covering the fight thought I had been given the works.

Tommy spent the whole evening running backwards and I had to force the fighting every inch of the way. I had him groggy at the end.

The referee, Dave Miller, gave four rounds to me, one to Loughran and called five even. Phil Collins, one of the judges, gave the fight to Loughran, calling the rounds 5-4-1. Eddie Klein, a restaurant owner in Chicago, who acted as the other judge, did not give me a single round. His vote decided it.

The defeat cost me a chance to match Bob Fitzsimmons who, weighing no more than 165 pounds, held the middleweight, light-heavyweight and heavyweight titles.

When I returned to Rumson, I learned that I had lost more than a fight; I had lost my wife, too. Maude had walked out taking four-year-old Mickey, Jr., with her. She left a note saying she was going to live with her sister in California. She was sick and tired of my doing as I pleased, staying out nights or days at a time, running around with dames, getting drunk every other night, shirking all family responsibilities.

I sure hadn't been a model husband but I hadn't thought anything like this would happen. I loved them both and now that they were gone, felt lost without them. I took Maude for granted, figuring marriage was a one-way ticket. I could break the rules and egoist that I was, thought I could get away with it. I provided a good home but wasn't in it very much. I knew the fault was mine.

That was bad but the worst was to come. The President of the Rumson Bank called me the next day, asking me to stop by. I did and he told me that Maude had been there a few days before and had emptied the vault. Since all the securities were made out in both our names, she could cash them in. In all, she took almost half a million dollars, of which $350,000 was in stocks and bonds.

I was cleaned out . . . no wife and no money.

My money troubles had begun to mount up earlier in the year. The million-dollar pile which I'd built up to crash Society had shrunk. I had blown a bundle when my gambling luck went bad. Slow horses, cold dice, fast dames and ridiculously high living cut me down; Maude got the rest.

The shock was too much for me, more than I could take. I broke down and, as you might figure, turned to the one thing which could help me forget—whiskey.

CHAPTER TWENTY

I had been a heavy drinker before, but nothing like this. In the weeks that followed I became a sot. I roamed from bar to bar, drunk all the time, not caring a hoot who saw me. At first, Kearns knew nothing about it. He had gone out of town to line up a fight for me with Leo Lomski, a top-ranking light-heavyweight from Philadelphia.

Lomski was another fighter in the stable of Bill Duffy

and Owney Madden. He had cleaned up most of the boys in the light-heavy division and his managers figured a victory over me would put him in line for a shot at Loughran's title. The match was made for July 29, 1929, in Philadelphia's Baker Bowl. The promoter was Max "Boo-Boo" Hoff, a Philadelphia beer baron.

Making the match was one thing, Kearns discovered—but finding me was another. He learned how I was carrying on almost the moment he arrived from Philadelphia. Word came to him from all directions that I had gotten loaded in Red Bank, Rumson, Shrewsbury and Asbury Park. He made the rounds of all the joints, but just couldn't catch up with me; I had either left or hadn't been there yet.

During my drunken soirées, I met one Johnny Malone, who was secretary to Mayor Hague, the powerful political boss of Jersey City. Johnny and I made a good team. We decided that between us we could drink every joint on the Jersey shore dry. We gave it a good try.

Searching parties were sent out for us. The Jersey City police, on orders from Mayor Hague, were on the lookout for Malone. Kearns, by this time, had hired a couple of private detectives to find me. It took them two weeks to catch up to us. We didn't go home but slept in the back of the cafés and clubs, like common bums.

Finally, I tired of it. Not the drinking, but living like a hobo. I was sick, worn out and filthy, and I just had to get one good night's sleep. The only place I could get that was in my own home, which was empty now.

My buddy thought it was a good idea. We managed somehow, despite our condition, to get to Rumson but we made such a racket getting into the house that we woke my neighbor. She had been keeping a watch on the house, having promised my mother to contact her the minute I showed. She telephoned Mom in Elizabeth, who immediately called Kearns. He had been keeping in constant touch with her.

The next morning, there was more commotion in my house than on Times Square. My mother was the first to arrive. She found Johnny stretched out on the couch in the living room, fully dressed. I was asleep in my bedroom. Mom shook Johnny awake, grabbed him by the collar and yanked him off the couch. She was all set to heave him out of the house.

Hearing the ruckus, I managed to stumble down the stairs, in time to hear her scream at Johnny:

"You no-good tramp! You're making a bum out of my son!"

Just then two Jersey City police cars pulled up and four cops stormed into the house. It was a lucky thing for Malone. They grabbed Johnny and whisked him off. I learned later that somehow he had managed to talk himself back into the good graces of the Mayor.

I had sobered up by the time Kearns arrived, but was in terrible shape. Kearns did all he could to get me into some kind of decent condition, but I had neither the will nor the heart to train. I just moped around the training camp. When the day before the scheduled fight came, I was in such a pitiful state that Kearns had to ask for a postponement. Hoff, the promoter, reluctantly agreed, but insisted the fight had to be held no later than August, while the weather was still favorable for an outdoor show.

Kearns had hoped to have the fight called off permanently. He didn't think I'd be able to eliminate all the booze I'd consumed, and work myself into condition by

August. But Boo-Boo had spent a lot of money promoting the fight and refused to call it off altogether. He needed the fight to get out of the red.

Hoff and Kearns finally reached an agreement. Hoff somehow convinced Kearns that Lomski would give me no trouble. Doc on the other hand promised that I would go easy on Lomski. That was a laugh considering my condition. Even if the fight ended in a draw, nobody would be hurt.

In Philadelphia in those days, as in many other parts of the country, the referee cast the only vote. There were no judges.

Kearns had a heart-to-heart talk with me. He reminded me that I was broke and that unless I made an all-out effort to get in condition, I would be through as a top attraction and a big money-earner. He warned me that if I didn't get into shape, he would break up our partnership. He added I'd probably wind up in the gutter, without him to look after me.

"Mickey, how much longer do you think you can get away with it?" Kearns asked. "You've done everything possible to ruin yourself. You've got to train seriously— starting right now. Unless you put your mind to it, we're through."

Kearns was right. I took the lecture to heart and went to work. It was torture because I had gotten so far out of shape. But inside of three weeks, I had driven myself back into top condition. Even Kearns was amazed.

"You've got a wonderful body, Mickey," he said. "I don't know how you did it. I don't know of any other man who could have done it."

When finally I climbed into the ring with Lomski, I charged out of my corner in the first round determined to flatten him. And I almost did. I won the round easily. Leo was a good fighter, but his style was made to order for me. When I got back to my corner, I noticed that Kearns was nervous.

"Don't worry, Doc," I said, "I'm in great shape. I'm going to take him in this round."

"That's what I'm worried about," Doc muttered.

I didn't get it.

"What are you talking about?" I asked. "This guy's my meat. I'm going to flatten him in this round, I tell you."

"Mickey," Doc said earnestly, "if you do, you and me are in for a lot of trouble. I promised that you would go easy. Owney Madden is sitting right behind Lomski to see that everything comes out as planned. The referee is going to call the fight a draw unless there's a knockout." The only reason Doc consented to the scheme at all was because he figured I'd be in such woeful condition, I might have gotten badly hurt fighting a man of Lomski's caliber.

"Now, I want you to go out there and take it easy. Carry him if you have to. But don't make him look bad."

What could I do? I had to agree to go easy.

I carried Lomski the rest of the way. You should have seen it. If Leo and I had been entered in a waltz contest, we probably would have won first prize. The action was so slow that the fans tried to boo us out of the ring. We should have been thrown out.

I pulled most of my punches. But a few landed, and when one did, I prayed that Lomski wouldn't go down. No matter how hard I tried to take it easy, I still managed to stay far in front of him on points.

The fight over, referee Pop Lewis, announced his decision. The crowd booed so loudly, I couldn't hear him. Finally, Lewis came over and held up my hand. Madden and Duffy, seated behind Lomski's corner, were fuming.

Doc and I didn't wait to see any more. We hurried to the dressing room. I dressed quickly and we sneaked out of the park as fast as we could. We didn't breathe easy until we were out of Philadelphia. Even during the train ride to New York, we kept a lookout for Owney, half expecting him to pop in on us at any moment.

Several days later, Doc received a message from Madden: "I'll be at the Cotton Club at noon today. I'll be waiting for you."

Doc figured he'd better be there, so at twelve o'clock he was in Madden's private office in the Club (which is now the Latin Quarter) on Forty-ninth Street and Broadway.

Kearns began talking as soon as he arrived, but Madden wouldn't listen.

"My guy could have knocked yours out any time he wanted to, but he obeyed orders and took it easy," raged Madden. "You pulled a double-cross on me and you're going to pay for it."

Kearns saw that Madden meant business and resorted to all the cunning he could muster. During the next twenty minutes, Doc put on a one-man talking act the likes of which few had ever heard before. He explained how I had fooled him by getting myself into excellent shape; how he had ordered me to hold up on Lomski when I told him I was going to knock him out; how I agreed to go easy. Even as tough a guy as Owney was convinced.

"I still think my guy can lick yours in an honest fight," growled Madden. "Okay, we'll forget about what happened if you will agree to give me a return fight. And this one will be on the level. This time my guy won't have the handcuffs on him."

His courage up by now, Doc agreed, and he went Madden one better.

"Owney," he said, "if you're so sure your man will beat Mickey, how about a side bet of, say, ten thousand dollars?"

Madden agreed.

My purse for the first Lomski fight was $25,000. My drunken spree had cost me $23,000 in I.O.U.'s. When I got through paying off, there was nothing left. Kearns didn't take a quarter.

The return bout with Lomski took place in Detroit and I got a $25,000 guarantee. We couldn't possibly go back to Philadelphia after stinking up the place. This time Doc made sure I stayed in shape. He never took an eye off me. When there was real dough at stake— particularly a side bet which was made as a matter of personal pride—Doc permitted no fooling. Mickey the playboy became Mickey the slaveboy.

In perfect shape, I had no trouble with Leo. I could have knocked him out any time after the third round but I held him up for the distance out of friendship for Duffy.

Madden took the loss calmly this time. His pride was hurt in that he'd had the bad judgment to back a loser. But the loss of the ten grand didn't make much difference to him. He was still king of the bootleggers and had his paws in all kinds of rackets.

True to his word, Kearns gave Ace Hudkins another crack at my middleweight crown. The match was set for Los Angeles on October 29, 1929. The entire West Coast was excited. This was the biggest fight to hit California in a long time.

Doc opened camp six weeks before the fight. Training quarters were set up in Long Beach, not far from Los Angeles and Hollywood.

Of course, Doc had to publicize the camp opening in typical Kearns fashion. Whenever the good Doctor did anything, he made sure the whole world was aware of it.

First, he lined up sparring partners for me. Then he invited all the sports writers and radio men in the area to witness my first workout. Newsreel cameras, too. Then, milking the thing for more publicity, Doc announced he would treat the Press to a special sparring match. "Gentlemen," he announced, "you're going to be privileged to witness a stirring two-round exhibition between Joe Benjamin, movie actor and former contender for the lightweight championship, and Mickey Walker, the present middleweight champion of the world."

It was strictly a gag, of course, and I went right along with it. Benjamin had been a good fighter in his day. He once boxed the great Benny Leonard. But he had quit the ring in 1925, and the years of living in Hollywood had softened his muscles and dulled his reflexes.

As I waited for the gong, I was thinking I would have to be extra careful. Benjamin was my pal. I didn't want to hurt him.

My intentions were good; but not Benjamin's, the rat. After a minute of sparring, in which I was doing a good job of pulling my punches, Joe suddenly reached back and hit me with a right that came by way of third base. The punch caught me flush on the chin and lifted me off my feet.

I flew backwards, clear out of the ring.

I wasn't badly hurt, but what a picture it must have made. Mickey Walker, the middleweight champion of the world, hit with a sucker punch and sent flying through the ropes by a flabby, washed-up lightweight who hadn't worn boxing gloves in years.

I felt like sinking into the ground. Instead, wild with anger, I jumped up as fast as I could and climbed back into the ring. Now I was going to let the double-crossing son-of-a-bitch have it. What a pal. Hitting me on the sneak. When I was through with him, he wasn't going to be able to stand up for a week.

"C'mon, you sneaking bastard," I gritted through my teeth, "come and get it."

I moved in ready to rip him with both hands, but just as I was about to let go with a punch, he dropped his arms to his sides and stood there, grinning widely.

I was steaming. "Let's fight, damn it!"

He continued to grin, then turned his back on me and walked to a corner of the ring. There he extended his hands to have one of the seconds take off his gloves. I stood simmering, not understanding what was going on. The gloves off, Benjamin turned toward me once more. He was still grinning.

"I don't fight with bums," he cracked and laughed as he climbed out through the ropes. I was left standing in the middle of the ring feeling like a fool.

Kearns, realizing this would make bad publicity, asked the assembled experts to be good guys and forget it. They were decent about it and the incident never got into the papers or on the air.

After that fiasco, I buckled down to serious training for my fight with Hudkins. I couldn't take a chance on not being ready.

The fight was easier than I expected. It took me less than a round to find out that Hudkins was not the same fighter who had extended me so much in Chicago. I felt him out in that opening round and realized that I would be able to take him pretty early in the fight. I nearly knocked him out in the second. He gave me no trouble at all. I had more trouble with Kearns, between rounds.

After the second round, I came back to my corner and said, "Doc, I can take him any time."

Kearns cautioned, "Don't take any unnecessary chances. Don't get careless. He may be playing you for a sucker."

I always listened to my manager during the course of a fight, but this time I just couldn't understand him. Without saying it in so many words, he was telling me to carry Hudkins. Why? I knew damn well that Hudkins wasn't putting on an act.

But I did as I was told. After three more rounds of being cautious I tackled Doc again between the fifth and sixth rounds.

"He's my meat, Doc," I said. "I can put him away right now. Why can't I go out and finish him?"

"I want you to go the distance," he answered. "You need the work."

I knew that was a lie. I tried to figure his angle. Maybe he was looking ahead to the third fight between us. Maybe he had made a deal, as he did with Owney Madden in the Lomski fight. But that couldn't be. I knew he couldn't fix this referee, Jack Kennedy, whom I had first met when I visited with President Coolidge in Washington some years back. Kennedy was then with the government and was one of the most honest men I've ever known. He became a commander in the U. S. Navy when the Second World War broke out.

I let Hudkins go the full ten rounds. I won easily, but I was not satisfied. I was so burned up at Kearns that I wouldn't speak to him in the dressing room. I kept trying to figure out why he hadn't let me finish Hudkins.

After awhile, I put it out of my mind. We went to a night club in Hollywood to celebrate. Some of the people in our party were Kearns's friends and insiders in the fight racket. From their remarks about the fight, I put two-and-two together and it added up to this: Doc was going to play it safe. Realizing that I was growing out of the 160-pound class, and wanting to go after bigger game, Doc had decided he'd hang on to the middleweight crown. So he was negotiating to buy Hudkins' contract.

He figured that if Hudkins beat me, he'd have the champion, anyhow. Should I win he would own the Ace, who looked to be the best in his division when and if I gave up the crown. The big thing, therefore, was to have Hudkins make an impressive showing in the fight.

No wonder he wouldn't let me kayo Hudkins. The more I thought of it, the sorer I got.

"You're a dirty, good-for-nothing double-crosser," I yelled, jumping up from the table. "I'm going to belt you on the chin."

Doc didn't scare.

"Why, you goddamn bum," he shouted back. "I'll lick you any day."

The nervy son-of-a-gun was ready to back up his words, too. He stood up in a fighting pose. It struck me very funny. Instead of popping him, I burst out laughing. There he stood, the bantam, a bag of bones, weighing maybe 125 pounds. I couldn't stop laughing. As usual, Doc had won another round, and I stuck out my hand.

"Let's have a drink on Hudkins, Doc. I hope you make him a champion, too."

CHAPTER TWENTY-ONE

Doc Kearns never got around to making Hudkins a champion and sold his contract after a few months. He found he couldn't give Hudkins the time and attention Ace deserved because he was too busy handling me. That was my busiest year in the ring. I fought often because I needed the money and I also wanted to get my mind off family troubles. Fighting was an outlet.

Before the Hudkins fight, Maude slapped me with a divorce suit early in 1930. Even though she was pregnant again, she was determined to go through with it. She entered the action in Pasadena, California, charging everything but adultery. She charged cruelty, accused me of being bad-tempered, an excessive drinker, of paying attention to other women.

She testified that I started to go wrong when I took off for Paris and ordered her to stay home and mind the house while I was gallivanting with other women. She claimed I was unfit to have custody of our children. She also charged I received love notes from women. She quoted some of these notes:

Mickey, you're a peach. You're the finest person I ever knew. With packs of love. Dotty.

I was so lonesome the other night that I went out with another man. There is never a day that I don't think of you, Mickey. With lots of love and kisses. Mae.

I denied the charges. But I finally gave in and let Maude have her divorce. It became final a year later.

The financial arrangements were settled out of court. She kept the real estate and securities which were worth $234,000, and also the bonds valued at $216,000. I'm glad now that she took them because they provided the children with good educations. I probably would have squandered the dough away.

The divorce final, I turned all my attention to the ring. Easily the most memorable of the sixteen fights I had that year was with Paul Swiderski on May 16th, on the eve of Derby Day in Louisville. It was the year Gallant Fox, ridden by my friend, Earle Sande, won the Kentucky Derby and went on to capture racing's Triple Crown with victories in the Preakness and Belmont.

Fight promoters used to try to make a quick payday from the Derby crowd by staging a boxing show on the eve of the traditional race. Eventually they discovered people were too busy with mint juleps and track touts to bother about prize fights. However, they kept going for several years before they tossed in the sponge. It was only in the late fifties that Derby-eve fights were revived.

The first time we met, Kearns had promised that some day he'd make me the heavyweight champion of the world. I had my heart set on it and kept reminding Doc of his promise. It wasn't until 1930 that he started taking me seriously and really went after the heavyweight title.

Max Schmeling was champion. He won the title on a foul in the elimination bout with Jack Sharkey. Kearns didn't waste any time with tune-ups. To get me a shot at the title as quickly as possible, Doc signed for a fight with Johnny Risko, a leading heavyweight contender. Why Louisville? I believe the only reason was that Kearns, who loved the race track, wanted to see the Kentucky Derby. He had never seen one.

A couple of days before the fight, Risko got sick and Jack Hurley, the promoter, had to find a substitute. The only available heavyweight he could find was Swiderski, who happened to be in town with his manager, Harry Lenny. They had come for the Derby.

Hurley didn't learn until the morning of the scheduled fight that Swiderski was an ex-sparring partner of mine. He got sore and wanted to call off the fight. Kearns argued with him until three o'clock in the afternoon. Doc didn't want the fight canceled because it meant we would lose a $25,000 guarantee. Finally, seeing he was getting nowhere with Hurley, he threw up his hands and said to me:

"Okay, Mick. No fight tonight. Go out and have a good time."

They were still bargaining when I walked out of Hurley's suite. Downstairs in the lobby, I picked up a few New York newspapermen friends and went pub-crawling. Among them were Joe Williams of the *New York World Telegram*, Hype Igoe of the *Journal* and Jim Jennings of the *Mirror*. I had been behaving for some time and was disgusted that all the clean living had been for nothing, now that the fight was called off. So I really tied one on.

Meanwhile, back at the hotel, Kearns and the promoter reached a compromise. Doc agreed to take a $2,500 cut in the purse and Hurley okayed Swiderski. The settlement was made late in the afternoon but Kearns and Hayes couldn't catch up to me until eight o'clock. By then I was flying so high I was ready to take on ten Swiderskis. And believe me, when I climbed into the ring about an hour later, I thought I saw that many Swiderskis.

Before bringing me to the park, Kearns and Hayes had half-carried me to the hotel and thrown me under a shower in a desperate attempt to sober me up. They worked on me with ice packs, but it did little good. When they got me to the Louisville Stadium at nine o'clock, I was dried out all right, like a stale prune, but I was still a long way from being sober.

Swiderski was a brute of a man. He stood six feet, three inches and he weighed 220 pounds. He knew all my tricks, having picked up most of them from sparring with me. Any fear of the fight being fixed was dispelled by the first punch. It was a right hand thrown by Swiderski. I never even saw it. It caught me flush on the chin and almost knocked me senseless.

I have only a faint recollection of the fight, but I read the next day that I was knocked down eight times in the first round and fourteen in the first three. I think that might be an exaggeration. I believe I was knocked down only ten in all, five times in the first round. Anyhow, I never felt a punch. I can't say the same for Swiderski. He had the misfortune to be sober. I knocked him down sixteen times, all coming after the third round. If the newsboys were correct, there were thirty knockdowns in the ten-round fight. That must be some kind of a record.

My brain was in a whirl from the first punch. Only instinct got me up after each knockdown. I was on one knee, after a knockdown in the opening round and the referee had reached the count of nine when the bell rang. There were still thirty seconds remaining in the round but Kearns picked up the water bottle, reached out and slammed it against the timekeeper's gong. I didn't know of this, of course, until Kearns told me about it later.

My mind was fuzzy, but I dimly remember Doc leaping

into the ring and dousing my head with a pail of ice water. Swiderski, mad at seeing his big chance to establish himself as a leading contender for the heavyweight title slip away because of a ruse, lost all his senses. He dashed across the ring and hit me a terrific punch on the nose as I was trying to scramble to my feet.

That should have disqualified him because he hit me while I was still on one knee, and after the bell. The ring had become a madhouse by then, and no one knew right from wrong. Truthfully, no one cared.

Teddy Hayes, my trainer, who had jumped into the ring after Kearns to help drag me back to my corner, whirled around and slugged Swiderski. By this time, Harry Lenny, Swiderski's manager, also was in the ring and he threw a punch at Hayes. Within seconds, the ring was filled with police and handlers. Everybody was pushing and shouting.

I was on my feet by then, but I didn't know where I was. Somehow, I thought I was in a street fight. I made up my mind to sock the first guy that got in my way. Seeing all those faces, brass buttons and clubs, I wound up a roundhouse swing right in the middle of them. Who did I pop? Doc Kearns, of course. He was trying to revive me with cold water and smelling salts. He had reached me, just as I let go. The punch landed on his chin. When the ring finally was cleared the only person on the canvas was Kearns. They told me later that it was I who dragged him to my corner, instead of the other way around.

The extra time didn't help me much in the next two rounds. No sooner was the fight resumed when Swiderski floored me again. I was struggling to get on my feet when the ring lights suddenly went out. Somebody had thrown a switch. Precious time was used up until they got the lights to work again. By then I had begun to be myself.

I took charge from the fourth round on and won the decision. The only round I remember clearly was the last one. I had Swiderski down a couple of times and I was eager to finish him in the next round. Strangely, I thought it was only the second round. Doc had a tough time convincing me the fight was over.

I was always known as a murderous body puncher and in that tenth round I remember Swiderski pleading with me, "Please, Mickey, lay off my stomach. I can't breathe."

I took more punches in that fight than in any of the more than two hundred I was in, but I didn't have a mark on me. Kearns, hit only once—by me—had a bump on his jaw as big as a duck's egg.

As usual after a fight, we had a party. Doc felt pretty badly about that bump on the jaw and I didn't smooth his feelings any by pointing out that I was unmarked. That got him hopping mad and pretty soon we were calling each other all kinds of names. During the height of the argument, Swiderski walked into our suite.

He accused Doc of paying off the electricians to put out the lights. That only made Doc madder, and he was ready to take on Swiderski himself. I had a tough time keeping them apart. Such a thing as throwing a switch in a stadium before thousands of people sounds incredible but in those days you could get away with a lot more than you can now. And there was nothing Kearns didn't try.

The next day was Derby Day. Doc and I were guests of Colonel Matt Winn, general manager of Churchill Downs. He invited us to sit in his box with several newspapermen. Damon Runyon, William Randolph Hearst's top sports columnist, was there. So were Hype Igoe, sports writer for the *Journal,* and Joe Williams, the columnist who now is sports editor of the Scripps-Howard newspaper chain.

We didn't go to Winn's box immediately, deciding first to go to the Clubhouse bar for a drink. We pooled a good-sized chunk of dough and gave it to an attendant to place a bet on Gallant Fox with Earle Sande riding. Gradually most of the sports writers drifted out, but we stayed on. One drink led to another and pretty soon we forgot about the Derby. After a while, somebody suddenly remembered the race and cried out, "Hey, you guys, it's about time for the Derby. Let's go out and watch it."

We made our way to the box, with difficulty. We weren't too steady on our feet. Although my mind was far from clear, I became aware that the park was half empty and wondered about it.

This Kentucky Derby can't be such an all-fired, red-hot event like they all say it is if they can't draw more people than this, I thought to myself. Why, I've had much bigger crowds come to see me fight.

The race got under way just as we found our seats. I pulled myself up and began cheering for Gallant Fox. "Come on, Gallant Fox! Come on, Sande," I screamed hoarsely, almost falling into Doc's lap as I tried to jump up. I knew Gallant Fox was carrying blue and gold silks and when a horse with those colors came racing across the finish line in front of the others, everyone in our crowd cheered madly.

"Boy, can I pick 'em, can I pick 'em," I kept repeating happily, as I half-ran, half-reeled to the payoff window. It was there at the window that I learned for the first time that the Derby had been run thirty minutes before.

Gallant Fox had won the big race all right, but the one we had been watching and yelling our heads off about wasn't the Derby at all; it was the next race. Gallant Fox was by then back in his barn.

Doc decided we better head back for New York that night because I had a fight against Charley Belanger in Detroit a week later. By the time we arrived at the station in Louisville, we had drunk up a pretty good part of our winnings. While waiting for the train, Doc took off his patent-leather shoes and placed them on the seat next to him.

"My feet are killing me," he complained, closing his eyes for a quick cat nap.

Some minutes later, a newly married couple came running down the platform with a horde of friends close behind, yelling, laughing, and flinging rice after them. By the sound of their voices, I could tell it was an Irish wedding.

I've always loved Irish weddings. One of the customs at Irish weddings is to throw shoes at the bride and groom. As this couple dashed by, I reached down for Doc's shoes and flung them after the fleeing pair. My aim was pretty good. One of Doc's brogans hit the groom squarely in the back. He stopped, looked around and saw the shoes lying at his feet. Before I could make a move, he grabbed up the shoes and dashed off after his bride.

Doc arrived in New York in his stocking feet, and I don't believe he ever knew the difference.

I fought Swiderski again that year, in Newark, four months after our first battle. After the exciting brawl in Louisville, promoters were competing with each other to stage the return go. Doc made them bid against each other and we got $25,000 for the fight.

I was in good shape because I was fighting about every three weeks. I just didn't have a chance to get out of condition. Even drinking made no difference.

I had Swiderski down in the first round and not even his mother would have bet on him to go the distance.

Back in my corner, Kearns leaned close and whispered something in my ear. I couldn't believe I heard him right. I asked him to say it again.

"Don't knock him out," Doc whispered again. "You've got to carry him."

"Nuts to you," I growled. "I'm going to knock this palooka right in your conniving lap."

This was a grudge fight as far as I was concerned. Swiderski had made me look bad in our first fight, and I was going to pay him for that.

"Is this another of your tricks, Doc?" I asked. "Don't tell me you're going to manage him too? Is this another Ace Hudkins job?"

"No, Mickey, I'm on the level," Kearns insisted. "If you don't think so, just look behind us. There's a big gorilla sitting there and look at what he's carrying."

I turned around and looked past Doc. Sure enough. There was this fat slob sitting in the first row behind the press section. He kept his right hand inside his coat which was partly open and even from where I sat I could make out the big black rod peeking out. It was pointed in my direction. When I finally was able to turn my eyes away, I nodded to Doc.

"Don't worry," I said. "Swiderski's going the distance."

He did, but it must have seemed a pretty dull fight to those who had seen our first one.

I was taking my shower in the dressing room after winning the easy decision when Harry Lenny, his manager, poked his head in.

"Nice goin', Champ," he said with a big grin. "I won a bundle that you don't knock out my boy."

So that's the way it was. I could win, all right, but I wasn't supposed to knock him out.

One of the toughest and gamest fighters I ever fought was heavyweight Johnny Risko. He was never a champion and I doubt if he was even close, but few of the top contenders wanted to be matched with him because of his reputation as a "spoiler." If he didn't beat you, at least he had the satisfaction of making you look bad.

I fought Risko three times. I licked him in our first two meetings, but he got the referee's decision in our last one. It was a typical home-town decision and it led to one of the few real battles I had with Kearns.

It wasn't until I licked Risko the first time, on November 7, 1930, in Detroit, that they began taking me seriously as a heavyweight contender. That was the fourteenth of my sixteen fights that year, all against the best heavyweights Doc could get me. I won all sixteen, failing to knock out only five of my opponents. Kearns was maneuvering me closer to the heavy crown.

I met Risko two months later, in Miami, Florida. It was a good money fight. We got thirty thousand dollars for it. Kearns decided to go swanky and had me do my training at the Hollywood Country Club, a few miles north of Miami.

The principal stockholder in the club was Al Capone. He was also the behind-the-scenes owner of one of the most exclusive hotels in Hollywood, Florida, and liked to spend several weeks a year there. He always had bodyguards. I don't remember ever seeing him alone.

Capone enjoyed seeing me work out. We had a ring set up out in the open and Al and his torpedoes occupied the ringside rows. Vacationers who used to attend my work-outs must have thought it odd to see these men, always wearing coats, buttoned from top to bottom, no matter how hot the weather. And some days it was 95 degrees. I've often wondered how those good people would have felt had they known what these goons were carrying under their coats. Most of those people had never seen a shoulder holster, except in a movie.

A few days before the fight, Kearns decided to give me a day off. Capone was disappointed. He was always looking for action. Then he got a brilliant idea. Gathering his gunmen together, he formed a team and challenged me and my camp to a baseball game. I wasn't turning down challenges, so I got up a team among my sparring partners and trainers.

Doc Kearns was the umpire.

A crowd came out to watch the game. One of the rules I laid down was no guns; they all had to be checked before their owners came to bat. Capone's men agreed reluctantly. Al took one of the bat bags and made them stash their guns inside. That's the first and only time, I bet, that a baseball bat bag was used as a gun bag.

The game was supposed to go the regulation nine innings, but it ended much sooner. It started out as a gag, but before one inning, everybody was taking it seriously. Those guys really played for blood.

I played shortstop for the Walker All-Stars; Al was the second baseman for the Capone All-Hoods. Scarface, a nickname he hated, wasn't much of an athlete but he played as if his life depended on it. He argued with Doc over practically every decision and, naturally, his hoods took up the argument even when they had no idea what it was all about.

Their constant quibbling over the umpire's calls got under the skin of some of my sparring partners. A couple of times, one of my guys got set to land a haymaker on one of Capone's noble athletes when suddenly he remembered the bat bag and went back to his position, happy to be in one piece.

Doc was having a hell of a time umpiring. Every time he made a decision against the Capone team, he found himself surrounded by mobsters. Finally, fearful that trouble might break out, Kearns called the game after six innings.

"Game called on account of darkness," announced Kearns, although the sun was shining brighter than ever. "I declare the game a tie."

Doc was a terrible mathematician. According to the scorekeeper, my team was ahead 28-6.

Anyway, I won that second Risko fight easily, and Doc agreed to let my third fight with him take place in Cleveland, Johnny's home town. Doc took an awful chance, putting me on in a city which was then known for home-town decisions. Beating Risko in Cleveland was a virtual impossibility.

We fought twelve rounds and at the end, the referee raised Risko's hand. I should have known this would happen, but I couldn't help being surprised. I honestly thought I had won that fight easier than the first two with Risko.

Later that night, Kearns and I engaged in our customary argument during a drinking bout. I accused him of not protecting me in the Risko fight.

"You're a lousy manager to let McGinty steal the decision," I shouted.

"And you're a lousy fighter to let Risko stay twelve rounds," Doc shot back.

I was furious. I wanted to pop him one on that yackety-yack chin of his, but how would it look for a fighter—a champion at that—to hit his manager in public? Instead, I just got up and left him sitting there by himself. I was so mad I didn't even bother to go back to the hotel to get my luggage and check out. I hailed a cab and headed straight for the airport.

I had no clothes except those on my back. But I did have money in my wallet and a bottle of Scotch.

It was a foggy night and when I arrived at the airport I was told that all planes had been grounded. That only made me feel worse. For no reason at all, I began to tell off the clerk behind the ticket counter. The poor fellow had nothing to do with my being grounded, but I wanted to get out of Cleveland so badly that I just took it out on the nearest target.

A fellow standing nearby heard me griping, and came closer.

"Aren't you Mickey Walker?" he asked.

"Yes, and what of it?" I growled, ready to give him a piece of my mind.

"I'll fly you where you want to go," he said. "I've got my own plane."

I didn't believe him. I thought it was a joke. I looked around, half expecting to see Doc Kearns hiding behind a pillar.

"I'm serious," the man said. "I got her at a hangar nearby. Where do you want to go?"

I told him New Jersey and he said it would cost me two hundred and fifty dollars. I said okay.

He had a plane all right. It was a two-seater. I sat next to him. He strapped a parachute on me, but as soon as I got in I knew I shouldn't have. I wanted to jump out, but didn't want him to think I was scared. I was! Lucky thing I had that bottle.

The minute we took off, I had a healthy swig and handed the bottle to the pilot. He turned out to be a good drinking partner. We passed the bottle back and forth until it was empty.

The flight took five hours. It should have taken three. The plane was tossing like a kite. What a combination. A 60-mile wind and a 90-proof pilot. We were flying, in more ways than one. I looked out of the window and all I saw were trees. We were flying so low that it seemed I could reach out and touch the branches.

I remembered the parachute. Suddenly I got the urge to try it out to see if it really worked. I told the pilot to try and keep the plane steady because I was going to jump out. That sobered him up in a hurry. He grabbed me with one hand and held me tight in my seat. With the other, he guided the plane. What a time he had, trying to keep me and the plane on an even keel at the same time.

We finally arrived at Casey Airport in Shrewsbury. It was eight in the morning. Amazingly, my buddy made a good landing. But no sooner did we hit the ground than the motor stopped. The plane was fresh out of gas and we couldn't have flown another tenth of a mile.

After I paid him off, I tried to get the pilot to come home with me, but he shook his head.

"I can't," he said. "I've got to get back to Cleveland. I'm getting married tonight."

CHAPTER TWENTY-TWO

To this day, I still don't know whether my pilot friend arrived in time for his wedding. As a matter of fact, I don't even know whether he arrived at all. I've never heard from him since.

I didn't wonder about him very long. Doc Kearns arrived the next day with my luggage and we resumed our relationship as if nothing had happened between us. That's the way we both are . . . what happened yesterday is past; it's today that counts.

I wasn't back in Rumson long when I became aware of a coolness on the part of my neighbors. Town folk who used to consider it a privilege to stop me and say hello, now avoided me. I didn't have to be a genius to figure out why; it was the divorce.

Before the divorce, there wasn't a day when I was home that at least two or three kids wouldn't drop over. The younger ones would come to ride the pony I had bought for Mickey, Jr., and the older fellows would come just to be around me. I was their idol. We still had the Walker A.C. and each spring I would buy new uniforms for them. On days when there were no games, I'd pile the gang into my car and take them fishing or swimming.

After the divorce, the kids stopped coming. Even the little ones who used to come just to ride Mickey's pony. I couldn't understand it. One day I spotted one of the youngsters in the street, a boy named Red Salmon. At first, Red didn't want to tell me why the kids didn't come any more. He finally broke down and told me that the mothers had forbidden them to visit me. They didn't want their kids to have anything to do with a divorced man. The mothers went even further. They ordered the boys to turn in their uniforms and disband the Walker A.C. ball team.

I was terribly hurt but I couldn't see why the kids should be the losers.

"Look, fellows, you don't have to disband," I told them. "Just bring the suits into Eisner's and have them rip off Walker A.C. and replace the letters with Rumson A.C."

That's what they did.

Something took place a month later that made me leave Rumson. I wasn't much of a church-goer, but I've always respected the Church for the good it does. When the local Catholic church was built around 1928, I offered to donate a chalice, but I was told someone else already had supplied one so I gave a sanctuary lamp instead. Donating that lamp was one of the greatest satisfactions I had ever had. After Maude divorced me, they took down the lamp.

That affected me as nothing else could have. I had given the lamp in good faith and it had been accepted in the same way. Forgetting its intrinsic value—it may have cost two or three grand—what sense was there in discarding a fine religious object because the donor had gone away from the Church?

To me, that was a narrow-minded act, the very opposite of the Christian charity which the Church teaches. Whatever punishment I must eventually sustain for my sins would be assessed by the Almighty and so it seemed senseless to deprive the parish of a holy adornment because I had fallen by the wayside. Would they have torn down the church if my money had helped build it?

Don't get me wrong. I wasn't right, in my way of living, from the point of view of religion or society. I played loose with morals and was guilty of breaking the laws of the Church.

I never claimed I was right and the Church wrong, in regard to morals. I respected my religion even though I didn't live up to it. I gave the lamp because I felt some desire to help out, materially, even though I was not a good Catholic. I wasn't trying to persuade God or the pastor that I could redeem my soul with a worldly gift. I know the Catholic religion too well for that. I was merely trying to help the parish with a gift, not to gain a favor.

A man may yield to the attractions of the earth and lose his formal religion, but no true Catholic ever rejects the Faith.

Maybe I was being too egotistical, but I felt that this act was uncalled for. So I moved out of Rumson and bought a home in Shrewsbury, a few miles southwest.

I plunked down $120,000 in cold cash for the house. I bought it from Tommy Secrest, then chief of the circulation department of the Hearst syndicate. It was during the depression period and Secrest, like many other people, found himself in a tough spot for cash. Oddly enough, the depression affected me very little. Within that first year after Maude left me, I was back in the chips again. I was fighting more than ever before and was getting big purses.

The house and the property surrounding it—about fifty acres—were worth a quarter of a million dollars. The house was colonial style, large and stately, with a dozen rooms, including six bedrooms and three baths. There were horses, cows, chickens and all sorts of farm equipment.

215

The help, a cook, a maid and a farm hand, agreed to stay on and I decided to become a gentleman-farmer!

The mansion—that's what it was, all right—was well over one hundred years old and originally belonged to the son of William Livingston, the first governor of New Jersey. It was built with pegs, walls a foot thick and hand-cut oak ceiling beams. The house had a wine cellar with a dungeon underneath it which was reached by secret stairways. If you ever got lost down there you'd rot before anyone found you. I had the wine cellar converted into a modern taproom which I used for parties when friends came down for weekends.

While the house was being done over, I stayed in Sea-bright, a resort town on a strip of land between the Shrewsbury River and the Atlantic Ocean. I always have been a bug on swimming as a body builder and for my money there isn't a finer place to swim in the whole United States than the Jersey shore. I am a strong swimmer even today.

I also spent a good deal of time in Highlands, adjoining Seabright. Highlands was a colorful place in those days. It was a favorite playground for athletes, show people and New York bootleggers. The most popular hotel then was Connors, owned by Herman Black. He named the hotel after his wife, Marie, whose maiden name was Connors.

It was at the Connors Hotel that I met Clara Hellmers. She lived in Jersey City but was spending her vacation at this resort town, with a girl friend named Dotty Dabb.

I fell hard for Clara. She had a sweet face and a fine figure. She was a blonde and I've always been partial to blondes. She was ten years younger than I was. I saw her practically every minute. We'd go swimming together during the afternoon and dancing in the evening. I bowled her over. She was nineteen and was overwhelmed by my fame and attention.

Three months after Maude divorced me, I married Clara at St. James Church in Shrewsbury. The Reverend Edgar Waite tied the knot. Kearns was my best man and Dotty Dabb, Clara's closest friend, was her maid of honor.

We held the reception at the big house and it was a gay, boisterous affair. In addition to Clara's friends and my own from Elizabeth and other Jersey towns, there was a big crowd from New York, including Bill Duffy, Morton Downey, Bobby Clark, Mike Jacobs, Dan Healy, Fanny Brice, Helen Kane, Billy DeBeck, Larry Fay, Senator Bill Lyons and Texas Guinan. The place was jammed, too, with newspapermen and boxers, fight managers, promoters, and just plain hustlers.

The party lasted until the wee hours of the morning. Some of my guests were in no condition to go home and they stayed over. I was determined not to get pie-eyed . . . not this night.

My new mother-in-law was staying with us, too, but I finally managed to get her to go to bed. At three o'clock, I had everybody in bed with one exception . . . Doc Kearns. Trying to outlast him was like telling a cannibal to lay off you on account of it was Friday.

"Be a pal, Doc," I pleaded, "go to sleep. Clara is waiting for me."

"Shay, Mick," he asked. "I thought you were a champ. Are you a champ or are you a champ? Tell me, who'sh the boss around here? She or you?"

"That's silly, Doc," I said impatiently. "You ought to know who's the boss in my house. It's me."

"Says you," Doc jeered.

He looked at me in that funny way of his and right away I knew I was in for trouble.

"If you're really the boss," he needled, "how about scramming out of here and really having ourselves a good time?"

"Okay," I blurted out before I could check my big mouth.

We sneaked out and headed for the Pleasant Inn, in Red Bank. That was only the beginning. For two days and nights, Kearns and I spent my honeymoon in one joint after another. We finally ended up in New York. Neither Doc nor I slept a wink for forty-eight hours. Kearns weighed all of 130 pounds in those days but he was made of iron. It was nothing for him to stay up four or five days at a time.

It was early in the morning when we returned to Shrewsbury—just in time to find my new bride and her ma packing their clothes. I had to do some tall talking to get them to unpack. I made Kearns the villain, laying the entire blame on him. He had gotten me so drunk, I claimed, that I didn't know what I was doing. It wasn't very difficult convincing Clara, but my mother-in-law was another proposition. Even when she finally agreed to unpack, she made it plain that she didn't believe my story.

"Young man," she said, pointing an accusing finger at me, "what you did is unpardonable. You are lucky indeed it is my daughter you married, and not me."

I sure am, I thought to myself.

Clara and I had been married only about a week when I received some disturbing news. A reporter from a Newark paper called me to ask if I had any comment to make regarding a story in the newspapers that Chancellor

Edward R. Walker, no relation, was threatening to prosecute me for bigamy.

It seemed that my divorce from Maude would not be final until the middle of May and I could not marry again until the final decree had been granted. In other words, Clara and I weren't legally man and wife. That was the first I heard of it. To me, a divorce was a divorce. Since I was free and in love, I could see no reason why I shouldn't marry again.

While trying to figure out how to get out of this latest mess, I woke up one day to learn the situation had become even worse. Kearns, taking charge as was his custom, gave out a story that my marriage to Clara had been annulled. It wasn't, of course, and both Clara and I quickly denied it the next day. But nobody would believe us. To the world, at least, we were living in sin.

Fortunately Judge Walker never went through with the prosecution, probably because of the time element. Six weeks later, May 6th, the final divorce decree came through.

I was content to let things go on as they were, but friends kept telling Clara that she still wasn't legally married, and she began to believe it. She kept after me for us to remarry. I put her off until I learned she was pregnant, then to relieve her mind and eliminate any doubt, Clara and I were married a second time on December 5, 1931. This time there was no doubt it was legal.

Clara and I enjoyed living in Shrewsbury, but the house was just too big so Mom and my brother, Joe, came to live with us. Mom still kept her home in Elizabeth, though.

I decided the house needed a new look, so I hired Uncle Joe Higgins, my first trainer, who had since become a painting contractor, to paint the house, inside and out. He and one of his workmen, a fellow named Buck Leonard, started painting in May, and they were still painting in September. I'd go to Detroit for a fight, or to St. Paul, or Baltimore, or Buffalo, and when I'd come back, they'd still be painting.

I remember one night after a party, when everybody had left, even Kearns. Uncle Joe and his helper—who still hadn't finished their painting job—were too drunk to go home. I was loaded too.

Uncle Joe and Buck had painted the taproom the day before, but I didn't like the job they'd done. I told Uncle Joe and he was offended.

"Why don't you do it yourself if you're not satisfied with the way we did it?" he growled.

"Okay," I yelled back, "I'll show you how it should be done."

I told my brother Joe to bring me some paint and a brush that we kept in the garage. Joe knew that in my condition I wasn't going to stand for any arguments, so he got the pail and brush.

I grabbed the brush, dipped it into the pail and began to paint. Uncle Joe, Buck and my brother sat down and watched. It took me three hours to do the job. Then I stood back to admire my work.

"See the difference now?" I said, turning to Uncle Joe. "That's the way I want it."

Uncle Joe got up for a closer inspection. He nodded admiringly.

"It does look a lot better, Mickey," he said. "I didn't know you were such a good painter. I learned something watching you. I promise you I'll paint the other rooms the same way. You won't have any more complaints."

The next day, when I was fully sober, my brother spoke up.

"Mickey, I've got something to tell you, but first I want you to promise me you won't get sore."

"Okay," I said.

"Remember the beautiful paint job you did last night? Well, there was no paint in that pail. I filled it with water. All you were doing was wetting the walls."

The whole thing struck me as so funny, that instead of getting angry, I just laughed.

CHAPTER TWENTY-THREE

Some of the whackiest things happened when I was drunk. Like the time the electric stove first came on the market in 1931. Mom had her heart set on owning one. On a weekend when she was away, I bought one for her as a surprise. It was real fancy, with a dashboard of dials and buttons.

As usual, Kearns and I got loaded during a weekend party. The talk turned to target shooting. Typically, Doc declared he was the best shot and of course I insisted I was better. The argument continued long after everybody had left. It was five in the morning and we were both blind.

I suddenly remembered that I had a 30-30 Winchester hunting rifle in the basement. We selected our target . . . the knob on the kettle on top of the new stove.

Doc and I took turns with the Winchester. After several cockeyed shots, we quit. Neither of us hit the kettle, let alone the knob. However, the brand-new stove was full of holes and the wall behind it looked as though it had chicken pox.

Mom came home the next day. When she saw the damage, she was furious. Naturally, she blamed Kearns. Her son, Edward, couldn't do anything wrong in her eyes. Doc knew beforehand he would be blamed and beat it out the back way. He didn't show up again for days—till the new stove he ordered was delivered and installed.

Not all the parties were in my house. One time Doc and I were invited by Herb Wynn, my rich polo-playing friend, to a party at his home in Little Silver. Among Wynn's other guests were polo stars Cecil Smith and Rube Williams. I had just purchased some polo ponies and that gave me an excuse to talk about the sport with these pros.

Kearns, of course, had to butt into the conversation. He knew even less about polo than target shooting, but that didn't stop him. First he claimed that Eastern polo ponies were just farm horses compared to those in the West. Then he bragged that he was a better horseman than anyone in the house, including Smith and Williams. The only horses Kearns knew anything about were running at Belmont. I told him so.

"I can outride you any day," I challenged.

We argued who was the better rider all through the party and the argument continued during the trip to Shrewsbury.

When we got back to the farm in the wee hours, we made straight for the barn where I kept a couple of nice, gentle plow horses that nobody, to my knowledge, had ever ridden before.

"Now we'll see who's the better rider," I shouted. "We'll race ten laps around the corral."

"It's a deal," barked Doc.

He climbed on one of the horses and I got on the other. If I wasn't sure whether these horses had even been ridden before, I learned soon enough. The moment I landed on the back of my horse he let out a whinny that rattled the roof. I whacked him on the rump and he reared high into the air, then leaped forward. As I went up, my head hit a beam and I fell to the ground, landing in a heap in the stable-floor muck.

Kearns had better luck. He managed, somehow, to get his nag out of the barn. He galloped around the corral yelling like a Comanche. John, the caretaker, hearing the noise, jumped into a pair of pants and came dashing out of the house in his nightshirt.

He came out just in time to see Doc's horse suddenly jam to a complete stop, causing Doc to sail clear over his head, into a hogshead of water. Doc landed head first and he might have drowned if John hadn't rushed over and pulled him out of the trough, feet first.

I didn't know any of this, of course, since at the time, I was out cold on the barn floor. After drying Doc out, John carried me to the corral and dunked my head into the trough. After we were revived, Doc and I staggered, with John's help, into the house for a nightcap before hitting the hay.

Kearns ribbed me for a week about having been thrown by a plow horse. He ignored altogether the fact that his horse had flung him into the drink. When Herb Wynn found out about it, he let me have it, too. That bothered me even more than Doc's ribbing and I became determined to prove my horsemanship.

223

I owned a big, vicious white horse, which nobody dared ride. I got so steamed up over the kidding that I bet Wynn I could ride that white horse from my house to his, a distance of about five miles. He took me up on it.

I got on the brute's back one afternoon and steered him along Sycamore Avenue toward Little Silver. He made no protest. We did fine except when cars passed us. Each time one did, he reared and raced back toward the house. I had a devil of a time getting him turned around again. It must have happened a dozen times.

We'd go along about a mile or so, a car would pass and whoa, Whitey would rear up on his hind legs, neighing loudly, and head for home. Sometimes, he'd be almost back to the house before I'd get him turned in the right direction again.

It took me half a day to get to Wynn's place. When I arrived, I was battered and bruised. I could hardly get out of the saddle but finally did and tied the horse to a Cadillac parked next to Wynn's house.

I had been at Herb's about an hour when we heard banging on the front door. It was Wynn's neighbor. The fellow was hopping mad. He could hardly speak. He just stood there in the doorway pointing and sputtering.

The guy's Cadillac was almost a total wreck. Whitey had kicked the hell out of it.

While I was living it up, Doc Kearns hadn't forgotten that we wanted a shot at the world's heavyweight title. The best heavyweight around at the time was Jack Sharkey, who then held the heavyweight title in New York State. Doc was determined to close a match between me and Jack. The biggest obstacle, even bigger than Sharkey's manager, was the New York Athletic Commission.

"It's preposterous," scoffed Jim Farley, the chairman. "Why, Sharkey is one of the most dangerous men in the ring. I'm not underestimating your fighter, but Sharkey is at least six inches taller than Walker, he has a greater reach and he must outweigh him by thirty pounds. I couldn't possibly sanction such a match."

Doc wasn't one to give up easily. He kept badgering the Commission and through the newspapers, challenged Sharkey every day. Sharkey's manager, Johnny Buckley, ignored the challenges, and the Commission continued to lend a deaf ear.

Then we got a break. The Hearst newspaper syndicate annually stages a sports event with proceeds going to the Free Milk Fund for Babies. They decided a Sharkey-Walker fight was just the attraction they needed and undertook to sponsor such a fight through one of their papers, the *New York Journal.*

The pressure applied by the newspaper was too much for the Commission, and finally Farley announced his group would sanction a Sharkey-Walker match provided I would relinquish my middleweight title. I hadn't defended my title since 1929, when I whipped Ace Hudkins for the second time and I was still under suspension in New York for not defending my crown within the six-month time limit.

Buckley wasn't hard to convince. Especially when Kearns agreed to let Sharkey have 30 percent of the gate to my 20 percent. With the fight figuring to draw around a quarter of a million dollars, that meant Sharkey's share would be at least $75,000. Not bad when you considered the fight appeared to be an easy one for Sharkey. So Buckley thought.

I was elated. I knew deep down in my heart that I

225

could lick Sharkey. Not that I didn't think Jack was a good man. Despite his temperament, which was more like that of an opera star than a boxer, he was a helluva good fighter. But I felt he was made to order for me. Jack was a strong puncher and he liked to fight at long range. I knew if I could get inside his guard, I'd be able to wear him down with a body attack. And I had no doubt that I'd be able to get to him.

The newspapers—all except the *Journal*—called it a bad match. They said it was bad at the box office because it seemed to be one-sided and unattractive; bad for Sharkey, who had nothing to gain even in victory; and bad for me because a licking by Sharkey would end my hopes of ever winning the heavyweight title.

We fooled 'em, though. Almost from the beginning, the fight caught on. The newspaper boys hadn't counted on two things: one, the fight fan is always curious to see whether a good little man can beat a good big man; and two, people knew they would get a good fight from Mickey Walker, win, lose or draw. The advance sale assured a financial success weeks before the fight.

This was to be my first big-money shot in New York in five years and Doc was going to make certain I'd be ready for it. He decided a tune-up fight would be just the thing, so he matched me with a fellow called Bearcat Wright— the biggest man in the ring outside of Primo Carnera.

The fight was set for Omaha, Nebraska, and on the way, the train stopped in Chicago, where we were joined by a bunch of boxing writers. I knew most of them and invited them all for a drink. By the time we arrived in Omaha it was eight o'clock in the morning and I still hadn't gone to bed. Full of booze, without sleep, and the fight only fourteen hours away, I was hustled to the hotel and put into bed by Teddy Hayes. I still had a hangover when my trainer woke me at three o'clock for the weigh-in.

I was still sick when I climbed into the ring that evening —and I got sicker when I saw the guy I was going to fight. They said the Bearcat weighed 260 pounds and was six feet, four inches in height, but to me he looked as big as the Chrysler Building and just as heavy.

"Move around and keep out of his reach," were Kearns's last-minute instructions as he shoved in my mouthpiece. "Don't slug with him, just box him."

I carried out Doc's orders in the first round. But I underestimated Wright's reach. From about six feet away —I thought—he suddenly reached out and slugged me with a right. The blow landed on top of my head and I took a perfect nose dive. Honest, the first part of me to hit the canvas was my nose. I didn't know what to grab first, my head or my nose. I was sure both were broken. Lucky thing he didn't hit me on the chin. I'd never have gotten up. At that, I didn't struggle to my feet until the referee had counted nine. Then the bell came to my rescue.

I was dizzy for seven rounds from that sock, but managed to stay out of the Bearcat's reach after that. Luckily, he was slow and clumsy. I also managed to sneak in a number of good body punches which slowed him up even more. From the third round on, I was actually fighting myself back into shape. By the eighth, I knew he was mine. Near the end of the round, I leaped up and reached his chin with a left hook that had the whole Walker family behind it. The Bearcat went down like a stricken rhinoceros. The ring quivered when his shoulders hit the canvas and for a minute I thought it was going to collapse. Wright managed to beat the count but he was all through. I won the fight easily.

It was a close call and I decided to stay away from liquor after that . . . at least until after the Sharkey fight. I trained the last six weeks at Gus Wilson's camp in Orangeburg, New York—no joking, no fooling around.

The experts were still skeptical. Most of them picked Sharkey, declaring that I didn't belong in the same ring with him. He was just too big, too strong. The book-makers tabbed Sharkey a 3 to 1 favorite. Bill Corum, writing in the *New York Journal,* said Sharkey should be 10 to 1 instead of 3 to 1.

". . . Sharkey has a 30-pound pull, much better of it in reach and is a better boxer," Corum wrote. "Sharkey is better conditioned, lives by a calisthenic manual, is a cleaner liver and a harder puncher . . .

"Now, tell me," he concluded, "on what are you going to make Walker beat him?"

Dan Parker, *New York Mirror* boxing expert, wrote: "If Sharkey doesn't knock out Walker, he ought to quit the ring. Mickey has flirted with the bright lights too long."

Wrote Paul Gallico of the *New York Daily News*: "Walker has lived high, wide and handsome since he has been in the chips. Sharkey ought to be able to beat Walker badly. Walker is a fine little fighter, a ripping, hooking puncher, but he doesn't belong in the same ring with Sharkey."

Sharkey himself was quoted: "I'll knock him out . . . Honestly, the odds ought to be 20 to 1. I think I could almost name the round. They say nobody living can keep Walker on the floor. This time he will be spread for keeps."

Writers who visited my camp actually expressed sympathy for me. I told them what they could do with it. The day of the fight I was sharp, eager and confident.

I fought Sharkey on July 22, 1931, at Ebbets Field, then the home of the Brooklyn Dodgers. More than thirty thousand people were there and the gate was $238,831. The odds, for some reason, had gone down to 2 to 1 on Sharkey. Maybe my confidence had rubbed off on some people.

Sharkey was six feet, and weighed 198 pounds and had a seventy-three-inch reach. I was five feet, six inches, and my reach was sixty-seven inches. While my weight was anounced at 168 pounds, I actually weighed 162 at weigh-in time the morning of the fight. The promoter thought my low weight might scare off some people and cut down the gate.

As usual I was a bundle of nerves in the dressing room, cranky and excited. I couldn't wait to get into the ring and get going. Kearns, as he did before every fight, gave me last-minute instructions to make sure I remembered the way we planned the fight. I only half listened. I had gone over it all day: stay in close . . . don't fight at long range . . . watch the right, his best punch . . . dig the left into his body . . . keep on top of him all the way.

Sharkey towered six inches above me as referee Arthur Donovan called us together under the glaring lights in the center of the ring. He gave us the last-minute talk about a clean fight and then we shook hands.

While waiting in my corner for the bell, I shuffled my feet in the resin and listened to Kearns.

"Okay, Mickey. This is it. You know what you have to do," Doc reminded.

I nodded.

Right from the start, I fought according to plan. I

229

rushed him, boring in with lefts to the body. I had no trouble getting inside because Jack was a stand-up fighter. I ducked his left jabs and stayed in close, working on his mid-section.

Sharkey was so busy trying to keep me away from him that he couldn't set me up for his right hand, which was his big punch.

I had the edge in the first three rounds and had him groggy in the fourth. I missed by a hair with two rights when I had him on queer street. I should have knocked him out then.

Another fighter might have gone for good. But Jack was too ring-wise and had too much class. He hung on smartly, clinching and mauling me as I tried to get free for a kayo punch. He weathered the round.

Jack never let me get that close again. He used his weight and reach to keep me away after that. I didn't stop boring in. I never let up and gave him an awful lot of punishment to the body. I can still see those left hooks ripping into his stomach.

I didn't mind getting hit as long as I got my punches across and Sharkey got in some good punches of his own. But he never hurt me because he couldn't get set with his long, powerful right hand.

This was the pattern for all of the fifteen rounds. Although he was heavier and bigger, I was stronger in the clinches. When the fight was over, I was fresher by far than he was. He looked disgusted, as if he thought he had lost. I was sure I had won.

As I waited for the decision to be announced, I thought to myself, I made it; I'm the heavyweight champion!

The fight was for the world's heavyweight title, as far as New York was concerned. The State Athletic Commission recognized no man as champion. Max Schmeling had beaten Sharkey the year before, winning the title on a foul but the Commission had taken the crown away from him when the German refused to give Sharkey a return bout.

The announcer had gathered the slips from the two judges and the referee, and the timekeeper was banging away at the bell to quiet the crowd down so that the verdict could be announced.

"Ladeez and gentlemen," bellowed Joe Humphreys, "referee Arthur Donovan gives eleven rounds to Walker and four to Sharkey."

I could hardly hear the tail end amidst the crowd's roar of approval. I looked at Doc and he was grinning.

The timekeeper had to hit the bell several times to quiet the crowd. Humphreys continued: "Judge George Kelly gives eight rounds to Sharkey and seven to Walker."

Now there were mingled cheers and boos. I was stunned. You should have seen Kearns and Hayes. They shouted protests and hopped around the ring gesturing wildly.

"Judge Charles Mathison votes seven rounds for each man with one even . . . The decision is a draw."

A draw? How could they? The referee, the third man in the ring, had given me eleven of the fifteen rounds and all I got was a draw. I could hardly believe it. Kearns was like a madman. He screamed all over ringside that we were robbed.

The crowd thought I was robbed, too. People stood up and booed the decision until Sharkey and I left the ring. Even those who bet on Sharkey couldn't believe it when the decision was announced.

The writers had been certain I had won the fight. That's

what they reported in their papers. Paul Gallico, one of my biggest critics among the boxing experts, wrote the following day:

". . . Walker won the Sharkey fight but didn't get it," the article read. "When he was matched with Sharkey, I recall that I led the pooh-poohing. In fact, I pooh-poohed from the housetops that it was a case for the ASPCA, a crime and a cruelty and ought to be stopped because Sharkey would kill the little man. Did I live to eat those words? You saw me eat every one of them. Sharkey couldn't do a thing with Edward Patrick except cut his eye in the later rounds and so sway the Judges to give a draw to him to which I did not think he was entitled. . . ."

Kearns and I were terribly disappointed but there was one consolation. The contracts called for a return match. But Buckley shattered that hope when he refused to go through with it.

It was understood that the winner would fight Schmeling and clear up the heavyweight muddle once and for all. Since there was no winner, it was up to Joe Jacobs, Schmeling's manager, to make the choice. He chose Sharkey. Jacobs, a smoothie, wanted no part of me. He knew I had licked Sharkey and he thought Jack would be an easier opponent for his man. As it turned out, Sharkey fooled him by beating Max easily and became the undisputed heavyweight champion of the world.

Joe Jacobs had promised Kearns that Schmeling would give me a shot at his title after Max had disposed of Sharkey. That's the only reason Doc had let Sharkey run out of the rematch with me. As it turned out, Max had no title after the Sharkey fight, but Jacobs kept his word, and signed Schmeling to meet me. Schmeling and I had one thing in common. We both wanted another crack at

Sharkey, and the New York Athletic Commission ruled that Sharkey must defend his title against the winner.

CHAPTER TWENTY-FOUR

The year 1931 was a big one: the Empire State Building and the George Washington Bridge were opened; Mahatma Gandhi presented his peace plan to the world in Geneva; Knute Rockne, the great Notre Dame coach was killed in a plane accident; the roof of the Vatican collapsed and precious art treasures were ruined; Congress was having hearings which led to the repeal of the Eighteenth Amendment.

It was also the year Doc Kearns entered the state of matrimony.

The bride was Lillian Kansler, a tall, beautiful girl, of tremendous charm. The daughter of a Kentucky colonel, she was much younger than Doc (who was in his fifties), but was madly in love with him.

I was best man at their wedding. It was held in my Shrewsbury home, a couple of weeks after the Sharkey fight. Doc's marriage to the southern belle was his second. I never knew his first wife.

Kearns's wedding far outstripped mine. Everybody who was anybody in show business, boxing and the newspaper business was there. It was a night to be remembered. It wasn't until four o'clock the next morning that the last of the celebrants had either left or had been put to bed. There were just two left—Doc and me.

All night long, no matter how much I drank, I kept one

thing in mind. The time had come. For two years I had been waiting for this night. I was not going to flub my chance to get even.

Kearns knew what was coming and he beat me to the punch.

"I suppose you're waiting to see who's going to be the boss in my family?" he asked with a touch of sarcasm.

"That's right, wise guy," I grinned.

Doc didn't say another word. He just put on his hat and coat and walked to the door. He looked over his shoulder to see if I was following.

"C'mon," he growled.

We walked right to the garage, got into my car and took off for New York. For two days and nights we hit as many hot spots as we could in the big town. The last stop, of course, was the Pleasant Inn in Red Bank. We couldn't go to bed without a nightcap.

We got back to the house just in time. Doc's bride, after two days and nights of crying, was about to pack up and leave. She would have left sooner except for Clara who, in a year and a half as my wife, had become accustomed to these escapades. Clara persuaded her to remain. Once we got back, it wasn't too difficult for the sweet-talking doctor to square himself with Lillian and pick up the belated honeymoon.

The marriage lasted long enough for them to have two sons, of whom Doc is very proud today. He and Lillian were later divorced. Doc doesn't have as much guts as I do, because he never married again.

Married life didn't change Doc, any more than it had changed me. He and I spent more time with each other than with our wives. We raised hell the rest of that year, letting the fun be interrupted only once—for an August fight with a Canadian, Jack Gagnon. That was in Buffalo and I shuffled him off to sleep in one round.

It wasn't until the following March that I fought again. I won a couple of fights by knockouts and was matched with Kingfish Levinsky in Chicago. The Kingfish was a big clown and not much of a fighter but he could punch. His sister, Lena, was his manager. I spotted Levinsky 23 pounds and handed him a shellacking.

A few days after that fight, I became a father again. Clara gave birth to a seven-and-a-half-pound boy. We named him James, after Jimmy Walker, the New York City Mayor, whom I admired. My brother Joe was the godfather by proxy for the Mayor, who couldn't attend.

My next fight was against Paulino Uzcudun, the heavyweight champion of Spain. This was another of the Milk Fund bouts sponsored by the *New York Journal*. Uzcudun had become prominent here by beating Max Baer in twenty rounds in Reno.

The fight was held in Madison Square Garden in May of 1932. While I was training at Madame Bey's, a carbuncle formed on the back of my neck. It became infected and I had to undergo surgery three days before the fight. A three-and-a-half-inch incision was necessary to remove the thing. I still have the scar today.

The wound was still open when I climbed into the ring to fight Uzcudun, but I won easily.

After the Uzcudun fight I didn't let myself get too much out of condition for I knew I had to be sharp for my fight with Schmeling in late September. At thirty-one, it is hard to get back into fighting condition after you let yourself go.

I trained hard and a week before the fight I was down to 158 pounds, my best fighting weight. Kearns thought

I was too sharp and feared I'd be stale by fight time. So he ordered me to take a day off from the training grind at Madame Bey's.

"Go anywhere, do anything," he advised. "I don't care what you do as long as you don't work. Relax, have some fun, even take a few beers. It'll do you good. You're too keyed up. I don't care if you put some pounds back. You've still got a week to get them off again."

I hung around the camp all morning doing nothing. I became bored and suggested to Kearns we play a round of golf at a nearby course. He thought it was a good idea. Since Kearns had said it would be all right for me to have a few, I figured I might as well make the most of it. No beer, though. Instead, I had a case of champagne delivered to the camp and we took it to the golf course.

I had my caddy carry the basket of champagne with my clubs. Doc and I played eighteen holes. Before it was over I not only carried a few more pounds, but a pretty good load. Near the end of the match, I was swinging at two golf balls. We managed to finish without incident, however . . . if you call losing a dozen golf balls and almost skulling a caddy, trivial.

On the way to the car, Kearns insisted on taking the wheel, claiming I was in no condition to drive.

"You're drunker than I am," I told him. "Why, the condition you're in, you couldn't drive a baby carriage."

Doc was insulted. We were in the parking lot and he began walking along the cracks in the concrete, trying to demonstrate his ability to walk a straight line. Of course, I had to show that I could do it, too. This led to another argument. Kearns claimed I was weaving from side to side and I yelled back that I was doing better than he was.

Kearns pointed to a picket fence at the far end of the parking lot. It was about four feet high with each board pointed at the top.

"See that fence??" Doc said. "I'll bet you I can jump over it."

Without waiting to see whether or not I'd take him up on it, Doc made a run for the fence and cleared it with room to spare. Naturally, I couldn't let him get away with that. Anything Doc could do, I could do better.

I took a running start and made my leap, using a belly-roll as I had seen some of the high-jumpers do. I made it all right, but in the act of going over, one of the pointed uprights scraped my forehead and opened a huge gash over my left eye. I bled like a stuck pig.

My cut was so bad the fight had to be postponed two weeks. I was disappointed. I had trained hard to get into top shape and the prospect of three more tough weeks of conditioning did not appeal to me. I had reached a peak and I knew that it would be impossible for me to retain that peak.

Sure enough, three weeks later, you wouldn't have recognized me as the same man. I was fat and out of shape. I just neglected training altogether. I came into the ring against Max Schmeling weighing 174 pounds, my heaviest ever. I had gained 16 pounds, mostly around the middle. This should give a clear indication how quickly I ballooned in those days when I let myself go. Nobody picks up pounds as quickly as I do, even now.

I'm not trying to take anything away from Schmeling. Max deserved his reputation. He might have beaten me even if I were in good shape but certainly, in my condition, I was no match for him.

The fight was held in the old Madison Square Garden

Bowl in Long Island City. Through the first seven rounds, it was close. In fact, the judges had me slightly ahead on points. Their cards showed I had won the third, fourth, fifth and seventh rounds. Schmeling hit me with a right in the first round, closing my left eye. In the fifth, I almost bent Max in half with a terrific left hook to the stomach.

Then came the eighth—it turned out to be a nightmare for me. Schmeling had landed a hard left late in the seventh round that almost closed my right eye. At the start of the eighth, he hit the eye again and this time it closed completely.

It was almost impossible for me to see.

Schmeling opened up then and gave me a terrific shellacking. It was the worst beating I ever took in my life. One punch knocked my mouthpiece to the canvas. Another dropped me for a five-count. I got up, but was floundering around helplessly. Twice more I went down, each time for a nine-count.

Max didn't want to hit me any more. He appealed to Jack Denny, the referee, to stop the fight, but the official wouldn't listen. I must have been a ghastly sight by then. My eyes were mere slits. The left side of my face was swollen and shapeless. My mouth was cut and bleeding. I was paralyzed when the gong finally ended the eighth.

Doc helped me back to my corner. He slapped me in the face and talked to me, asking if I knew who he was and where I was. I told him not to worry, that I was all right. He knew differently. He'd decided not to let me go out for the ninth round.

The best description of the fight was written by Paul Gallico in the *New York Daily News:*

". . . In case you missed the eighth and last round of that fight in Long Island City last night between Mickey

Walker and Max Schmeling, you might run down to the slaughterhouse on First Avenue and 44th Street and watch them dress beef. If you want to know what it was like, it was like the slaughtering of an ox, a desperate little ox. Once Herr Schmeling, the German butcher who appeared to be fixing up a side of beef for the trade, remembered who he was and where he was, that he had human attributes, and signaled to the referee that he thought the beef was well-dressed, and would he not end this horrid, bloody, inhuman dream? The referee, however, was for more slaughter.

"Walker was a study in pain in that last round. Can you imagine how he must have hurt? His mouth was cut. Both eyes were shut. One of them was cut, his lips were smashed. He had nothing but a smear for a face. And into that smear, Schmeling kept driving his fists."

That beating ended Kearns's dream of having a second heavyweight champion, but it brought out in him qualities that no one ever suspected, a touch of sentiment and sympathy. With Doc, the fight game always had been strictly a cold, hard, merciless business. The ring has no place for gentleness.

With Kearns, a man could fight or he couldn't. If he couldn't, he didn't belong in the ring. Doc might like a fighter personally, but when the bell rang, he dismissed all thoughts of sentiment. If his man came back to his corner "snoring," or cut and bleeding, it was Doc's duty to revive him as much as possible, not give him sympathy.

Ice-cold and pitiless in a corner, slitting open a closed eye with a steady hand, slicing off a chunk of hanging flesh from a lower lip, cuffing a half-unconscious fighter awake: that was Kearns—until that night in the Garden

239

Bowl when I was half-carried, half-dragged back to my corner at the end of the eighth round.

As the bell rang to start the ninth, Kearns signaled to the referee. He couldn't stand seeing me punished any more. He had brought me a long way—through the middleweight title, into competition with light-heavyweight and heavyweight contenders, and he had convinced both himself and me that we could win the big title. Kearns saw the dream fade in that fight with the "Black Uhlan of the Rhine" and admitted it by his sign to the referee.

I was going to hang up my gloves after the Schmeling fight. Doc disagreed. He thought I could still beat most of the fighters around, even if I couldn't handle the top heavyweights. He wanted to take me out to the West Coast and start fresh. I needed time to think it over. I had taken a bad beating and all I wanted to do was to stay home and rest. Doc thought it a good idea.

I had been home a month when I got the urge to fight again. My wounds had healed. I felt good. I telephoned Kearns and told him I was ready for another fight. Inside of a week, he had arranged a match in Los Angeles with the Belgian heavyweight, Arthur DeKuh.

Before leaving for the West Coast, I had to take care of an important matter. It was Mom's birthday and I was determined to make this one she wouldn't forget. In other years, I had always bought Mom a gift on her birthday. One year it was a diamond-and-ruby-studded necklace, another it was a white ermine evening coat, and once I bought her a Cadillac.

Mom had little use for these expensive gifts. The diamond necklace she gave to Aunt Maggie and the car she gave to Uncle Joe.

I decided I was going to do something different this

time. Instead of buying her a gift, which she probably wouldn't appreciate anyway, I decided to take her out for a night's entertainment and show her the time of her life. Mom was going to be my date on her birthday. We were to be driven around by my old chauffeur and buddy, Jimmy Duryea.

It was wild. I got Mom a new dress and a new hairdo. After a round of joints, we wound up at a classy place along the Jersey shore frequented by the social set. It was about midnight. We drank only champagne and Liz was high and happy.

Mom requested the orchestra leader to play "Trees" and asked the soloist to sing it. The singer wasn't too good, but Mom didn't care. A group of fraternity kids from Princeton jeered and heckled the soloist.

Mom became angry and asked me to quiet the kids down. I went over, saw they were youngsters having a good time. They recognized me and asked me to join them. I did and ordered a round of drinks. The talk turned to boxing and one of the boys, who had seen the Schmeling fight, started re-creating it, with gestures.

Mom, across the room, misunderstood his fist-swinging. She thought her Edward was in trouble and yelled for Duryea, who was at the bar and loaded. Jimmy looked over at me and disappeared. A minute or two later he lurched back with a gleaming .45, which he brandished wobbily in both hands.

"Stand back, Mickey," he roared. "I'll get 'em all . . . every last son-of-a-bitch!"

The place all but blew apart. Customers dashed for exits, upsetting tables and chairs while I grappled with Jimmy and took away the rod. Mom was crying. The manager had the presence of mind to call the police. It took some time for the cops to quiet things down. Just when everything appeared settled, the manager began squawking about the damage. Mom didn't like his tone of voice and bashed him over the head with her pocketbook.

The upshot of it all was that Mom, Jimmy and I were hauled off to the station house, where I was socked with a five-hundred-dollar fine. That was Mom's special birthday party. It was the last one we ever celebrated together.

I left for the West Coast in mid-November, ten weeks after the Schmeling fight. I won my first comeback fight, knocking out DeKuh in one round. The knockout victory gave me a little more confidence but I was only kidding myself. I was through as a big timer, only I didn't know it yet.

I had a couple more fights in the East, winning one, losing another. But I'd started going downhill after the Schmeling fight. I wasn't getting those big, fat purses any more. Things weren't so good financially.

Doc was becoming involved in California politics and persuaded me to make another trip to the West Coast with him. This time I took Clara and little Jimmy with me. We stayed there nearly four months. But Kearns, busy campaigning for a man who eventually became mayor of Los Angeles, paid little attention to me. Politics didn't interest me. I had had my fling back in 1925 and it wasn't exciting enough for me.

Doc seemed to have lost all interest in boxing—and in me. All the time I was in California, I saw no action. Our expenses were mounting and with no money coming in I was getting worried. I began looking around for some business to enter, but couldn't find anything I was fitted for. I finally made up my mind to split up with Kearns.

Doc was on a drunk one night. He became boisterous

and got into a heated argument with a café proprietor. A cop was summoned, but he couldn't quiet Kearns. The cop threatened to pinch Doc. That made him even more belligerent.

"Nobody can pinch me," Doc bragged. "I'm a friend of the mayor. I'm the guy who put him in office."

Kearns not only was taken to jail, but was fined $250 for disturbing the peace.

After this escapade, I made a break with Kearns. It had been four months since he'd gotten me a fight, and I was going broke. Doc was willing. He knew he wasn't doing much for me, anyway. I decided to take Clara back East, and this time Kearns remained behind. Our partnership of eight years was ended.

CHAPTER TWENTY-FIVE

I needed a good stake quickly and I was lucky to get an offer to fight Maxie Rosenbloom for the world's light-heavyweight title. My name still drew a good box office. Frank Bachman, Maxie's manager, figured I was only a shell and that his boy could take me easily. Rosenbloom was called "Slapsie" because he lacked a kayo punch and pawed with an open glove, but he was a good fighter.

Since I didn't have a manager, I handled my own affairs. The purse of twenty thousand dollars wasn't bad. I knew this was probably my last big-money fight if I lost. So I put in some hard training at Atlantic Highlands.

I had a frequent visitor at the training camp, a dapper guy who called himself Count Lustig. He claimed he was a rabid fight fan. He never missed a day of my training.

The Count—that's the only name I ever knew him by—had a magnetic personality. He had gracious manners and spoke with a flavorful German accent. He dressed impeccably, in dark business suits, a homburg and bow tie. He was quite a dandy.

I was relaxing after a stiff workout one day when the Count asked me what I was going to do when my fighting days were over.

"You can't fight forever, you know," he said. "How would you like to open a café in New York?"

Before I could answer, he went on, "I have a wealthy friend who would be happy to have you as a partner in one of New York's better places. You wouldn't have to invest any money. All that would be needed would be your occasional appearance."

I was interested. I agreed to meet the angel, who was going to back me in the café business. The friend turned out to be a woman, May Sobel—the Count's sweetheart. She had an expensive apartment on Park Avenue.

We held a business meeting every day for two weeks, always in May's Park Avenue apartment. Each day she'd introduce me to another one of her men friends. The Count didn't seem to mind.

Count Lustig and I always traveled by train from the Highlands to New York and back. I suggested we use my car, but he claimed it made him carsick. The Count never was without a small suitcase and every day he'd find some excuse for me to carry it as soon as we entered the station. He never took it back until he reached May's apartment.

In the meantime, negotiations were progressing well. We reached the point of actually selecting a spot for the night club, on Forty-ninth Street and Broadway. I got in touch with Uncle Dan Higgins, the architect, and got him to draw up some blueprints. Uncle Dan liked the set up and had plans drawn for it.

Early one morning, I was at home enjoying a day off from training when there was a knock on the front door. Clara was out with the baby and I was all alone. I opened the door and saw two tall fellows standing there. They had the look of detectives.

"You Mickey Walker?" one of them asked pleasantly enough.

"Yes, come in."

They were FBI men. I was wanted for interrogation by the New York office. I asked why, but they wouldn't tell me.

"Okay," I said amiably. "I'll be there first thing tomorrow morning."

"You'd better come with us now," one of them said quietly.

The way he said it, I knew there was no use arguing. Also, I was beginning to suspect that this might involve something serious.

I didn't ask a single question during the ride to New York. I knew it would bring no answers. Nobody spoke throughout the entire trip.

It was eleven o'clock when I was ushered into the New York office of the FBI. I still couldn't figure it out. I must have cooled my heels for about ten minutes when a tall, well-built, middle-aged man entered. He introduced himself as Earl J. Connolly, head of the New York office.

"Are you a friend of Count Lustig?" he asked.

"Sure," I said, "we're good friends. He's a real nice fellow in spite of his appearance."

"Do you know his business?"

"Sure, the café business."

"Do you know what else he does?"

"No."

Connolly looked at me, doubt in his eyes. He arose from his chair and stood over me.

"You mean you don't know that Count Lustig is a notorious counterfeiter?" he asked.

I shook my head.

"One of the best in the world," he said. "Internationally known and sought. He's an artist in his work, making money that is almost perfect. We've been trailing him for months. We've watched the two of you for weeks. We could have picked him up long before this, but we wanted to catch him red-handed. We finally did and we've now got him under lock and key."

I stared at the man, not knowing whether to believe him or not. Count Lustig a counterfeiter? It sounded impossible. But FBI men are not known to play jokes.

Connolly hurled question after question at me. How about those daily trips with Lustig? Where were we going? What about those suitcases I was carrying? Did I know what was in them? Did I ever ask what was in them? Who did he give them to? Did I know that they contained thousands of dollars in counterfeit money? Did I know that Lustig had his headquarters and printing press near my camp?

Did I know that May Sobel was a madam who was in league with the Count? And did I know that the men I was meeting every day were accomplices who peddled the phony money, twenty cents on the dollar?

Each time I shook my head, the FBI chief shot another question. I had a heck of a time trying to convince him I didn't know a thing about it.

I was kept in the office all day. Connolly had lunch brought in for me. The grilling lasted, on and off, for twelve hours. I answered every question as truthfully as I could. I had nothing to hide. At first, the FBI agent couldn't believe that I didn't know a thing. I just couldn't be that naïve, he insisted. He thought I was in cahoots with the counterfeiters and was trying to protect them. I finally became irritable and weary from all the questioning.

"Look," I said, "I've told you the truth. It might be hard for you to believe, but it's the truth. I've told you everything I know and I can't tell you any more. I don't care if you shoot me, but if you don't let me go, I'm going to punch somebody in the jaw."

The chief gave me another long, searching look. Then he arose from back of his desk, came over and extended his hand.

"Okay, Mickey, I'm convinced," he said at last. "But you've been a chump."

Brother, was he right. What a spot I would have been in if I'd opened the joint and it turned out to be a front for counterfeiters. And we were ready to open. In fact, the finishing touches were almost completed and I had booked Rudy Vallee for my first show. He had been out of the limelight for a while and this was to have been a comeback for him.

Lustig and May Sobel were found guilty and sent to jail. The Count went to Alcatraz for a ten-year term, but he died after four years of prison life. I corresponded with him for a time. Even though a crook, he was a charming guy.

A few days before my fight with Rosenbloom, I had

another visitor in camp. Who else but Jack Kearns? He wanted to hook up with me again.

The doctor was in my corner the night of the fight, but it didn't do me any good. Maxie beat me easily. I was rusty. I had no pep. I had a chance to knock him out in the ninth round—I had him groggy, but couldn't put him away. I had lost the killer instinct that had inspired the Toy Bulldog nickname.

As far as I was concerned, that was it. Fifteen years of fighting was enough. When I told Doc, he just laughed.

"Quit?" he snorted. "What for? There are too many bums around for you to quit now. You can still take most of them. Hell, Mickey, you can still fight. You should have licked Rosenbloom. It's my fault that you didn't, not yours. If I had been here to take charge of your training, you'd have been in better shape and you'd have beaten Maxie easy. We'll get him again and next time you'll lick him."

I thought maybe he was right, and decided not to hang up my gloves just yet.

I rested a month, then bowled over some bloke in Newark. In January of 1934, Doc got me a match with Bob Godwin, a pretty good heavyweight, in West Palm Beach, Florida. I took the match because it gave me an excuse to spend a short vacation with Clara in Florida.

A day or two after the fight, I received a telephone call from my brother Joe. He advised me to come home—Mom was very sick. I had just purchased a brand new Lincoln. Clara and I had driven to Florida. But we packed immediately and headed back north. We figured that—taking turns driving—we should arrive in New Jersey in twenty-four hours.

Everything went well until we reached Virginia and hit snow. Clara was driving and she was tired. I was getting ready to take over when the car skidded off the road—at 60 miles an hour. We banged into—of all places—a sheriff's home. The car hit the outhouse and knocked a corner off it.

Miraculously, neither Clara nor I was hurt although Clara was slightly shaken up. The car, however, was badly damaged. I didn't mind that because it was insured. But it would take at least twenty-four hours to have it repaired.

The sheriff was sympathetic. Also very cooperative. He not only overlooked the damage to his outhouse, but he arranged for us to board a bus to Washington where we took a train to Elizabeth. I left the car in Virginia, of course, and I never did pick it up. I never heard from the sheriff, either. To this day I don't know what happened to my 1934 Lincoln. I can't even remember the name of the town where we had the accident.

I knew I was going to lose Mom the moment I saw her. She knew she was going, too. She had stayed alive for days through sheer will power alone; she just had to see her son Edward once more.

Mom died the day after I arrived.

Just before she went to Heaven, Liz beckoned me to her side, gathered up what strength she could, and whispered into my ear, "Edward, always be a good boy. The Lord will look out for you."

Three months after mother's death, Kearns maneuvered a rematch with Rosenbloom in Los Angeles. This time I was in shape, a strong 158 pounds.

I whipped Maxie handily but no title went with the victory. Rosenbloom had refused to give me a return until I agreed to a non-title bout.

Champion or not, I was encouraged. The Toy Bulldog may have lost some of his bite, but he could still handle himself in the ring . . . against the best. All I had to do was keep in fighting shape.

I can still remember Rosenbloom's words in the first round right after my left hook to the belly had made him grunt in pain.

"Mickey," he gasped in surprise, "you're not the same guy I fought six months ago."

Three months later, I fought Young Corbett in San Francisco. Corbett was the local favorite. I felt that I licked him, but they gave him the decision. I found out later that nobody beat Corbett in San Francisco.

Doc and I needed money badly when he made the Corbett match. But in the chips or broke, Doc always lived to the hilt, so he took a big suite at the St. Francis, San Francisco's best hotel. He had to make an impression.

Lilyan Tashman and I were good friends at the time and through her, Kearns and I were invited to a party. It was quite a social gathering and because I was a sports celebrity, they made a great fuss over me. Soon I was on a first-name basis with most of the guests.

One of the guests owned the Steambeer Brewery. We were drinking and somehow or other I wound up buying the brewery for $100,000. I told this fellow my cash was tied up and therefore I couldn't give him a down payment for a few days. He said it was prefectly all right as long as I would sign some papers, promising to make payment at a stipulated time. The whole thing ended with him advancing me $10,000 to go to New York and consult with my lawyers.

We were no longer broke. The ten grand helped to pay hotel and training camp expenses. My purse for the Corbett fight was $20,000, but I collected only half of it. The brewery owner's lawyers had attached the other half of the purse. The ring was full of lawyers after the last round.

Kearns and I split up for good after that fight. We parted good friends. The decision to break up our partnership was made in his Los Angeles home. We were sitting in the library. Both of us knew my best days were past.

"Mickey, we've been through a lot together," Kearns began, "but the time has come for us to part."

I was prepared for this. Kearns had been paying less and less attention to me. He had long ago become convinced that he would never regain the heavyweight championship through me. I was going downhill. I was thirty-three and an old man, in ring terms. I was no longer an asset. I knew Doc's thoughts: find some eager, ambitious, hungry fighter with the recklessness of youth. Start fresh. Teach him everything you know, and hope he develops into another Jack Dempsey or another Mickey Walker.

Doc was talking again. I turned to listen.

"I think it's time you hung up your gloves, Mick," he was saying. "You're old and slow. Your spark is gone. You don't love it any more. Your heart isn't in it. Get out before you get hurt. I'd hate to see anything happen to you. Quit while you've still got your senses. I don't want to see you walking on your heels, your eyes sunk deep in their sockets, your brain scrambled."

There it was—the thing I thought would never happen to me. Doc was letting me have it with both barrels. He didn't try to spare me in the least. He must have been thinking of this moment for a long time. He must have rehearsed this for weeks, maybe months.

"You've been lucky," Doc continued. "You hardly have any marks on you, except for scar tissue over your eyes.

Your brains are still intact. Your tongue is not thick. Your head is clear and your body is strong. Hang up your gloves, Mick, and go into some business. You're not too old for that. There's still time."

I listened without a word. I wasn't bitter; I wasn't even disappointed. Sure, I didn't like to hear it, but deep down inside I knew Doc was right. He made a lot of sense, as he always did. I got up to go.

"I retire as of now, Doc," I said. We shook hands on it.

I went back East determined to stay retired this time. I was going on thirty-four. I was a man. I knew all the angles. I knew even better than Kearns that age had caught up with me. I could tell it when I was in the ring. It came home to me every time I missed an opening, just a fraction of a second late; I knew it every time my Sunday punch landed, and the other guy didn't go down.

Again I tried to turn to something else. I considered going into real estate, architecture, engineering. I thought about those things, but that's as far as it went. Maybe ten, fifteen years before, I could have done it, but not now. I was no longer equipped for it. I was equipped for just one thing . . . fighting for a living. Nothing else. Fighting was my business. Why kid myself? Fighting was the only way I knew to make a buck. Somehow, I guess I had known all along I wasn't going to quit.

I still had my home in Shrewsbury, and I had to have quick money to keep it up and provide for my family. Although I no longer had any title hopes, I could still attract sizeable purses. I had grown too used to the good life—and big money. I had to go on.

So I went back to managing myself again. But not for long. I received a visitor at my home one day. It was Bill Duffy. He didn't waste any words.

"I just learned that you and Kearns have split up," he said. "I've always wanted to be your manager, but I didn't want to interfere with Kearns. Now that the partnership is dissolved, I'd like to manage you. I believe you can still fight. You're only thirty-four. Bob Fitzsimmons was thirty-five when he knocked out Jim Jeffries for the heavyweight title."

I let Duffy talk me into making another comeback . . . with him as my new manager. He didn't have to argue too much; I was looking for an excuse to remain in the fight game.

The first match Duffy made for me was against Natie Brown in Washington, D.C. I had insisted on a good fighter and Brown was a good one. He had just gone the distance with Joe Louis, giving the Brown Bomber a good fight. We fought a draw. I felt good. I hadn't gotten hurt. I picked up $6,500. I was back in business. Funny what one good showing will do for a washed-up pug. I thought I was back in the groove again, but I was kidding myself . . . any excuse just to continue fighting.

A month later I fought Paul Pirrone in Philadelphia. Pirrone was an up-and-coming young light-heavyweight, a good puncher. I lost a ten-round decision. Three weeks later, after I had whipped a fellow called Tait Littman in Pittsburgh, I took Pirrone on again.

Duffy wanted this one for fifteen rounds. He remembered that I had rallied in the last two rounds of our previous fight and thought I would have won if the fight had gone longer. What Bill didn't realize was that I was fighting on instinct alone, and giving it a dying man's last gasp. He still kept thinking of me as Mickey Walker, the young and fearless Toy Bulldog of the old days.

I knew fifteen rounds would be too much for me, and I wanted the fight limited to ten rounds. We finally compromised at twelve. It turned out I was right. Pirrone knocked me out in the eleventh. It was the first time a referee had ever counted ten over me since Phil Delmont kayoed me in my first year of fighting.

Even a knockout failed to shake Duffy's confidence in me. He still nursed the belief that I had the potential to challenge for the heavyweight title. Max Baer was now the champion, having knocked out Primo Carnera in eleven rounds. I knew differently of course, and this time I refused to listen.

I made up my mind to call it quits.

Duffy didn't try to persuade me. Instead, he offered me a partnership in a saloon he planned to open on Forty-ninth Street and Eighth Avenue, across the street from Madison Square Garden. I jumped at the chance.

We opened in February, 1935. Duffy named the place The Toy Bulldog. Kearns, in California, sent me a telegram at the grand opening. It read:

REMEMBERING A GOLF COURSE IN LONDON WHERE YOU MET A KING IN HIS LINE AS YOU ARE IN YOURS. THOUGH UNABLE TO BE WITH YOU, MY HEART IS WITH YOU, PAL. YOU ARE THE GREATEST FIGHTER IN THE RING AND IN LIFE. THERE'S ONLY ONE MICKEY WALKER.

(SIGNED) JACK KEARNS.

CHAPTER TWENTY-SIX

The saloon did a flourishing business from the start. It became one of the most popular places off Broadway. The only trouble was, it made a bum out of me. I spent practically all of my time there, meeting and mingling with tough characters, dating dolls who hung around the place, and drinking myself silly. I loved Clara, but she was a fine girl and didn't fit in with that fast crowd.

I've got no excuses. I just didn't go home nights. I went on drunks regularly, sometimes for weeks at a time.

My brother Joe took care of me every time I went on a toot. He was working for the Catholic Youth Organization at the time and had use of that group's station wagon. It had a shield on one side which read "Cardinal Hayes CYO."

Every time I'd come down the stretch on a bender, my bartender, Mike Burns, would telephone my brother at the CYO.

"Hey, Joe, better come over and get Mickey."

Up would come the station wagon and Joe would pack me into it and drive me home to Shrewsbury. This happened on the average of two, three nights a week. Pretty soon the CYO would receive telephone calls from people wanting to know why a Cardinal Hayes station wagon would park in front of a saloon every night. Joe had a lot of explaining to do at headquarters.

The trouble with me and drinking was that I'd feel

three drinks as much as thirty. Once I got started, I was on my way.

I stayed retired exactly eight months. Duffy kept after me and I did need the dough. Starting in July, I fought nine times in 1935, winning seven.

Duffy, the eternal optimist, was getting ideas again. One day he gave me the "wonderful" news that he had agreed to a match with Joe Louis. I didn't want to fight Louis. I knew I didn't stand a chance against him. Even in my best days I knew I couldn't have licked him.

Joe was twenty-one and I was thirty-four. He was unbeaten. Of the twenty-five opponents he'd faced, he had knocked out twenty-one. His latest win had been a four-round kayo over Baer, three months after Max had been stripped of his heavyweight title by Jim Braddock.

Duffy pointed out that the Louis-Baer fight had drawn $240,000. He felt that a fight between Louis and myself would draw maybe half a million; that meant I would clear about $150,000. Bill honestly felt I could beat Louis. He claimed I had the style with which to do it. He said Louis had never met a low, bobbing-and-weaving fighter like me and would have trouble solving my style.

I had my doubts, but agreed to the match. I would have gone through with it, too, if it hadn't been for my fight with Eric Seelig on November 29, 1935. Seelig was the European middleweight champion and the fight took place in St. Nicholas Arena. This was supposed to be a tune-up for me.

For six rounds it looked like it, too. Seelig wasn't much of a fighter. My eighteen years of ring experience was too much for him and at the end of the sixth round I was far out in front.

While waiting for the start of the seventh, I thought

to myself, This is it. I'll finish him in this round. I rushed out of my corner, readying my Sunday punch. But Seelig must have had the same idea. He must have known that his only chance was a knockout. We collided in the center of the ring, our heads butting. The blow opened a big cut over my left eye. It slit my forehead wide open. Blood spurted all over. I couldn't keep it out of my eyes. I could hardly see. The blood covered both of us as well as the referee, Johnny MacAvoy.

MacAvoy was an old friend of mine. It was he who had supervised my training for the championship bout with Jack Britton back in 1921. Now, fourteen years later, Mac-Avoy was in the same ring with me, as referee.

Mac didn't want to stop the fight. He was hoping I could last out the round and maybe my handlers could stop the flow of the blood in the minute rest period. But a member of the Boxing Commission, sitting at ringside, motioned for him to call a halt. The Commission doctor came into the ring to examine me. One look, and he ordered the referee to stop the fight.

I stormed around the ring, raising a heck of a row, but it did no good. As MacAvoy made the announcement, I rushed at him and threw a punch at him. Johnny ducked and grabbed me around the waist.

"Mickey," he whispered hoarsely, "I hate to do this, but it's for your own good."

My anger subsided as quickly as it had flared up. I knew Johnny was right. I nodded my head, but couldn't stop the tears coming to my eyes.

"Johnny," I said, almost choking, "you've seen me in my last fight. Thanks for doing me the favor."

It was my last fight. I made no more comebacks.

I was lucky. Had I won, I probably would have fought

257

Joe Louis and he might have killed me. What good would the hundred-fifty grand have done me then?

I didn't miss the ring half as much as I thought I would. I gave most of my attention to my saloon on Eighth Avenue, which had become a hangout for sports fans, fighters and ex-fighters, bookies, tough guys and newspapermen.

Hardly a night went by that I wasn't challenged by a drunk at least once. I had a number of fight pictures over the bar. A customer, after a couple of drinks, would look up at the picture of John L. Sullivan or Jack Dempsey at one end of the bar. After a while, he would begin imitating the pose. Another drink or two and he'd move down to another picture, maybe of Gene Tunney or Angel Firpo, and he would imitate that pose. By the time he got to the end of the bar, he was ready to take me on. When that happened, I'd have to scram out of the place. The customer was always right. He could lick Walker with one hand tied behind his back.

Hype Igoe, the *Journal* fight writer, was a frequent visitor to my place. When he was drinking, he got the damnedest ideas. One night, after tanking up at Jack Dempsey's saloon a block east of mine on Broadway, he staggered into my place with a kid's top and claimed he was the champion top-spinner of the world.

After a few rounds, I told Hype I could outspin him. Ignoring the other customers, I tried spinning the top on the bar and they gave me the horse laugh when I couldn't make the damned thing whirl. Undaunted, I decided I was an "outdoor spinner," and challenged Igoe to go over to Broadway with me where I'd show him some real spinning.

"I can throw it a full block and make it spin," I boasted. We kept arguing and drinking and, by closing time, both

258

of *us* were spinning. Up we went to Broadway, lurching and holding onto one another. When we got there, I took a big windup like Bob Feller and let fly. The top did go far—right through the front window of Dempsey's place.

A cop grabbed us. I tried to tell him who we were, but he took one whiff and dragged us off to the Fifty-second Street police station. Dempsey was notified but he refused to press charges. He just laughed when I offered to pay for the window.

"Like hell, you will," he said. "I'll get even. You never know—some night I might get drunk enough to smash your window."

My marriage to Clara was slowly but surely going on the rocks. She stood for plenty. It got so bad that I'd be home one night a week, maybe. Joe was engaged to be married, now, and didn't have time to take care of me when I went on a bender—which was often. I had a room at the Belvedere Hotel on West Forty-ninth Street, a few doors from my saloon. I spent most of my nights there.

Clara took as much as she could. But when she began hearing stories that I was going around with other women, she gave up. In the winter of 1936, she packed her clothes, took Jimmy, now four and a half, and moved in with her folks in Jersey City.

I couldn't blame her. She had tried her best to make a go of our marriage. I was all right until I took a drink. One always led to another . . . and another . . . and then I was gone. The saloon I half-owned didn't help things either. In fact, that was the real cause of our break.

After Clara left me, I closed my Shrewsbury home and set up bachelor quarters at the Belvedere.

It was just about this time that I made my first serious venture into show business. I was open for anything at that time and when Alfredo Salmaggi, director of the Hippodrome Opera Company, offered me a role in *Carmen,* I accepted. I had the part of a bullfighter and I appeared on stage just once . . . riding into the bull ring on a horse.

But that was enough for me to become smitten with the acting bug. I made up my mind to become an actor.

There's a little bit of ham in everybody. I always had what they call stage presence and could tell a pretty good story; I inherited the gift of gab from my mother, I guess. On my wildest nights, I could reel off a pretty good buck and wing and I used to wow them at the Silver Slipper and Guinan's with an imitation of George Raft or of Bojangles Bill Robinson in the soft-shoe routine.

I went on the stage for the first time as a kid, aged twelve. Annette Kellerman, the nautical beauty, appeared at Proctor's Theater in Elizabeth, in 1913. They had a diving contest on the stage and a bunch of us kids would enter it at every performance. It was a good excuse to crash the gate.

They had a big glass tank on the stage. All of us kids were good swimmers. We had only one trouble: we were accustomed to swimming in our birthday suits most of the time. One day I stole Uncle Dan's bathing suit. He was a husky, muscular guy, twice my size.

When I jumped off the high dive, I jumped right out of my suit, too. There was a gasp in the audience, and the stagehands hurriedly dropped the curtain. They fished me out—and pitched me out in the alley, throwing my clothes after me.

Then there was the vaudeville appearance at the Old Howard Burlesque in Boston with Jack Bulger, after I had won the welterweight title. That was a joke routine followed by a boxing exhibition.

When I was middleweight champion, Kearns made a deal with Universal Pictures Corporation for me to make a series of pictures in Hollywood. I didn't have any desire to be in the movies then, but Kearns insisted. So they gave me a screen test with make-up and all.

I had a face like an eggplant sauté even then, and the first time I saw myself on the screen, I got a sinking feeling. My first and only movie was a stinker.

The producer, Kearns and I were watching the preview. I looked like a roughneck made out to look like a pansy. Kearns, trying to impress the producer, kept referring to my natural acting ability. "Just look at that youthful charm," he kept saying.

"Youthful charm, my ass," I exploded, jumping out of my chair. "You can take the picture and shove it."

I had signed to do a dozen three-reel pictures at a thousand dollars a week, but I refused to go through with the contract. All of Kearn's oratory couldn't make me change my mind. The movie company filed suit against me for $25,000 for breach of contract but Judge George V. Mullen dismissed the case.

I did a vaudeville turn in 1931 before the Sharkey fight, an act with Ben Blue, the Hollywood comedian. As usual, we wound up the act with a boxing exhibition. While clowning with Blue during a show, I accidentally forgot to pull a punch. Even with those big gloves, the blow knocked him back against the ropes which weren't very strong. The ring collapsed and he fell through the scenery. That was the end of that act.

Now, after the bit in *Carmen*, I teamed with Bobby Barry, a good local comic from Elizabeth. We played the Keith Albee circuit, which was tops in those days. We opened at the Gaiety Theater in Washington, D.C. In each city, I held a press conference and gave the boys enough stories to provide them with columns for a week.

When we finished the vaudeville tour, I continued as an entertainer in night clubs. As a master of ceremonies, I was able to get from $750 to $1,500 a week, depending on the size of the place and the business it did. I told stories and danced and I wasn't too bad, either—if I do say so myself. Booking agents were after me.

Although I was making out okay working in night clubs, and business was good in my joint on Eighth Avenue, I kept looking for my own night club. I wanted a large place where I could be boss and make the big money. I soon heard that such a spot was available—in Keansburg, New Jersey.

It was called the Wagon Wheel. I rented it, sight unseen, by phone. I thought it was a high-class place with big-time entertainment. I went down there to take over a few days before Memorial Day, 1938. Beforehand, I hired help and entertainers. I had good contacts. I got Lupe Velez, the Mexican Bombshell.

I also brought Willie Lewis, the bartender, and a couple of waiters from my New York place.

We took a boat from New York to Keansburg and only had to walk a block from the boardwalk to the Wagon Wheel. I nearly died when I saw it. I had expected a big, beautiful place that I could be proud of . . . and which would make a lot of money. This was a hole-in-the-wall, dingy, old, run-down, and it seated only two hundred people. It sickened me. I was embarrassed.

"Well, I loused things up," I apologized. "You see what I've got here. It looks like I won't make enough money to pay you off. You can get out of your contracts if you want to."

262

My people huddled to discuss it and decided to stick with me and take what I could afford to pay—for awhile, anyway.

I was so grateful that I decided to give them a treat.

I went next door to a Greek restaurant and borrowed a case of liquor. The first drinks in the joint were on me.

I never did stop buying drinks in that place. I was still America's host. But I did one smart thing. That was to bring an old friend of my father's, Tim Corbett, down to manage the place for me. I thought I was doing him a favor by giving him a summer job. It turned out that I was getting the favor. If it hadn't been for Tim, nobody would have been paid off.

I was constantly drunk. I sure had the opportunity. We were open every minute of the day that the law allowed. We did the best business that any place in Keansburg had ever done. Nobody in town went thirsty if I could help it.

My New York friends came down on weekends or on their nights off. Entertainers, I mean. They'd put their talent out for me free and give my customers shows that topped anything on Broadway.

A skinny little kid named Frankie used to hang around and volunteered to sing. I gave him a chance and he turned out to be a terrific entertainer. Nobody had ever heard of him and he'd sing for nothing, just for the chance to be heard.

Even though he was puny, he was tough. He never ducked a fight and he got into a lot of them. Drunks and show-offs would pick on him because he looked anemic. Rather than take the ribbing, he'd fight all comers.

He could sing, too. The way he belted out a song was sensational. A real personality kid. He was only seventeen

263

then but I could see what a future he had ahead of him. And to think I never paid a red cent to Frank Sinatra.

CHAPTER TWENTY-SEVEN

Love bit me again that summer. One evening, I was sitting in our little office in the rear of the place when the bartender buzzed for me. Sitting at the bar were two girls, each about eighteen.

I walked up to the bartender and he whispered, "Mickey, I can't serve these kids. They're too young."

"I'm sorry," I told the girls, "but we are not permitted to serve minors. You'll have to leave."

They didn't put up an argument and I walked out into the street with them. I asked the prettier one, a honey-blond, her name. I wanted to know her. Eleanor Marvil was her name and she came from Jersey City. She was in Keansburg on vacation and was staying in the same hotel where I lived.

"Do you like to swim?" I asked.

She loved it, she said.

"Then suppose we meet on the beach tomorrow morning?" I suggested. She agreed.

Eleanor turned out to be a good swimmer and we spent a lot of mornings and afternoons together. It wasn't long before I took her out evenings, too.

I continued seeing Eleanor after her summer vacation was over and she returned to Jersey City, where she lived with her parents. We were in love. Clara and I had been separated for more than two years and our marriage was on the rocks. Finally, she sued for divorce early in 1939 and I didn't contest it. In the settlement, I let her have the house and land in Shrewsbury. She later sold it to Jack Delaney, a restaurant owner in Greenwich Village. He cut up the fifty acres into a housing development.

Two months after the divorce, Eleanor and I drove to Virginia and were married.

I didn't renew my lease on the Wagon Wheel in the summer of 1939. I didn't think that type of environment —late hours and a honky-tonk joint—was for Eleanor. We lived at the Belvedere, but I intended to move back to Elizabeth.

This was my fourth marriage, counting my double marriage to Clara back in 1931. I wanted it to last. I knew that my own personal faults—excessive drinking and carousing—were responsible for the breakup of the others. I was thirty-eight and realized if I didn't settle down, I probably never would. I had paid too high a price for my fun. My drinking had cost me the loss of friends and self-respect. If I continued this way, my health would be the next to go.

I became ashamed to have Eleanor see me drunk so often. I could see the hurt look in her eyes when she had to take care of me after a bad night. There must have been times when she was ashamed of me, but she never complained. She knew I was too bullheaded to try to reform me. My brother and others had tried and failed.

The problem was mine. I had to lick it myself. But it wasn't easy. I cut down, but continued to drink. I just couldn't cut it out altogether.

I tried to keep busy with other things. I even became a legitimate actor. I got a small part in a play by Marguerite

Herter called *Hi Angel,* at Woodstock's Maverick Theater in Newark. The show closed in two weeks.

I went back to night-club entertaining. I worked at the Blue Moon in Newark for a fat week's salary, plus a percentage of the gross. The fellow tending bar was Jackie Gleason. He used to come out from behind the bar and help me in my act. He was very funny, even then.

I was asked to make a personal appearance one evening in Brooklyn at a dinner in honor of an old friend, Johnny Summers. I had fought him back in 1921, taking a ten-round decision. After the affair, I intended to go over to my brother's house in Elizabeth, since Eleanor was visiting with her folks in Jersey City.

The party for Summers was in a night club and lasted most of the night. I didn't get to Elizabeth until eight in the morning, by which time I was carrying a good package. Once again, my good intentions went to hell.

I drove my big Pierce Arrow from Brooklyn to Jersey without getting into any trouble, though I can't remember how I did it or how long it took. It was almost a complete blank, but I must have partially sobered up while driving.

It had been a long time since I'd seen my old pals in Elizabeth and I got the idea to drop in on Eddie Coakley, who ran a café. I figured I'd have a nightcap before going to brother Joe's.

Coakley was just opening up and there was only one customer in the place, a skinny little guy who I knew had to be one of those hollow-legged barflies. I'd never seen him before.

I ordered a drink and bought one for this guy, too. After a while, some of my old pals came in and, of course, I bought rounds for them.

Every round included the little stranger. I kept buying

and drinking as the day wore on. By early evening, I began to get sleepy and wanted to go to bed. But more and more friends who had heard I was there came by to say hello and I had to have a drink with every one of them.

Finally, I just couldn't take it any longer. I was sick from so much drinking. I announced that I was going to leave. I'd had too much liquor, even for me. I had been drinking steadily in this joint for nearly twelve hours.

When he heard I was going, this rum-soaked character grabbed me by the sleeve.

"Buy me one more drink," he croaked. "One more drink."

"Sorry, Mac, I'm busted," I answered. "And I'm tired. I'm going home to sleep."

He looked at me in disgust, blinking his bloodshot eyes.

"Why, you cheap son-of-a-bitch," he snarled. "Here I've been keeping you company all day, and you won't even buy me one last little drink. That's the thanks I get."

My Irish temper came up and I cocked my right arm to bust him on the jaw. But I held back, stopping the punch in mid-air. Suddenly I saw myself as this weasel must have . . . a lush, a sucker for a touch, a washed-up pug, a drunken sot ready to sprawl in the gutter.

I shuddered. For the first time in my life, I was utterly fed up with myself. I knew now why others had become disgusted with me. The full meaning of it hit me with a terrific impact.

What a sight *I* must have been down through the years. How much trouble I had caused through drinking to excess—the broken marriages, the problems I created for others who had to take care of me. I recalled it with loathing. What a miserable mutt I must have been on the drunken orgy with Mayor Hague's secretary, sleeping on saloon floors and in back rooms; the heartbreak it must have been for my good mother and my wives . . . the rotten example I had been to my children. What a fool I was. How repulsive I must have looked to poor Joe when he had to come and drag me out of a cheap bar.

What good had it all been? This self-degradation, this reckless ruination, those days and nights in an alcoholic fog?

I never fully realized before what a sorry-looking sight I had made. It took a drunk to point it out to me.

It was like looking into a mirror.

I stared at this shriveled-up, drunken bum—and I saw myself.

"Thanks, friend," I said. "You don't know it but you just did me a hell of a favor."

I called the bartender.

"Eddie," I said. "Lend me twenty bucks and give everybody in the house a drink. It's on me. And make mine a small beer."

I picked up my beer and turned to the crowd.

"Gentlemen," I said, raising the glass high as if making a toast. "This is my last drink. I'll never take another as long as I live."

The date was September 1, 1939—the day Hitler marched into Poland and exploded the second great war on the world.

I haven't had a drink since.

CHAPTER TWENTY-EIGHT

By the time I got to Joe's house, I was feeling a little better about things. I was tired, but I didn't fall asleep for a long time. I lay in bed thinking. Where was I going? What had I accomplished? I had made a lot of money, but what had I to show for it? My weakness for the bottle and for broads had led to brawls, in and out of the courts, damage to my reputation and loss of respect.

I had reached the heights dreamed of by so many but scaled by so few and all I had to show for it was the loss of two fortunes, two homes and two wives.

Before falling asleep I determined to start a new kind of life.

Early the next morning, I set about finding out if there was anything left of Mickey Walker. I had an idea and was going to give it a try.

The first thing I did was to sever all connections with the Toy Bulldog saloon in New York. That was easy. I just decided I'd never go back to the joint. Let Duffy do whatever he wanted to with my half-share. He could have it—as a present.

Next, I sought out two pals. One was "Kinch" Kintchner, a bartender at Eddie Coakley's. The other was Frank Terrill, an accountant who had gone to pot because of the same malady I had . . . excessive drinking. As long as I was in a reforming mood, why not reform my friend Frank, too? I was broke so I borrowed twenty bucks from Coakley. That made it forty I owed him, including the twenty for that last round of drinks.

Having picked up Kinch and Frank, I drove to Jersey City for Eleanor. I told her of my idea. There was a fellow I knew who had a big café up in Fort Montgomery, New York, near West Point. He once had told me that any time I wanted to become his partner, he'd be glad to take me up on it.

Eleanor, happy that I had decided to give up my dissipated way of living, was delighted. She assured me of all the help she could give.

Except for my brother Joe, his wife Mary, and Frank and Kinch, I told no one of my plans. I just packed up and left. I was determined to get away from my old haunts and start from scratch in a place where no one knew me.

My café-owner friend at Fort Montgomery was happy to take me in as a partner. He settled Eleanor and me in comfortable living quarters in a motel he owned, next door to the café.

Business picked up considerably soon after I joined him. I was host, official greeter, and bottle-washer. I engaged Kintchner as an extra bartender and Terrill took charge of the books. I brought in entertainment, direct from Broadway, and took over as master of ceremonies. With top-notch shows, our café soon became a popular spot.

Some of my best weekend customers were cadets from West Point. We ran a respectable place and the future generals always behaved themselves like future generals.

I met an old friend there, Billy Kavanaugh, a former fighter and referee who had become boxing coach at West Point. Billy invited me to watch some of his boxing classes and occasionally I helped with instructions.

After two months at Fort Montgomery, I had to make

an important decision. Kavanaugh retired and recommended that I succeed him as boxing coach at the military academy. I was offered the appointment but turned it down. I wasn't afraid of it, but felt I wasn't for the job. I couldn't take orders; I couldn't stand discipline; I knew I'd break every regulation in the book. At West Point, a man on duty couldn't even breathe cockeyed.

Drinking had nothing to do with my decision. I had been off the bottle for months. And strange as it may sound, I didn't miss it. From the time I gave up drinking, more than twenty years ago, I have never once had the urge to take a drink. It isn't a question of will power. I just thought it all out and convinced myself that drinking was no longer for me. I had to quit for keeps—and somehow, I have never wanted even a taste of it since.

Six months after we arrived at Fort Montgomery, two events took place almost simultaneously. First, Eleanor became pregnant. I took her back to Jersey City so she could be with her folks when the baby came. Second, Bill Duffy found me. He had been looking high and low for me ever since my disappearance. Finally he got the idea I might be up in the country. This used to be his territory and he knew I had always enjoyed my visits with him.

Bill pleaded with me to come back.

"This is no place for you," he argued. "Quit the sticks, Mickey, and come back to New York."

I hadn't the faintest notion of going back. I hadn't been so content in years. Finally he realized he was just wasting his time.

"What will I do with the Toy Bulldog?" he asked. "The joint's gone down since you left. I've been busy. There's nobody to take care of it."

"I don't care what you do with it," I said. "Give it away, for all I care."

That's just what he did. He gave it to a friend of ours, Johnny Rock. Johnny's dead now and the Toy Bulldog has changed hands since then but they still keep the name.

Kerry was born in the spring of 1940. I now had at least one child by each of my wives: Mickey, Jr., and Pat with Maude; Jimmy with Clara, and Kerry with Eleanor. They've all turned out fine. I'm very lucky to have such wonderful children.

My partner was doing better than he ever dreamed. Business was good—too good, in fact. He got ideas. He became involved in deals that I didn't like. I told him I'd leave him if he continued. We argued. My mind was made up for me a few days later when the police became suspicious and started investigating. I figured I'd had enough and walked out.

I had somewhere to go. A fellow in Kingston, only a few miles north of Fort Montgomery, had been after me for some time to manage his café. He had split up with his partner. I took the offer.

I stayed there a year and did well. But my wanderlust overcame me again. I never could stay too long in one place. A friend tipped me off to a café in Poughkeepsie which he said I could buy cheaply. I liked the looks of it and bought it.

I had saved up a little money, for I had two jobs at the time. In addition to the restaurant, I had become a radio sports commentator, conducting a show five nights a week. The station was located in Poughkeepsie, a major consideration in my moving there. I interviewed local sports celebrities, read the sports news, gave the weather and occasionally the general news.

The place clicked and I should have made a lot of money, but I didn't. I just couldn't seem to hang on to the profits. I spent five thousand dollars remodeling it, for example. And I trusted too many people who turned out to be dead beats.

Another man would have become rich, another Toots Shor, maybe.

Oh, the business netted me a fair living, but that was all. I had no feeling for it and began to feel my feet itching again. I became moody. The joint annoyed me and I was getting tired of it. I felt imprisoned and wanted to break out. Something was bothering me, but I couldn't figure out what it was.

I had a visitor one day, my brother Joe. It didn't take him long to sense that something was wrong.

Joe insisted I take the day off and go out to play golf with him. I didn't want to leave the business, but he persuaded me. We drove to a golf course in Elizabeth.

Joe invited a couple of his friends and we played as a foursome. It was the most relaxing day I had spent in a long time. I enjoyed myself immensely even though it was the first time in years that I played through eighteen holes of golf without having my caddy follow me around with a case of champagne or beer.

Later, as we were showering in the clubhouse, my brother spoke up.

"You know, Ed, I don't remember when I've seen you so relaxed."

"Yes," I agreed. "I'm really enjoying this. It sure feels good being back with old friends in my old home town."

Suddenly, I knew what was wrong.

"Joe," I said, "I'm coming back. Back to my home town. I've missed it. I miss the old gang."

"What are you going to do with your café in Pough-keepsie?" asked Joe.

"Leave it . . . give it away. I don't know."

"What's the matter with you, Ed?" Joe demanded. "Are you nuts? You just sank five grand into the place."

"I don't give a damn. I'm coming back to Elizabeth."

"But, Ed," Joe pleaded, "you can't get up and leave a good business just like that. You've got a big investment up there. Think it over."

"I have thought it over. Find a place in Elizabeth that's for sale. I want to come home."

Two days later, I was back in Elizabeth. I got out of a ten-year lease in the Poughkeepsie place by giving up the fixtures and improvements to the owner. Of course, I didn't get any money.

Joe found a spot . . . a café that was making out poorly but looked good to me if it were run right. The owner was in debt and I agreed to give him fifteen hundred dollars and take over the bills. Impulsive as ever, I didn't even check the books. Whew! What a shock. It turned out that he owed twelve thousand dollars to the landlord and to food and liquor wholesalers.

Luck was with me. It was in the summer of 1941 and already there were many servicemen in the area. We weren't at war yet but the draft was on and the Army was building up. I called my place The First Round, which had a double meaning: as the first round of a fight or the first round of drinks.

It was a money-maker from the beginning. Besides the GI's, there were many defense plants in the area—and those defense workers had the dough to spend.

Since I had abandoned the bottle and Broadway, my life was different. I spent more time with my family. My reformation was complete. I gave up the old friends of the saloon set and completely divorced myself from the sporting crowd. The only contact I kept with boxing was to serve as a referee in fight clubs in the East.

The adjustment wasn't easy. No excitement, no parties. It was quiet and at times downright boring. For entertainment, Eleanor and I visited friends, went dancing and took in a movie occasionally.

One evening, brother Joe and his wife, Mary, Eleanor and I went to see *The Moon and Sixpence* at a theater in Elizabeth. The picture was based on Somerset Maugham's book on the life of the French painter, Gauguin, in Tahiti. I didn't know who Gauguin was but I had read some of Maugham's books. I had met the writer at Billy DeBeck's apartment years earlier during the Roaring Twenties.

The picture had a strange effect on me. I was disturbed but I couldn't quite understand the feeling. I couldn't get it out of my mind and slept little that night for thinking about it. I had never been thrilled like this by a movie before. I just had to see it again, alone. I went back the next day and got the same impression—a tingling sensation which I couldn't figure out. I went back a third day. I was in the theater when it hit me—I envied this guy who could paint so beautifully. I envied his way of living. I pictured myself in his place. If I could only paint like that, I thought. Suddenly, I wanted to be an artist. I wanted to paint. That's the way it was with me in those days. I made up my mind on the spur of the moment. I jumped from my seat, impulsive as always, and rushed from the theater. The picture wasn't half over but I knew now what I wanted.

I headed straight for Kramer's art store on Bond Street. "Give me everything an artist needs," I told the clerk.

I wound up with an easel, palette, canvas sketch board, oil tubes, and a fistful of brushes. That set me back about two hundred dollars. Included was a primer for beginners. As I was about to leave, I turned to the clerk.

"Don't tell anyone about this," I warned him. "If I find out that you did, I'll break your jaw."

I had always felt artists were sissies and didn't want to be laughed at by my friends.

I had no idea how to begin. A thousand questions came to my mind, a thousand problems confronted me. All I knew was that I wanted to paint. This was a challenge. I knew it would be tough, maybe harder to lick than anything I ever tried before. But that wasn't going to stop me.

Compared to this, fighting was easy. It came natural to me. Painting didn't. The most important thing I had going for me was desire. Looking back now, I think this feeling for painting was a suppressed desire, unconsciously a part of me for many years.

Having made up my mind to be a painter, I rushed into it with both hands, so to speak. I set up a small studio at home. I read the primer thoroughly and then started to paint. But I couldn't. I still had no idea.

I thought of an old friend, Maxwell Simpson. He used to work out with me at the YMCA in Elizabeth back in 1919. I became a fighter; he went to Paris to study art. Today he is one of America's leading artists.

Maxwell lived only a couple of blocks away. I told him of my ambition and he saw that I was serious. He agreed to help and gave me lessons in private. I still didn't want anybody to know. I put in all my time, outside of business, learning to paint. I went to Simpson's home once a week . . . sometimes oftener if I became confused or discouraged. I would sneak out the canvas under my coat, so nobody would know.

I improved under his guidance. There were times when I became discouraged and was down. Simpson kept after me, however. He thought I showed promise. I was painting for the mere joy of it and felt happiness and contentment while doing it.

It wasn't easy. I had to feel my way, to get my own expression. But Simpson encouraged me. He kept telling me that it was in me and that it would come out.

Soon, nothing else mattered. I painted at every opportunity, and I was no longer bored. I had the feeling I was beginning a new career. Painting had become a happy obsession with me.

All this time, nobody outside my family knew I was painting.

I thought nothing could stop my fervor but something happened which made me put aside my brush and palette for a while.

On December 7, 1941, the Japanese attacked Pearl Harbor.

Of course, I wanted to get into the war. I had been too young for the first one, but I felt sure I could help in this one. Like most Americans, my blood boiled against the Germans and Japs.

I was in Boston to referee a fight between Freddie "Red" Cochran and Garvey Young. Red was from Elizabeth and Young was a Bean-towner. In talking to the promoter a couple of days before the fight, I told him, "This is my last refereeing job, Sam. I'm going into the service. I'm going to join up."

"What branch of service are you goin' to enlist in?" he asked.

"I don't know," I answered. "Maybe the Air Force."

I knew they wouldn't take me as a pilot because of my age, but I hoped they'd take me as a bombardier or a gunner. I had read that older men from the movie and entertainment fields had been accepted for these jobs.

"Why not join up here?" Sam suggested. "I can get you a lot of publicity and I'm sure the story will help the fight [box office]."

I agreed. The next afternoon, I went to the Navy recruiting office and told them what I wanted to do. Photographers and reporters from Boston papers were there to cover my enlistment.

The officer behind the desk interviewed me after I filled out the application form. He noted my age. I was going to be forty-one in a few months. He looked up.

"All right, Mr. Walker. When the Navy gets around to your age limit, we'll call you. This is a young man's navy."

"What is the age limit for fliers?" I asked.

"Twenty-six," he answered, trying to keep a straight face.

The newspapermen laughed. "You better win the war with the USO, Mick," one cracked.

The story was in the papers the next day, having gone out on the Associated Press wire.

One of the head men in the USO read it in a New York paper and it gave him an idea. His job was to line up entertainment for our men overseas. He recruited champion athletes in various fields to demonstrate their talent in athletic shows. I signed on as master of ceremonies for a show he had in mind.

He got together a fine troupe of wonderful guys. Jack Redman, a trick-shot golfer, was one of the star performers. One stunt of his wowed the audiences. He'd tee up a golf ball and take a full swing at it as if driving it out into the audience. The soldiers would duck and yell, only to see the ball go straight up into the air and come down in Jack's hand.

We also had Bobby Walthour, a six-day bike rider who did tricks on his wheel. There was Lou Pagliaro, table tennis champ, and his partner, a red-headed Irish girl from Brooklyn. She was the best woman player in the world and they always gave a great performance. Joe Pasco, champion bag-puncher, also was with us. He was over fifty but he could make a punching bag talk once he got his hands moving. One cute stunt of his was to have the GI's sing popular songs while he punched the bag in time with the rhythm.

We were assigned to tour bases in South America, Africa and the Mediterranean areas. Once we had a show to do at a camp in Africa and as we were landing at Dakar air base, I spotted a native village nearby. I was intrigued by the large grass huts of cone-shaped design. There also were smaller shacks with red roofs.

I borrowed a jeep one afternoon and drove over to the village. I took along my pastel crayons and a sketch pad and spent several hours sketching the scene. I became so engrossed in my work that I forgot the time. It wasn't until the light began to fade that I realized I had to rush back to the base to do the show.

Painting had taken such a hold on me that I plunged back into it when I returned from overseas. I didn't have to spend too much time in The First Round. It was a good money-maker; saloon keeping was a very good business during the war. I was back in the chips and with the money rolling in I could devote most of my time to painting.

I painted every day without letup. I went right to the easel as soon as I got up in the morning. Sometimes I even got up in the middle of the night when the desire to paint came over me. In my zeal, I even missed meals. I had no daily schedule. I just worked, worked, worked. My subjects were mostly portraits, landscapes and still life. I never seemed to lack for inspiration.

One day my friend Bill Corum, the sports columnist, called me at home and said he was coming over. By that time, I had done about thirty paintings and many of them were hanging on the walls of the living and dining rooms.

Before Bill arrived, I took down the canvasses and hid them in closets.

After dinner, Bill sat in the living room with a drink and a cigarette. As we were talking, I saw him staring past me at the wall. I turned and saw that I had forgotten to take down one painting, a six-by-ten-inch landscape.

I tried to distract him with conversation but he refused to take his eyes off the painting. Finally, he arose and walked over for a closer look. He noticed my signature in the bottom right-hand corner.

"Did you really paint that?" Corum asked.

"I did," I admitted sheepishly. "It's just a hobby, Bill, that's all."

I tried to laugh it off but he wouldn't believe me.

"Hobby, my eye," Bill snapped. "I'm no art expert but this looks like a professional job to me. How long have you been at this?"

I had to tell him that I had been painting for a few years. He asked whether I had any others around to show him. He made me show him the rest.

Corum was astonished. He kept shaking his head. He was especially impressed with one painting of two fighters

280

in a ring. It depicted one man down for the count as the referee raised the right arm of the victor. I called it "Ten and Out."

"What a story," he kept repeating. "What a great story this would make."

"Please, Bill," I appealed to him. "Don't give me away. If you do, I swear I'll punch your head off. I don't want this thing to become a big joke in the fight racket. People would think I had gone soft in the head . . . an ex-pug interested in painting."

"You're wrong, Mickey," Corum said. "They won't look at it that way. This work is too good to be hidden in the closet. Others should see and appreciate it."

I could see Corum's mind working. He snapped his fingers.

"I know what I'm going to do," he almost shouted, "I'm going to give you the greatest art exhibit any man ever had."

I guess my vanity was tickled. I went along. I told Bill I'd leave everything in his hands.

Corum wasted no time. Within a month, in May of 1944, he set up a one-man show at the Waldorf-Astoria Hotel and induced a magazine called *Click* to sponsor it. He helped to promote it with a column about my work as an artist—so everyone now knew.

Corum invited art critics and newspapermen. I couldn't ignore my old friends in Elizabeth, so I invited them. When my New York crowd heard that their old pal had gone artistic, they turned out to see what it was all about.

It was a strange mixture: Park Avenue critics and art lovers milling around with my Keighry Head and Broadway pals. There were fighters, Tenth Avenue dock wallopers, con men, jockeys and shills. Many borrowed or stole tuxedos, cutaways or other formal wear. Others came in sports jackets and turtleneck sweaters.

Corum, a born promoter, outdid himself. He even had newsreel cameras cover the exhibit. The Park Avenue clientele didn't mind mingling with the riff-raff. They rather enjoyed it; sort of slumming, you know. It was a funny sight to see those low-brow characters sipping champagne and trying to discuss art. Ninety percent of them had never tasted the grape before and I doubt that even one of them had ever been in an art gallery.

Unquestionably the *pièce de rèsistance* was a newsreel statement made by Tony Galento, the former heavyweight contender from New Jersey, who was a friend of mine and my guest. Galento, sometimes referred to as "The Human Beer Barrel," came wearing a monocle on a black velvet ribbon, a beret and a smock. It was all part of a gag, of course. Galento, posing as an art critic, had spent two hours rehearsing a couple of lines: "The perspective is distorted and the subordination of technique to composition is indubitably fatuous."

When the newsreel cameras lighted up, he became flustered and forgot what he was supposed to say. He used his own words and they were even funnier.

The whole thing turned out to be such a success that less than a year later, the Associated American Artists Galleries, at 711 Fifth Avenue, through the director, George Fortson, invited me to exhibit another one-man show. It attracted one of the biggest crowds the establishment ever had. This time my friends weren't there, just art "critics." My paintings drew admiring comments. Such adjectives as "stimulating," "interesting," and "true American primitive" were used.

What satisfied me most was that six of my canvasses

were sold, at prices ranging from seventy-five to one thousand dollars.

A couple of years later, just before Christmas of 1947, Doc Kearns pulled a stunt which helped me gain national prominence as an artist. He was opening a Lincoln agency in Chicago and asked me to send him one of my paintings. I thought he wanted to dress up his showroom.

I had just finished a canvas called "December Masquerade." It was a winter scene, a man carrying a pack on his back as he climbed a ladder. I sent him this picture. Instead of hanging it in his showroom, Doc entered it in an exhibition at Marshall Field Galleries, claiming it was Santa Claus delivering Christmas packages.

Ten days later, he sent me a sheaf of clippings from Chicago newspapers, some of which ran the story on the front pages and some on the sports pages.

Unfortunately, they kidded the work in gag captions with the Santa Claus interpretation. Actually, it was a scene from Murray Bay, Canada, where I had trained for some of my fights.

The painting took first prize in the exhibition. It was a great honor. I didn't know at the time that a five-thousand-dollar prize went with it.

I read in a newspaper, some years later, that Doc sold the picture for fifteen thousand.

CHAPTER TWENTY-NINE

With my painting and my business both flourishing, I had it good. But like many parents then, I had a daily worry.

My son, Mickey, Jr., was in the Marines as a bombardier and was going through the toughest action in the Pacific. He started out in the Navy as a pilot, but was so reckless that they grounded him. He then transferred to the Marine Corps. Thank God he came through it without an injury. He won the Silver Star.

Jimmy, then thirteen, was a regular visitor in Elizabeth. He lived in Brooklyn with Clara, who had by this time sold the house in Shrewsbury. She and Jimmy were with her folks. Because of Jimmy, Clara and I saw each other quite often.

Seeing Clara so frequently rekindled the spark in me. I discovered myself falling in love with her again. It got to the point where I decided I had to have a serious talk with her. I told her I loved her still and she said she felt the same way.

I was in quite a predicament. Here I was, married, but in love with my ex-wife. I finally decided to bring the whole thing out in the open. It was only fair to Eleanor that I explain.

Eleanor was very understanding. She thought it best for all concerned that she get a divorce. She got it in 1946 and I was free to remarry Clara.

Part of the settlement was that I'd maintain support of Eleanor and Kerry. In fact, they continued to live with me. I bought a huge house in Cranford, New Jersey, and set them up in a private apartment in one wing. Clara, Jimmy and I lived in the main part of the place. Clara and Eleanor got along very well.

When the war was over, Mickey, Jr., went to Cornell to study architecture. He spent the summer as well as Easter and Christmas vacations with us. So I had three of my four children with me much of the time. I was getting older and it made me feel good to have the kids around me. Only Pat was missing. She was with Maude, my first wife, in California, and I had never seen her.

Now my painting took up nearly all my time. I had little interest in anything else and once more, ironically, I began to neglect my family and friends. I was making a reputation for myself and was invited to join the American Contemporary Artists. My one-man exhibits were praised by art critics. I was so absorbed in art that I didn't realize a new rift was growing between Clara and myself. She had been a young artist herself when I married her the first time, but she had lost all feeling for it. She was opposed to my painting because she saw what it was doing to our marriage.

I neglected Clara woefully. I seldom took her out, and friends dropped in for visits only on rare occasions. They knew I'd be occupied with my work and they wouldn't be welcome. I just wanted to be at home alone with my brush and palette.

Clara did manage to tear me away from my easel long enough to take her Christmas shopping in 1947. After shopping we went to dinner, then to a movie. It was the first time in months that I had shown her any consideration.

When we came out of the theater, snow was falling heavily. That turned out to be the biggest snowfall ever recorded in the metropolitan area.

We were driving through the town of Garwood about 10:30 P.M. and I was fascinated by a snow scene. By then, I always carried sketch pads, crayons and artist's pencils in the car. I had promised Clara I wouldn't touch a brush until after New Year's, but as soon as I saw this scene, I forgot my promise. The glittering beauty of the white

285

snow and moonlight dazzled me. I had to sketch it. I put the lights on inside the car and sat there for an hour and a half, sketching.

Clara was cold, bored and disgusted. When we finally got home, she was so furious she went to bed without speaking to me. I didn't even notice. The only thing on my mind was the snow scene.

I couldn't get the scene out of my mind during the night. The next morning, I rushed to Swain's, bought a large canvas and laid out the drawing with charcoal.

I got so involved with this painting that I didn't even realize it when Christmas Eve arrived. Friends came over and Clara had to practically drag me from the easel. I couldn't wait to get rid of the guests and it wasn't a very Christmas-like atmosphere.

After the guests left, Clara and I got into a loud argument. A truce was finally agreed upon when I promised I'd take her out New Year's Eve. But when that holiday rolled around, I forgot my promise and stayed with the painting. I had also promised Clara a Florida vacation in January. But first I had to get this painting finished for an exhibition at the ACA Galleries. She decided to go alone to Florida.

I said I'd meet her in Miami, but she knew I wouldn't. I wasn't even thinking of Florida. The painting was the only thing on my mind, night and day.

Three weeks later, I received a letter from Clara. She was suing for a divorce.

"Painting is your only love," she wrote.

I guess she was right.

I finally finished the scene and it was accepted for the spring exhibition.

Clara got her divorce early in the summer of 1948. In

her bill of divorcement she charged: "Art is Mickey's new mistress."

With another marriage on the rocks, I decided to make the best of things and spend more time with the kids. Mickey, Jr., and I planned a vacation at Manasquan, on the Jersey shore, when he came home from Cornell for summer vacation.

I had begun another painting by then, a portrait of a teen-age girl. Mickey looked closely at the canvas.

"Gee Dad, you got a touch of Pat in that painting," he remarked.

I laid down the brush and we moved to the living room. I began to talk about Pat and reminded Mickey that I had never seen her, and that I had not seen their Mother, Maude, in eighteen years. I wanted very much to see my daughter.

I got an idea.

"Do you think your mother and I could hit it off again after all these years?" I asked my son.

"I don't know, Dad," Mickey answered. "But why don't you find out? Give her a call. I have the number."

I called Maude in Los Angeles. She hadn't remarried. We talked as though we hadn't been separated at all, almost as if I had been out with her the previous night. I described my conversation with Mickey and the purpose of the call.

"Would you like to give it a try again?" I asked.

She said it might be possible and agreed to come East to discuss it. When she arrived, we all went to Manasquan for a week's vacation. The years hadn't changed her much; she still looked pretty.

By the time Maude was to return to California, it was agreed that we'd marry again and that I'd move out to the West Coast. Maude had invested her money wisely and her business interests wouldn't let her leave California. I cut all ties in the East. I sold the house in Cranford and also got rid of my café in Elizabeth.

It took me a month to clean up all the loose ends. Then I took Kerry and flew to Los Angeles to remarry Maude.

Seeing Pat for the first time, I realized how much she looked like me. She had my blue eyes, my nose, my chin and the same mannerisms. She was full of life and fun. She had the same coloring and same stocky build. She even had a temper like mine. If she had been a boy, we would have another ring champ in the Walker family. I showed Pat more attention than I did her mother, I'm afraid.

Pat, Kerry, Maude and I lived in Maude's house in Beverly Hills. Many of the movie stars lived in the area, but the night life of Hollywood had lost its appeal for me. Twenty years before, when I was looking at it for the first time, I was a part of it and it seemed to have everything I would ever want. Now, it wasn't for me. This time I mingled with a different crowd, people whose private lives weren't splashed all over the news.

I continued to paint and spent most of my free time with Pat. I also had a sideline. Since 1948, I had been sports editor of the *Police Gazette*, a New York weekly devoted to sports and entertainment. I kept that connection while living in California.

Pat is a very religious Catholic girl and we weren't together very long when she began to get on me for not going to church. I hadn't been inside a church since she was born.

Pat kept after me about going to confession. I tried to tell her that as a divorced man I couldn't receive the Sacraments of the Church. Besides, I was afraid of confession. I'd never become a criminal but it seemed to me I'd committed practically every sin. Even if I did go to confession, I wouldn't know where to begin. I had so much to confess.

One day Pat and I were visiting Gene Fowler at his home outside Los Angeles. Another friend, Thomas Mitchell, the great character actor, was there, too. So was a priest, a friend of Gene's.

I remember it well because it was Thanksgiving Day, 1950. Fowler, a devout Catholic, had a special room in his home where he meditated and thought out his problems.

We were at his house about an hour when Fowler asked Pat and me to come with him. We followed Gene into his private quarters.

The first thing my eyes lit upon was a beautiful silver chalice. The windows of the room were open and the glow of the sun on the chalice gave it a holy look.

I stood there speechless. The room was so still, so peaceful. It made me think of Sacred Heart Church in the days when I regularly attended Mass. It made me think of my First Holy Communion. It took me out of myself.

Pat was the proudest girl in the world that Sunday as she stood beside me in church.

I kept busy, but unfortunately Maude got very little of my time. The old feeling between us had gone as suddenly as it had come and it couldn't be revived. From the start, Maude understood that this marriage wasn't going to be one bubbling with romance. She was aware that the real reason I married her a second time was to be back with the children. But this was supposed to be a marriage for companionship. It never turned out that way. We seemed to be in each other's way. I really had thought it would be different. Or maybe I just hoped so.

We never got into any real arguments; in fact, we rarely seemed to have much to discuss between us. We had few mutual interests, aside from the children. She liked to go out and have a good time; by then I found I would rather stay home with the children. That was ironic. Back in our youth, it was the other way around. After awhile, Maude didn't consider me good company and went out by herself. That was all right with me because my painting kept me busy. This went on for several years. She never complained; she just didn't care. As for me, as long as I had my children and my painting, I was content.

I guess it was about four years after Maude and I had remarried that Pat became engaged. I was happy for her because she was in love with a fine young man, but this marked the beginning of the end of my second marriage to Maude. Once Pat married and moved out, I knew there was no more sense in my hanging around. With Pat out of the house, I had no real interest or reason in being there.

So, a few months after Pat's wedding, I suggested to Maude that she get a divorce. She didn't object. In fact, I'm sure she was relieved. We had been together nearly five years but long before that we both realized we had made a mistake trying to grab something back from the past.

I packed up and returned East, taking Kerry with me. He was fifteen. Maude got the divorce in 1955.

CHAPTER THIRTY

I was fifty-four years old and I was determined to have no further serious dealings with women. No longer would they be part of my life. Three wives, six marriages . . . that should be enough for any man—more than enough. Painting was going to get all my attention from now on.

Kerry and I moved in with Aunt Maggie in Spotswood, New Jersey, which is near New Brunswick. Her house was large and she assured me we would have plenty of privacy.

I wasn't back East a week, however, when John Carney, President of the *Police Gazette*, phoned.

"Come to New York," he said, "I want to discuss an important feature series with you."

Carney had something else in mind. He had closed a deal for a restaurant and bar, and he wanted me as partner. I was to be the host and official greeter. What he really was after was my name.

I thought I had said good-bye to the saloon business when I sold my place in Elizabeth nine years before. I had expected to spend the rest of my years painting. But Carney was my friend. He had given me a job when I needed one. Now he needed my help.

The café was on Broadway and Fifty-first Street, opposite Lindy's. It was a small place with room for one hundred and twenty customers.

"We'll have to redecorate," I told Carney. "It will have to be given a new decor."

"Okay, Mickey," he said, "anything you say. We'll

panel the walls and hang up some of your paintings. This is going to be a high-class restaurant. We'll make it an attraction for the highbrows and the smart set as well as for the sports and entertainment headliners.

"As a matter of fact," he added, "I've got the name all picked out. We'll call it The Glove and Palette."

Opening night was a huge success. The joint was packed.

I was the master of ceremonies, of course, and I invited some of my family to come over for the opening: Joe and his wife, Mary, and two of my aunts, Maggie and Nellie.

Aunt Nellie was a straight-laced woman. She was warm-hearted, lovable and homespun—about the closest thing to a saint I ever knew. She was reluctant about going without her husband, a fireman whom she had married in 1919.

Now, more than thirty-five years later, Aunt Nellie was so pleased by the prospect of her first visit to a New York night club that she bought herself a new dress and a new hat for the occasion. The hat was a dilly. It looked like a deep soup plate, kind of Oriental-style.

Aunt Maggie, of course, was an entirely different type. She was dressed in the latest fashion, chic, high-toned and glamorous.

They arrived in Joe's Plymouth coupe, my two aunts in the rumble seat, Joe and Mary in front.

It was quite an evening. Aunt Nellie had never tasted liquor in her life. We told her that a Tom Collins was only lemon juice. She downed two or three in a hurry. Pretty soon her hat was on one side of her head. She sat at the table smoking a cigarette. She had never smoked before and she had about three-quarters of the butt in her mouth.

She was snapping her fingers to the music and calling to the waiter to bring her another "Phil Collins."

I introduced Nellie on the microphone, giving her a big buildup, like she was Marilyn Monroe. She got up and took bows as if the buildup was coming to her. She was really in high gear.

When the meal was being served, she insisted on meeting the cook. The waiter obliged her only because of me. Pretty soon Aunt Nellie and the chef were comparing recipes. She ended up inviting him to her house to taste her vegetable soup.

Aunt Maggie, getting a kick out of her, addressed Nellie as "Broadway Nell." This pleased Nellie.

"Tonight I'm Broadway Nell," she exclaimed. "Tomorrow I'll be plain Nellie again, so I may as well enjoy it."

She did.

My brother and I were the only sober ones in the party. When it got late, I suggested that he take the girls home. It was quite a job loading them into the car.

It was broad daylight when they finally got to Elizabeth. I followed in my car to make sure nothing went wrong. Nellie's husband, who was just about to leave for the firehouse, was furious when he saw her.

"Woman," he screamed at her, "you're drunk."

"You're darn tootin' I am," Aunt Nellie shouted back. "While you were sleeping your fool head off, I was having a whale of a time. I was Broadway Nell. What the hell were you?"

And this was our saintly Aunt Nellie.

From that first night, business was good and Carney was happy. But I wasn't. I had no time to paint and I also felt myself being drawn back to the old Broadway life.

Not that I had any temptation to drink. It was just that I was staying out until all hours and this wasn't my kind of life any more. I stayed on, though, because I didn't want to let Carney down. I felt my leaving would hurt the business.

One evening, Abe Attel, my old pal and former featherweight champ, came in with a blond young lady at his side. They sat in a booth near the bar. I couldn't take my eyes away from Abe's friend. She had blue eyes and when she smiled, which was often, she flashed the most beautiful white teeth I've ever seen.

I could hardly wait for an introduction. The old spark, the one I'd thought smothered forever, had been rekindled. The flame started at my feet and jumped to my head. I was a goner again. Forgotten quickly was my promise to give up women.

Her name was Martha Chudy Gallagher. She was a divorcee and had given up a promising career as a ballet dancer to get married. She was in her early thirties, but she didn't regard the difference in our age as a barrier. I was happier than I'd ever been in my life before.

On January 21, 1956, less than a month after the introduction, I was taking my marriage vows for the seventh time. I made another vow. This was going to be for keeps. She was going to be my last wife.

Judge John MacGuire, my brother's old friend and former would-be manager, performed the ceremony. Governor Robert Meyner of New Jersey was among those who attended the reception at the Essex House in Newark. Marci and I spent our honeymoon in Niagara Falls. It was my first visit to the Falls, and for the first time in my life I began to realize what real love was all about.

I left The Glove and Palette six months later. I took a fling at various other businesses, but none worked out.

One night at Toots Shor's restaurant I heard someone call me. It was my old playmate, Joe Benjamin, the former lightweight contender. After we were seated a few minutes, he asked what I was doing.

"Nothing much," I replied.

"How would you like to go into the liquor business?" he asked.

I shook my head vehemently. "No, Joe," I said quickly. "No more saloons for me. I've had enough."

"You don't understand, Mick," Benjamin said, "I mean selling liquor. You've got a good gift of gab and if you're still the same old personality kid I knew in the old days, you ought to make a good salesman.

"A friend of ours, Ben Ohlandt, is vice-president of National Distillers, the top-flight liquor house that distills such brands at Old Grandad, and Old Crow. I'll make an appointment for you to see him about a job as a public relations man. How about it, Mickey?"

It sounded good. I said okay.

The next day in a huge office on Park Avenue, we came to terms in less than five minutes. When Ben Ohlandt and I parted, I was the National Distillers' special representative.

That was in 1957. I'm still with the company and very happy. It's a good job. I go around the country, attending luncheons, dinners, community and social functions, father-and-son affairs and lodge activities.

I meet all kinds of nice people and learn to appreciate and understand the problems of others. My job is to promote National Distillers' products. I haven't touched a drop since 1939 and you may wonder why I sell something I don't use myself. It isn't so strange. I never induce people to drink liquor; I try only to convince those who drink that ours is the best product on the market.

I was in Washington recently on a business trip and had dinner at Goldie Ahearn's restaurant. Goldie promotes fights in the capital and we have known each other for many years. He stopped at my table and we naturally talked shop. First about the liquor business and then fights. We got to comparing the current fighters with those of my time. I told him I didn't think much of the present-day fighters with the exception of Floyd Patterson, Archie Moore and Ray Robinson.

I said that, even at my age, I could lick the current top middleweights like Paul Pender, Gene Fullmer and Carmen Basilio and a couple of others—provided, of course, that the bout was limited to two or three rounds.

Ahearn seemed to agree. Then he led me to another table and introduced me to a group of men. They were scientists and doctors in town for a medical convention and he related my theory about licking the current crop of fighters.

"Mickey, here, claims he could fight the best middleweights of today and whip them—although he doesn't think he could go more than three rounds," Goldie said.

I explained what seemed to be a boast. I told them that although I was sixty, I was in good physical condition and felt I had the body of a thirty-year-old. I gave Jim Londos as an example. Jim was the heavyweight wrestling champion when he was in his fifties—and that was when wrestling wasn't a vaudeville act. He was a clean liver and great believer in physical culture, proper diet and regular sleeping habits.

"Look at Archie Moore," I told these gentlemen. "He's

close to fifty, according to the record books. Well, I know he's fifty-four. It sounds incredible that a man of that age could be light-heavyweight champion of the world, but it is perfectly logical to me. He's a physical marvel."

The medical men agreed that it was possible for a man of sixty to give an acceptable ring performance, provided he was in perfect physical condition, had the ability and the knowledge, and the fight was limited to a few rounds.

One of the doctors went even further, including proper diet, exercise and rest. He contended he could get me ready within ninety days to fight for the middleweight title.

The wild idea excited me and I might have taken him up on it, except that I knew no boxing commission in its right mind would grant a boxer's license to a sixty-year-old. Still, I just can't help wondering how well I would do if such a thing were possible.

From this, you must get the idea that I don't think much of current fighters. Well, that's right. I'm not one of those good-old-days guys, but I feel that very few of today's fighters compare with the men of my era. Guys are fighting main events on your television screen who couldn't even get into Stillman's Gym to spar for free when I was fighting. Most of them are a pack of TV hams.

Boxers are rushed too fast these days. They never really learn their trade because they become television heroes and are accepted as good fighters. Take Chuck Davey, who actually fought for the welter title a few years ago. He was just a college kid out of Michigan State and had little ability. But the TV buildup got him into the ring with the champ, Kid Gavilan, and he was butchered.

Television is ruining the small clubs, driving them out of business. It is impossible for a small club to keep going because people will not go out and pay to see fights when they can stay home and see them for nothing. Boxers learn their trade in the small clubs. I fought for three years before I could get a bout in New York. The reason there are so few good fighters today is that there are not enough small boxing clubs.

Another factor which hurts the quality of boxing today is that there are too many other careers easily available. Most kids want an education and more people are financially able to send their sons to college. The accent is on specialization and professions.

As a rule, it is only the underprivileged kids from poor neighborhoods who turn to boxing. Look at the youngsters in the Golden Gloves tournaments. They're all kids from settlement houses or boys who have low-paying jobs in industry.

Whenever the general standard of living becomes higher, boxing gets worse. Good times lead to softer living and there are not as many kids willing to go through the drudgery and sacrifice which is demanded for a successful ring career. This generation and the ones to follow are becoming softer and softer. Everything is done by machine in this mechanical age. All things are made easier. I suppose it's progress, and you can't find fault with that. But it doesn't encourage fighters. Boxing is a manual art.

We ought to inaugurate a national program to restore boxing to the status it once had as a sport. The Army and Navy did something of that sort during the war years. Men like Gene Tunney, Rocky Marciano and Gene Fullmer learned to fight in the service.

European governments underwrite health and athletic programs as well as athletes in those countries that dominate international competition—as the Russians have in the Olympics. Countries far poorer than ours find the money for such programs. Sweden has a national health plan, with an accent on gymnastics. So has Switzerland, one of the smallest countries in Europe.

Such a plan could start in high schools and be continued in colleges. Perhaps, then, there would be fewer 4-F's and the country, generally, would be stronger and healthier. The most exercise the average youth gets these days is Rock 'n' Roll. A body built properly and early, lasts a lot longer.

I'm glad I'm not in boxing the way it is today. It is because I love it that I deplore the manner in which the sport has been cheapened. That's why I advised two of my sons, Jimmy and Kerry, against becoming professional boxers. Each had ability and the desire for a ring career.

It's difficult for an ex-fighter to completely divorce himself from the ring. I'm one of the fortunate ones who has been able to do it. My painting and my job have kept my life full. The ring is just a pleasant memory. I'm glad I was a boxer, but Marci and art have given me a contentment I never knew before.

Responsible art critics have been kind to me. I have been called a good artist. Some of my work has been shown in the Metropolitan Museum of Art in New York, in the Philadelphia Academy of Fine Arts and in the London Gallery. I've also exhibited at Carnegie Hall. I guess I've done about two hundred paintings, in all.

However, I'm no Rembrandt. I've still got much to learn. You can live ten lifetimes without knowing all there is to know about painting. Some day, I hope to do a painting so fine that it will be compared to Rembrandt and other masters.

People have asked me why I don't paint boxers. Maybe

it's because I know too much about boxing and too little about art.

Art is no longer a full-time mistress. I paint at every opportunity but it isn't the way it was when I first started to paint. I have learned, finally, that my family is important. I enjoy the time I spend with them.

CHAPTER THIRTY-ONE

Marci and I live in a comfortable apartment in Sutton Place, a quiet and fashionable section in New York City. Marci's daughter, Junior, lives with us. Like her mother, she's blond, beautiful and the brashest twenty-year-old you ever saw. Marci says that I've spoiled her and maybe I have but I love her like my own daughter.

I don't see my own children as much as I would like. Mickey and Pat, both married, live in California. Jimmy lives in New Jersey and Kerry is in the Navy.

Both Jimmy and Kerry had ring ambitions. Jimmy is a graduate of Miami University, where he played football and was a member of the boxing team. I had a more difficult time talking him out of boxing professionally than I had with Kerry later on. Both would have been good, too, but when I pointed out what they'd be up against, the comparatively short time they'd stay in the limelight and make good money, and the difficulties they'd encounter in settling down to the life of a normal citizen again, they agreed to give up the idea.

I remember Kerry was visiting us one evening when the telephone rang and Junior got up to answer it.

"Daddy," she said, "it's for you. Long distance from Los Angeles."

The caller was a friend, a Hollywood screen writer. He said a major film company was interested in making a movie of my life. Could I arrange to come out at once to Hollywood for a conference? They'd pay all the expenses. I said it could be arranged and I'd be out there before the end of the week.

My friend met me at the airport in Los Angeles and drove me to a hotel in Hollywood. He said he had made a dinner appointment for me with the producer that evening at Frank Lyman's restaurant. Frank is a brother of Abe Lyman, the famous band leader.

We took a cab to the restaurant but instead of driving up to the door, my friend told the cab driver to pull up in the parking lot nearby. I could see by the big neon lights that the lot belonged to the NBC Studios. I figured there must be a mistake but before I could say anything, bright lights flashed all around us. I was trying to avoid the glare when I heard a shout:

"Mickey, you're on 'This Is Your Life.' "

I didn't quite grasp the situation. It wasn't until my friend grabbed me by the arm and marched me on the NBC stage that I realized what was happening.

"Oh, hell," I blurted out.

It was a complete surprise. No movie studio was contemplating my life story. The whole thing had been concocted just to get me to come to Hollywood. I had been tricked from the very beginning. They knew that had I known the truth, I never would have come.

It's not that I don't approve of this television show. On the contrary, I think "This Is Your Life" is a dandy show, but I never had a desire to go on it. I used to confide to friends that they couldn't get me to go on that show for a million dollars.

I remember when Barney Ross, the former welterweight champ, was the principal, and also the night they did the life of Lillian Roth, the singer. The theme of these shows was sympathy. Barney and Lillian had sunk to the depths because of dope or liquor and had made comebacks. I know both well and admire both. Barney was a great fighter and Lillian was a wonderful performer. But instead of sympathy, I felt only embarrassment for them.

It depressed me to hear their stories on television. Their confessions sounded sordid. Oh, I agree it took courage and will power on their part to overcome their mistakes, but I cringed as they sat there while their private lives were laid bare to millions of televiewers. It was almost like being undressed in front of the whole world.

"No son-of-a-buck is going to do that to me," I swore to myself. "I don't want anybody ever to feel sorry for me."

Now, here I was in the same position as were Barney and Lillian. All I could think of was how to get the hell out of there. I might have done it, too, if Ralph Edwards, the director of the show, hadn't grabbed me by the arm and led me to a chair. I followed meekly. The audience was like a blur because of the bright lights.

Edwards didn't waste any time. He began his spiel at once. Sure enough, the theme concerned my drinking days, and how I conquered that old devil hootch. I didn't like it; I didn't like it at all . . . and was getting madder by the minute. I was seriously considering one of two things . . . whether to slug him or just get up and march off the stage. Wouldn't that have been something?

I was trying to make up my mind what to do when I heard a familiar voice. I would know that voice anywhere; it belonged to Aunt Maggie. I didn't know it then, of course, but she had been standing in the wings waiting to be called. But she couldn't restrain herself when she heard Edwards telling the audience what a heavy drinker I once had been and she barged out like a tigress.

"That's not true, Mr. Edwards," she screamed, pointing an accusing finger at the stunned director. "My Edward never drank like that."

I looked at dear old Aunt Maggie, ready to scratch Edwards' eyes out, and I burst out laughing. It was one of the funniest sights I ever saw. Aunt Maggie kept pushing forward and pointing that finger while Edwards kept backing off. I felt like getting up and applauding the old scrapper. I thought she was going to haul off and let the poor fellow have a fistful right on the kisser. I was half-hoping she would. The people in the audience didn't know what to make of it. They didn't know whether to laugh or be alarmed, because they didn't know whether it was staged or not.

Aunt Maggie ignored the audience.

"My Edward is a good boy," she shouted, "and don't you give anyone the impression he isn't."

Poor Edwards. For a couple of moments, he just stood helplessly, trying to recover his wits. He didn't know what to say. He had a script all prepared for the show, of course, but Aunt Maggie had certainly put a crimp in it.

I'll say this for Edwards: he made a good recovery.

"Now, now, dear lady," he said soothingly, "I have a great deal of admiration for Mickey. I would never say anything uncomplimentary about him. I think he deserves a great deal of credit for what he's done."

This seemed to satisfy Aunt Maggie and the tension

eased. Edwards, having regained some of his composure, introduced Aunt Maggie to the audience and led her to a chair at my left. I winked at her.

The show continued uninterrupted, but Edwards was careful not to make any more references to my drinking. Instead, we discussed some of my fights, talked about my children and devoted the major portion of the program to my painting. Ralph even exhibited some of my pictures. I wondered how he got them—there were about eight or ten canvasses—until he introduced my daughter, Pat. Of course, she was responsible; I had left a number of paintings with her when I went back East.

I don't know how much the audience was entertained, but I got a big bang out of the show. I saw friends and relatives I hadn't seen in years. Johnny Anthes, my first manager, was there. Old Johnny is gone now, the good Lord rest his soul. I was surprised to see Dominic Orsini, the boy I fought in my first professional bout. Lew Tendler, who tried to win my welterweight crown from me, was introduced. Lew, a good fighter in his day, is a successful restaurateur now, with places in Philadelphia, Atlantic City and Miami Beach.

Mickey, Jr., who is an architect in Los Angeles, was there, with his wife and four children. So was Pat. The last one to be called out to the stage, I think, was my brother Joe. He had helped arrange the entire thing but had never let out a peep to me.

It was a good show and a happy evening for me. But in no sense was it a portrayal of my life . . . not in the least. How could it be? How could you wrap up anyone's life in thirty minutes? How is it possible for anyone but myself to really describe what kind of a life I led? A few remarks . . . a few pictures . . . a few friends . . . a few relatives? These things and people were just part of my life.

Where was Doc Kearns, who probably knows more about me than any living person today? Why, he could have told the people more in five minutes than all the others could have in five days. But Doc, who was as much a part of my life as anyone, wasn't there.

Where was Jack Dempsey? Where was Teddy Hayes, my trainer; and Jimmy Duryea, my chauffeur?

Harry Greb, if he were still alive, could have told them about Mickey Walker. And Jack Bulger, my old manager, who was my tutor, my friend, my second father. And Mother Regina and Sister Anselma, who fretted and worried over me. Oh, if Mike, my old man, could have been there. Mike, who used to cuss me out for fighting—but stuck out his chest when he heard people talking about his famous son, the champion boxer. And Liz, my mother, who wanted the whole wide world to know that her son was the greatest—and did anyone want to make something out of it?

Some of my former wives could have told them a thing or two about Mickey Walker.

There were so many people . . . so many episodes . . . so many things to tell. There are so many things to remember. But that's all it is . . . a memory. Maybe it's best that way. You can't live with ghosts.

I wouldn't want to relive the past if I could. For me, there is only one way:

Live today, forget yesterday, and have hope for tomorrow.

ABOUT JOE REICHLER

JOE REICHLER has been baseball editor and a top feature writer for the Associated Press since 1942, but his contribution to baseball lore does not stop there by any means. He is the author of a number of books, including *It's Good to Be Alive*, with Roy Campanella, *The History of Baseball*, *Baseball's Unforgettable Game*, and *Inside the Majors*. He has also written many articles on sports celebrities for the *Saturday Evening Post*, as well as stories for *Sports Illustrated, Collier's* and *True* magazines.

Now a resident of Roslyn Heights, Long Island, Mr. Reichler was born in New York City. He attended St. John's University, where he studied law.